T0315002

Public Sociology series

Series editors: **John Brewer**, Queen's University, Northern Ireland and **Neil McLaughlin**, McMaster University, Canada

---

Public Sociology series addresses not only what sociologists do, but what sociology is for, and focuses on the commitment to materially improving people's lives through understanding of the social condition. It showcases the wide diversity of sociological research that addresses the many global challenges that threaten the future of humankind.

Forthcoming in the series:

Erich Fromm and Global Public Sociology
Neil McLaughlin

The Public Sociology of Waste
Myra J. Hird

Out now in the series:

*Public Sociology As Educational Practice:
Challenges, Dialogues and Counter-Publics*
Edited by **Eurig Scandrett**

Find out more at

bristoluniversitypress.co.uk/public-sociology

Public Sociology series

Series editors: **John Brewer**, Queen's University, Northern Ireland and **Neil McLaughlin**, McMaster University, Canada

---

International editorial advisory board:

Find out more at
bristoluniversitypress.co.uk/public-sociology

THE PUBLIC AND THEIR PLATFORMS

Public Sociology in an Era of Social Media

Mark Carrigan and Lambros Fatsis

BRISTOL
UNIVERSITY
PRESS

First published in Great Britain in 2021 by

Bristol University Press
University of Bristol
1-9 Old Park Hill
Bristol
BS2 8BB
UK
t: +44 (0)117 954 5940
e: bup-info@bristol.ac.uk

Details of international sales and distribution partners are available at
bristoluniversitypress.co.uk

British Library Cataloguing in Publication Data
A catalogue record for this book is available from the British Library

ISBN 978-1-5292-0105-5 hardcover
ISBN 978-1-5292-0107-9 paperback
ISBN 978-1-5292-0108-6 ePub
ISBN 978-1-5292-0106-2 ePdf

Cover design by Andrew Corbett.
Front cover image: photo copyright Andrew Corbett.
Bristol University Press uses environmentally responsible print partners.
Printed and bound in Great Britain by CMP, Poole.

Contents

Acknowledgements

Parts of Chapters 3 and 4 are drawn from an essay by Mark Carrigan, published by Discover Society under a CC BY-NC-ND 4.0 license. The original essay is available online at: https://archive.discoversociety. org/2019/05/01/focus-the-platform-university/.

Parts of Chapters 4 and 5 are drawn from a PhD thesis by Lambros Fatsis, 'Making sociology public: a critical analysis of an old idea and a recent debate', awarded by the University of Sussex in 2014.

Over the last decade we've had countless conversations with friends and colleagues about what public sociology is and could be. We'd like to dedicate our book to this community and hope it provides a platform for us to continue these conversations in the future.

Series Editors' Preface

Sociology is a highly reflexive subject. All scholarly disciplines examine themselves reflexively in terms of theory and practice as they apply what the sociologist of science Robert Merton once called 'organised scepticism'. Sociology adds to this constant internal academic debate also a vigorous, almost obsessive, concern about its very purpose and rationale. This attentiveness to founding principles shows itself in significant intellectual interest in the 'canon' of great thinkers and its history as a discipline, in vigorous debate about the boundaries of the discipline, and in considerable inventiveness in developing new areas and subfields of sociology. This fascination with the purpose and social organization of the discipline also reflects in the debate about sociology's civic engagements and commitments, its level of activism, and its moral and political purposes.

This echoes the contemporary discussion about the idea of public sociology. 'Public sociology' is a new phrase for a long-standing debate about the purpose of sociology that began with the discipline's origins. It is therefore no coincidence that students in the 21st century, when being introduced to sociology for the first time, wrestle with ideas formulated centuries before, for while social change has rendered some of these ideas redundant, particularly the Social Darwinism of the 19th century and functionalism in the 1950s, familiarity with these earlier debates and frameworks is the lens into understanding the purpose, value and prospect of sociology as key thinkers conceived it in the past. The ideas may have changed but the moral purpose has not.

A contentious discipline is destined to argue continually about its past. Some see the roots of sociology grounded in medieval scholasticism, in 18th century Scotland, with the Scottish Enlightenment's engagement with the social changes wrought by commercialism, in conservative reactions to the Enlightenment or in 19th century encounters with the negative effects of industrialization and modernization. Contentious disciplines, however, are condemned to always live in their past if they do not also develop a vision for their future; a sense purpose and a rationale that takes the discipline forward. Sociology has always been forward looking, offering an analysis and diagnosis of what C. Wright Mills liked to call the human condition. Interest in the social condition and in its improvement and betterment for the majority of ordinary men and women has always been sociology's ultimate objective.

At the end of the second millennium, when public sociology was named by Michael Burawoy, there was a strong feeling in the discipline that the professionalization of the subject during the 20th century had come at the cost of its public engagement, its commitment to social justice, and its reputation for activism. The vitality and creativity of the public sociology debate was largely fuelled by what Aldon Morris called 'liberation capitalism', created in social movements of political engagement outside of the universities in the years after the social turmoil and changes of the 1960s.

The discipline has mostly reacted positively to Burawoy's call for public sociology, although there has been spirited dissent from those concerned with sociology's scientific status. Public sociology represents a practical realignment of the discipline by encouraging a focus on substantive and theoretical topics that are important to the many publics with whom the discipline engages. Public sociology, however, is also a normative realignment of the discipline through its commitment to enhance understanding of the social condition so that the lives of people are materially improved. Public sociology not only changes what sociologists do, it also redefines what sociology is for.

Sociology's concern with founding principles is both a strength and a weakness of the discipline. Nothing seems settled in sociology; the discipline does not obliterate past ideas by their absorption into new ones, as Robert Merton once put it, as the natural sciences insist on doing. The past remains a learning tool in sociology and the history of sociology is contemporaneous as we stand on the shoulders of giants to learn from earlier generations of sociologists. We therefore revisit debates about the boundaries between sociology and its cognate disciplines, or debates about the relationship between individuals and society, or about the analytical categories of individuals, groups, communities and societies, or of the primacy of material conditions over symbolic ones, or of the place of politics, identity, culture, economics and the everyday in structuring and determining social life. The boundaries of sociology are porous and, as many sociologists have asserted, the discipline is a hybrid, drawing ideas eclectically from those subjects closely aligned to it.

This hybridity is also sociology's great strength. Sociology's openness facilitates inter-disciplinarity and encourages innovation in the fields to which the sociological imagination is applied. It also opens up new topics about which sociological questions can be asked. Sociology thus exposes the hidden and the neglected to scrutiny. There is very little that cannot have sociological questions asked of it. The boundaries of sociology are thus ever expanding and widening; it is limitless in applying the sociological imagination. The tension between continuity and change – something evident in society generally – reflects thus also in the discipline itself. This gives sociology a frisson that is both fertile and fruitful as new ideas rub up against old ones and as the conceptual apparatus of sociology is simultaneously revisited and renewed. This tends to work against faddism in sociology, since nothing is entirely new and the latest fashions have their pasts.

Public sociology is thus not itself new and it has its own history. Burawoy rightly emphasized the role of C. Wright Mills and broader frameworks allow us to highlight the contribution of the radical W.E.B. Du Bois, the early feminist and peace campaigner Jane Addams, and scores of feminist, socialist and anti-racist scholars from the Global South, such as Fernando Henrique Cardosa in Brazil and Fatima Meer in South Africa. Going back further into the history of public sociology, the Scots in the 18th century were public sociologists in their way, allowing us to see that Burawoy's refocusing of sociology's research agenda and its normative realignment is the latest expression of a long-standing concern. The signal achievement of Burawoy's injunction was to mobilize the profession to reflect again on its founding principles and to take the discipline forward to engage with the relevance of sociology to the social and human condition in the 21st century.

Despite the popularity of the idea of public sociology, and the widespread use of such discourse, no book series is singularly dedicated to it. The purpose of this Series is to draw together some of the best sociological research that carries the imprimatur of 'public sociology', done inside the academy by senior figures and early career researchers, as well as outside it by practitioners, policy analysts and independent researchers seeking to apply sociological research in real-world settings.

The reflexivity of professional sociologists as they ponder the usefulness of sociology under neoliberalism and late modern cosmopolitanism, will be addressed in this Series, as the Series publishes works that engage from a sociological perspective with the fundamental global challenges that threaten the very future of humankind. The relevance of sociology will be highlighted in works that address these challenges as they feature in global social changes but also as they are mediated in local and regional communities and settings. The Series will thus feature titles that work at a global level of abstraction as well as studies that are micro ethnographic depictions of global processes as they affect local communities. The focus of the Series is thus on what Michael Ignatieff refers to as 'the ordinary virtues' of everyday life, social justice, equality of opportunity, fairness, tolerance, respect, trust and respect, and how the organization and structure of society – at a general level or in local neighbourhoods – inhibits or promotes these virtues and practices. The Series will expose through detailed sociological analysis, both the dynamics of social suffering and celebrate the hopes of social emancipation.

The discourse of public sociology has permeated outside the discipline of sociology, as other subjects take up its challenge and re-orientate themselves, such as public anthropology, public political science and public international relations. In pioneering the engagement with its different publics, sociology has therefore once again led the way, and this Series is designed to take the debate about public sociology and its practices in new directions. In being the first of its kind, this Series will showcase how the discipline of sociology has utilized the language and ideas of public sociology to change what it does and what it is for. This Series will address not only what sociologists do, but also sociology's focus on the commitment to enhance understanding of the social condition so that the lives of ordinary people are materially improved. It will show case the wide diversity of sociological research that addresses the many global challenges that threaten the future of humankind in the 21st century.

These qualities are admirably represented in *The Public and Their Platforms: Public Sociology in an Era of Social Media* by Mark Carrigan and Lambros Fatsis. Coming as they do from sociology and criminology respectively, the volume both theorizes the very notion of the public as well as the social practices represented by contemporary platforms to address strategies and logics of social media interventions by what they call sociologists in public. In so doing, it explores the boundaries between public sociology, media studies and the political economy of platforms by addressing the publics, knowledges and practices that shape ideas in a social media saturated world.

The Public and Their Platforms is as much a critique of public sociology, as it advocates for the need for a deeper understanding of the institutional logics of social media platforms, what they call 'platform literacy', as a less doctrinaire focus on sociology's disciplinary interests and traditional forms of evaluation of scholarship. The authors emphasize what they call the 'personalism' in platforms as opposed to the 'objectivity' of scholarship. They put these theories into practice both as highly visible social media academics based in the United

Kingdom, while also being university researchers. The arguments advanced about platforms and their publics when understood through the lens of public sociology are global in their significance and impact. They add to our knowledge of social media practices as well as to our practice of public sociology.

The volume chiefly argues that sociology in public should be conceived as a form of dialogue occurring between citizens as well as scholars. In this volume, any worthwhile dialogue that occurs between sociologists in public and the broader civil society must be done in ways that are informed by a sophisticated theory about how the public has been constituted historically and how modern platforms operate. The volume is no self-help book for budding public sociologists, as it offers no easy answers to how one can do effective public sociology. It does, however, insist that we move beyond studying public sociology to doing it effectively, something both authors are known for having done themselves. Carrigan and Fatsis argue that effective sociology in public requires sociological and social theorizing along with practice, and thus the volume both fits with and expands our vision of public sociology.

This is a call for a public sociology put to use. It is public sociology that demands we theorize and understand the platforms that are re-shaping the intellectual world around us. By using the lens of public sociology, the volume seeks to challenge the practices of existing public sociology, creating a sociology in public that can effectively promote social change. As editors, we therefore very warmly welcome this volume to the Series.

John D. Brewer and Neil McLaughlin
Belfast and Toronto
December 2020

Introduction

You are holding a book of sociology about public life and the technologies that make it possible. But you are reading it during a period when our experience of *being public* is largely mediated through *being online*. This seems like the perfect moment to be thinking about the contents of this book. The pandemic has done much to challenge our conceptions and practice of what public life is, how it has been or can be understood sociologically and what role social media platforms play in enabling or compromising our ability to occupy, create and identify ourselves with or as a *public*. Just like a virus forced us to confront the ills of social life in pre-COVID times, while also prompting us to reimagine its aftermath in a more convivial, equitable, less extractive and more human manner, this book aspires to a similar reconstructive logic without leaving a trail of devastation in its wake. What we have put together in book form, therefore, is an attempt at throwing our ideas of public life, technological innovations and sociological scholarship up in the air; as an invitation to a conversation about how we can make such resources work for us as ingredients of a citizenship which traverses the conventional distinctions of 'online' and 'offline'.

Rather fittingly, this book's life has been shaped by some of the issues it addresses. Much of its content was mulled over in public or semi-public spaces – pubs, cafés and library courtyards – where its authors met to discuss how to rethink and write about public sociology as an endeavour that could be practised as a relationship between *intellectuals*, *publics* and *platforms* of communication. Both of us were ambivalent about how social media could stimulate public life, yet neither of us were satisfied with doing away with them, without attempting to understand how such platforms are designed or what the terms *public*, *sociology* and *public sociology* mean. As a result, we chose to place our dissatisfaction between book covers, resisting the temptation to fetishize offline life, malign online activities or pretend that (public) sociology has all the (right) answers about how to make social life (more) sociable. As keen social media users, active participants in our community and public sociology enthusiasts, we were convinced that digital technology, civic engagement and public-oriented scholarship can all be used together to achieve what we want from the tools we use, the world we inhabit and the stuff we teach and write; provided that we rethink our approach to and relationship with them all.

The Public and Their Platforms should therefore be thought, and read, as the result of a conversation between two academic sociologists which was sharpened by blog posts and Twitter exchanges, but also affected by the onset of a global pandemic which simultaneously challenged and reinforced our thinking about how to be public as sociologists who are committed to participating in, creating and sustaining associational life in all its variety, tensions, contradictions and pleasures. Owing its development to such (in)auspicious circumstances, much of the book reflects the concerns it describes, adding to our excitement of sharing it with you. Having hitherto talked about the book's life course without drawing up a road map for the journey ahead, the remainder of this Introduction will guide readers through each chapter to help you trace our argument bit by bit.

Chapter 1 offers a critical inquiry into the idea of *the public* as it has been theorized within and beyond sociology, while also pointing out how eloquently silent the debate on public sociology has been in discussing the public at any adequate length. After exploring some dominant themes that surround theories of the public which variously describe it through a language of crisis, the remainder of this chapter rethinks the public as an identity (something we *are*), as an activity (something we *do*) and as a type of space (something we *make*) that enables citizenship to take place, if not take root as a routine practice of everyday life. The spirit of this chapter therefore is positive and reconstructive, attempting to offer examples of how we can be public in ways that turn an otherwise abstract word into a physical, material reality that could be likened to a muscle that needs to be exercised rather than an abstract aura that is alluded to in vague and elusive ways.

Chapter 2 draws inspiration from such a direct, embodied and experiential approach to being public and attempts at identifying ways of using digital platforms as 'tools for conviviality' (Illich 1973) that can be used to manufacture real, human connection and build community rather than trap us into a digital grid where only mere connectivity and superficial networks are possible. The tone, mission and function of this chapter is exploratory, trying as it does to investigate how to humanize and publicize social media; without falling into their clutches as complicated online systems that keep us busy as addicted users of a digital treadmill that exhausts our public or civic energy, instead of exercising, nourishing it and propelling it forward.

Chapter 3 expands on this negotiation between the desire to be public and the limits and possibilities of social media to help us achieve such a goal, by exploring the relationship between publics and platforms. This relationship plays out on a very unstable ground, due to the constraints that the architecture of online platforms imposes on its users' ability to exploit them for our purposes as we wish, not as this online ecosystem dictates. The question of how or whether social media users can exercise agency independently of the restrictive design of such platforms take centre stage here, pointing at their addictive nature and its impact on our ability to stand on such platforms only to step out of them by exploiting them as resources for mobilizing people offline. What makes this challenging is the realization that it is not enough to know enough about such platforms to use them in ways that benefit us. Tapping, as social media do, into our desire to vie for the eyes and ears of our followers online, we lose sight of how much time we spend feeding such an attention economy (Marwick 2013, Tufekci 2013) that can easily turn utopian expectations about networked activism into dystopian fears of subjugation and submission to surveillance capitalism (Zuboff 2019).

Chapter 4 momentarily disconnects from the online world to explore the relationship between sociology and its platforms. Approaching platforms as positions from which to communicate that are facilitated by technological infrastructures, we also stress the obvious enough point that these can be digital *and* analogue. Rethinking the relationship between sociology and its platforms in this manner reminds us that sociology did not wait for the arrival of the internet to communicate its insights, but has always relied on other, earlier media technologies to do so. These include academic publishers as well as print and broadcast media that predate the emergence of digital technology and help us contextualize the radical transformations social media brought about as they became an institutional(ized) feature of academic life as dissemination engines and tools for generating publicity.

Chapter 5 offers a potted history of public sociology by describing it as an old idea which became a new debate, following Michael Burawoy's presidential address at the 2004 annual meeting of American Sociological Association. Tracing the public sociology debate, before it became so popular, allows us to reflect on the evolution of sociologists' anxieties about the public nature of our discipline, which are as old as sociology itself. This allows us to resist the temptation of thinking that sociology suddenly acquired a public deficit in the 21st century, arguing instead that our discipline has always been plagued by an existential crisis regarding its identity (what it is), purpose (who it is there for) and target audience (who it speaks to). By raising such questions in the context of sociology's disciplinary history, we also contemplate its future, digital or otherwise.

Chapter 6 explores ways of practising sociology online in ways that benefit rather than alienate the discipline from itself, its practitioners and its audiences. In doing so we discuss multiple challenges that sneak up on us slyly including our ability to translate sociological research into social media content, the allure of narcissistic self-promotion or institutional pressure to ply our scholarly wares online as enterprising brand ambassadors. More importantly and more optimistically, however, this chapter sketches out a plan for engaging with social media in ways that do not compromise sociological rigour or academic solidarity.

Chapter 7 offers a sociology of platforms which is aimed at making them 'public' through the way that we use them. While the spirit of this chapter is optimistic, highlighting how exciting social media are as objects of and tools for sociological research and thinking, we are also cautious about the limits that their political economy imposes on us. At the heart of such duality lies the realization that online platforms are not neutral, idle tools that we can use whenever or however we like but powerful systems that dictate how much we can do with and through them. The idea of platform capitalism (Srnicek 2017) becomes central here, as we analyse the function of social media as promising opportunities for connection, exchange and collaboration while also extracting our attention in ways that obscure the reality that we use social media as much as they use us, by conditioning out behaviour within them much like physical spaces determine the way we navigate them spatially.

Chapter 8 concludes our book by attempting to (re)assemble public sociology as a theoretical debate and a routine practice online and offline. Anchored in a desire to use both sociology and social media platforms to stimulate civic engagement and public participation, we organize our discussion around three main propositions. The first opposes the professionalization of public sociology through its institutionalization as a sociological subgenre. The second approaches social media platforms as digital (under)commons (Harney and Moten 2013) that enable participation inside and outside them. The third recruits the figure of 'the public intellectual' but recasts them as a less elitist and more sociable figure that speaks as much as they listen. In exploring and redefining sociologists' relationship with their 'public(s)', their platforms and their own discipline, an alternative way of engaging with all three is sketched out in theoretical terms that aspire to become ideas for action.

We invite our readers to *use* this book as a companion to thinking about public life, technology and scholarship at a specific historical moment where social, or rather physical, distancing has left us reliant on digitalization. Rethinking the limits and possibilities of being 'public' online, in physical spaces, in our scholarship and in our civic engagement lies at the heart of what we deem essential to meaningful social and scholarly life. We therefore offer this book as an attempt to speak to such issues, by articulating a vision for thinking and doing things differently in ways that empower us, instead of powering social media systems or academic institutions whose interests can and often do diverge from ours.

1

Defining 'the Public'

What does public sociology mean in an era of social media? Many answers to this question see social media as providing new tools for public sociology, promising the expansion of sociology's reach by communicating its insights to vast audiences. This book argues that such a response engages only superficially with what social media can and *cannot* contribute to public sociology, offering little insight about media platforms and their impact on sociology's scholarly and public expression. Worse still, much of the public sociology debate is remarkably silent on the question of what 'the public' is, means, or how it should be brought about. This leaves it ill equipped to account for how shifts in the means through which social life is mediated influence processes of public formation and the publics which ensue from such processes (Marres 2012). In the following chapters we attempt to address this deficit in order to reconstruct public sociology for an era of ubiquitous platforms. But first it's necessary to account for what 'the public' is and what it means to be *public*. In seeking to provide an answer, this chapter is a necessary prelude to what follows, resting as it does on our reconceptualization of 'the public' to discuss platforms as communication tools, while also interrogating their relationship to their users and the public context they shape and are shaped by, before concluding with our vision for a digital public sociology as a form of sociological practice that uses social media as what we call **assembly devices** to create public life online *and* offline.

In the 15-year period that public sociology has been hotly debated, its critics, sceptics and devotees have been drawn into a conceptual whirlpool of various ways with which to think about, refrain from or practise it. Astonishingly, much less of a storm has been brewing around the question of what the 'public' in public sociology means, or how it could be thought or brought about. Douglas Hartmann (2017: 9) perceptively pointed this out in his presidential address at the 2016 Midwest Sociological Society's Annual Meeting, where he admitted how 'struck' he was about 'how little sociologists have theorized the notion of "the public" in talking about public sociology'. Such a realization invites uncomfortable questions about why this adjective which imbued contemporary sociology with so much hope has been edited out of our thinking about public sociology, when so much of the term's meaning depends on it. Without wishing to cast aspersions on our discipline or proffer the pretence that the authors of this book have the answer, it would not be entirely unreasonable to suggest that the absent presence of 'the public' from the public sociology debate may have something to do with the shy and elusive nature of the word itself, which flies out of our reach not so much on a lexical but on a conceptual level.

Much of what follows in this chapter will grapple with this theoretical conundrum by tracing some of the dominant themes through which 'the public' has been thought within sociology and neighbouring social science disciplines, while also calling for its celebration as a useful metaphor and an active ingredient for citizenship. The purpose of this chapter is to make the term visible in discussions on public sociology, to highlight the dazzling diversity of ways in which 'the public' has been theorized, and (re)focus our attention on the *uses* of the term as a civic principle to aspire to and perform; as opposed to obsessing over its *meanings* as an empirical phenomenon to be forced into this or that sociological perspective. In doing so we intend to place less emphasis on what 'the public' is or does as an analytical concept, but rather stress what it can mean and do as a civic, associational identity with which to make and participate in public life. Having set out the intellectual agenda for this chapter, or rather the rationale behind it, we shall in turn explore what and who 'the public' is or may be, how it can come about, what it is made of, and what it looks like, while also offering our own account of how to rethink and revive it not just as a sociological concept but as a civic identity. This is important not only as an attempt to rethink 'the public' as something that we *are*, *do* and *make*. It is also a preliminary for this book's ambition to connect 'publics', 'platforms', and 'sociology' by understanding what these terms mean, how they have hitherto been thought about, as well as what they mean in relation to each other and how they can take place in public. Much of what follows, therefore, offers a springboard for reconceptualizing 'the public' in order to bring it to life as lived experience of social life rather than the nebulous abstraction which it often remains at present. The COVID-19 pandemic has thrown these questions into sharp relief, presenting us with the challenge of reinscribing 'publicness' after the civic trauma of lockdown and social distancing. While we can't do justice to the scale of a crisis which emerged while we were in the final stages of writing this book, we nevertheless believe that the questions we raise are timely when physical interaction has been problematized by this public health emergency, and social relations have come to depend more than ever on the affordances of digital platforms.

What/who is 'the public'?

Defining 'the public' inevitably tempts us into hair-splitting disputes about the term's meaning, orientation and use that may not be unique to this term alone, but are interesting to observe and participate in due to the word's centrality in the vocabulary of public sociology. In spite of this centrality it is a conceptual and empirical entity which often runs in the background of discussions without being noticed, articulated or analytically defined. It is instead assumed to simply exist as a *realm* that we refer to, often as a shorthand for democratic politics or civil society, without specifying or clarifying just what kind of sphere of activity we refer to or who it is represented by. Any effort to address the intellectual messiness that clutters the notion of 'the public', therefore, resembles what could be described as an attempt to know the unknowable or confront what Derrida (1992: 24–26) called the 'ghost of the undecidable'; given the difficulty of choosing how to approach, make sense, explain and refer to the way(s) in which collective life is staged and played out.

The best illustration of the term's 'undecidability' comes from a novelist's pen, namely Virginia Woolf,[1] who likened 'the public' to 'a vast, almost featureless, almost shapeless jelly of human stuff'. Echoing the ambiguity that the 20th century modernist writer expressed in her short, sharp, yet apt observation about the difficulty of fastening 'the public' into a single definition, the term draws much of its meaning from its routine association with words that often become synonymous with it: 'crowd', 'multitude', or 'the people'. These signifiers figure prominently in how social media has been greeted by social commentators: 'here comes everybody' as the cyber-utopian Clay Shirky (2007) put it in an influential early text (Couldry 2014, 2015). Even the more pessimistic literature which has emerged in recent years has tended to focus on the multitude, but with this framed as a dangerous mob whipped into a reactionary frenzy by an insurgent strongman who uses social media to manipulate the masses (Müller 2016, Žižek 2018). The mental links we make between the notion itself and the additional terms we use to describe it reveals how vulnerable 'the public' becomes to the meanings we intend to impose on it intellectually and politically.

This becomes evident in the main interpretations of it that cluster around two main recurring themes that flow back like a returning tide in the relevant sociological literature. The first of those themes is expressed in the tension between depictions of 'the public' as good, bad, and redeemable, while the second laments the loss of 'the public' as a casualty of an excessively growing individualism that leaves little room for collective life. Each has its correlates in commentaries on social media, even if the novelty of the technology and the social outcomes it has played a role in mean these themes have developed in new directions. Crudely put the first cluster of sociological motifs on 'the public' express ambiguity towards our ability and willingness to be public, while the second laments the disappearance of collective public life and its replacement with the private lifeworld.[2] Both will be replaced by a more positive and constructive argument which aims at demonstrating how 'the public' should be thought less as an essence to be distilled but rather as a relationship to be *created* through both analogue and digital platforms that have the capacity to create their own publics by the opportunities they allow for citizens to coalesce around matters of shared concern (Marres 2012). While digitalization has brought a change in what it means to make something public, with the simple fact of being 'out there' no longer sufficient for meaningful visibility, this merely strengthens the role of common concern in public formation as the focal point through which assembly takes place. This means 'the public' has more of a place than ever in an era of ubiquitous platforms, regardless of whether we see it as good, bad or redeemable. The problematization of co-presence entailed by social distancing makes it even more urgent that we confront the challenges involved in our reliance on digital platforms, as well as that we do so in a way which cuts through the cultural politics of utopianism and dystopianism which has tended to pervade discussions of digital change (Carrigan 2018).

The good, the bad, and the redeemable 'public'

Starting with the first of those themes, 'the public' seems caught in the pincer movement of two related yet contradictory interpretations, 'good' versus 'bad', the pressure of which is eased by hopeful revisions of the term that render it 'redeemable' or rescuable through rational democratic participation.[3] When it is conceived as virtuous, 'the public' is used to describe conscious members of a political community who strive for the *common good* by thinking and acting on the basis of interests that people have in common, thereby supporting institutions that are designed to serve such interests. When it is dismissed as embodying vice, 'the public' is depicted as a messy mass of unreliable *common people* who have no consciousness or identity as a political entity, and can be moulded into whatever political leaders wish them to be. As we will argue in a later chapter, this assumption lurks in the background of contemporary populism even if it often goes unexplained, with social media assumed to be the powerful tool which accounts for this manipulative capacity.[4]

When it is revived as a relational obligation that all citizens have to each other by caring for shared, common interests despite disagreements, 'the public' is understood as representing a *common cause* achieved through reasoned dialogue which can then lead to sensible decision making. Each of these interpretations are represented and depicted by idealized allusions to Classical or Periclean Athens for the *good* public, by reminders of barbarism and chaos for the *bad* public, and by the possibility of civility through deliberation for the *redeemable* public.[5] Each of these competing visions often combines elements from all approaches making them difficult to delineate or attribute to specific, separate and air-tight schools of thought that are uncontaminated by ambiguity, contradictions and overlap. What is often conceived and idealized as a *demos* – which 'hold[s] power' and 'exercise[s] rule' (Dunn 2005: 51) – is also dismissed as a *plethos* – a 'crowd' (Canetti 1962, Le Bon 1995, Tarde 2006), a 'herd' (Trotter 1908), a 'group mind' (McDougall 1927) – which is susceptible to propaganda (Bernays 1961, 1977, 2005), but also retains the capacity to fulfil the democratic *ethos* by organizing itself as a body of citizens who make collective decisions in dialogue through 'communicative action' (Habermas 1984). Contemporary treatments of platformized politics inevitably grapple with the same tensions in their engagement with the unfolding reality which is the context for this book (Papacharissi 2014).

This coexistence of contradictory visions of the public is captured well by Walter Lippmann's (1925) description of 'the public' as a chameleonic 'phantom realm' which is so intellectually flexible that it can easily become politically malleable both as a source of 'people power' and as a victim of 'populist reason' (Laclau 2005). In such a scenario, 'the public' is transformed from a collective agent which mobilizes around its common interest to effect change to a passive plaything of demagoguery which feeds on public support to satisfy self-interested political agendas. Could there be a more apt summary of the transition from the utopian hopes which originally greeted social media to the often dystopian fears of the contemporary 'techlash'? This highlights the potential of 'the public' to express both virtue and vice depending both on how the term is understood and on the intentions of those who exploit it to shape or steer collective action towards a desired goal. 'The public' can, therefore, be thought to denote virtue if and when it is used to imply and encourage political agency in a democratic polity, but it can also depict vice if and when that same 'public' is thought to behave uncritically or emotively. The empirical complexity and conceptual uncertainty surrounding social media and its political significance destabilize this yet further (Gerbaudo 2012, 2019, Tufekci 2017). It leaves us in a situation where the same term can be used with remarkably different connotations, the balance of which fluctuates as the political turmoil around us grows (Žižek 2009, Mason 2012, Frank 2018).

The tension between interpretations that exalt and deride 'the public' was illustrated with much literary flair by Bernard Mandeville (1970) in his depiction of humanity as a 'grumbling hive' or 'a compound of passions' where private vice and public benefit co-exist, but ought to be skilfully managed by social institutions and authorities. This unruliness of 'the public', according to Mandeville, serves as a boon to politicians who can and should turn our private vices into public virtues by appealing to the former to achieve the latter. One way of achieving this is through manipulating our emotions through praise or blame by using concepts such as goodness and virtue which flatter, tame and dupe us into conquering our selfish passions in order to help and live peaceably with others. In the following chapter we consider what Seymour (2019) calls the *Twittering Machine* as something which represents, at least in part, a machinery adequate to Mandeville's vision. It is one entwined within the fabric of social relations to an unprecedented degree as a result of the COVID-19 crisis, and it is essential that we grapple with the civic implications of this dependence on corporate platforms.

The disappearance of 'the public'

This proposed channelling of egoism and selfishness to sociable and even benevolent ends is approached with pensive sadness by the second bundle of interpretations of 'the public' considered here. The prevailing tone of these responses to 'the public' is one of contemplative melancholia which laments the gradual disappearance of public life due to the emergence and dominance of an acquisitive, consumptive society composed of passive, individualized consumers. The 'public' is thus seen as confronting its own loss, disappearance (Arendt 1998), fall (Sennett 2002) and eclipse (Dewey 1927). It is a 'lonely crowd' (Riesman 1950) which 'bowl[s] alone' (Putnam 2000), languishing in social relationships and interactions that are no longer characterized by common membership in a political community, but mediated, if not altogether managed, by the market economy (Skocpol 2003). Such a 'decline of the public' and the 'hollowing out of citizenship', as Marquand (2004) put it, reflects a gradual yet gigantic surge of economic, sociopolitical and cultural change(s) which transformed the public realm from a public open space for meeting people and discussing politics, to a large enclosed area for buying material goods with which to enrich the self, adorn the home, and support the family unit at the expense of civic life. Even this contracted sphere sat empty for long periods during the lockdown measures, which the COVID-19 crisis necessitated, with socioeconomic ramifications which are still playing out at the time of writing.

This withdrawal from the public sphere (*res publica*) and retreat into the private domain (*res privata*) is routinely interpreted as symptomatic of late-stage capitalism, with Habermas' (1989) contribution being vital here, but similar concerns have been voiced in pre-capitalist societies too. The language of loss and deprivation in which 'the public' is shrink-wrapped, therefore, may accurately describe an era of 'shifting involvements' with 'private interest' overshadowing 'public action' (Hirschman 2002). But this civic malaise is as old as the words that are used to describe it. The ancient Roman origins of the word 'private' (*privatus*) depict citizens that are withdrawn from, but also deprived (*privare*) of their association with public life, echoing the ancient Greek distinction between private persons (*idiōtes*) and citizens (*polites*) where the former are harshly dismissed as ignorant and idiotic, because they retire into a life of their own instead of participating in the life of the city (*polis*). We can see echoes of this in contemporary accusations that social media fuels an 'identity politics' which brings the fabric of private existence into public life, violating the historical separation between the two spheres (Papacharissi 2010, Marres 2012, Butler 2015). This historical reminder is important as it suggests an inability to be 'public' even during periods in human history whose vocabulary strongly disapproved of civic inaction. During such a historical era, one of its best known philosophers, Aristotle (1885: 30), writes: 'For that which is common to the greatest number has the least care bestowed on it. Every one thinks chiefly of his own, hardly at all of the common interest; and only when he is himself concerned as an individual.'

This dismissive comment may surprise readers for its critique of individualism, especially as it is written in an era that is yet unsullied by the possessive individualism that capitalist economy brought in its wake, and in a place where Western participatory democracy is supposed to be in bloom. Yet, Aristotle's dictum presages contemporary anxieties about 'diminished democracy' (Skocpol 2003), the 'fall of public man' (Sennett 2002), and 'the tragedy of the commons' (Hardin 1968) which are expressed in the same declinist language. It also presages contemporary anxieties about the loss of social skills and openness to conversation being driven by digital technology (Turkle 2016, 2017). The salutary lesson that we can draw from such mourning of an ever-shrinking 'public' and the excessive growth of privatism is to recognize the over-idealized place that 'the public' occupies in our imagination, without downplaying its decline or losing hope in bringing it about. Such a realization simply allows us to manage our expectations before we prematurely declare failure by reminding ourselves that 'the public' is not an unclaimed inheritance from the past or a once well-trodden path that now grows weeds, but an investment that we commit to make and a road that is paved as we walk it. This allows us to shift away from self-defeating narratives of doom, urging us instead to create the conditions for the flourishing of public life by rethinking how 'the public' can be thought about in a way that would allow us to rethink and reconfigure our relationship with it.

The remainder of this chapter will therefore approach 'the public' by drawing on what is most positive and constructive from the themes discussed earlier, with a view to rethink and re-introduce it as something that we are, can become and bring about as a reality and a routine practice, rather than a muddled and murky abstraction expressed in passive grammatical constructions. The following section will therefore call for a self-conception of ourselves as public persons, not just as individuals, and an understanding of 'the public' as ourselves by recognizing and realizing our capacity to *be* public and *make* publics through reclaiming collective life as an integral part of our everyday experience. Such an ambition also reflects the aim of this book as an attempt to illustrate how we, as citizens and sociologists alike, can become public through the affordances of digital platforms while carefully negotiating their constraints. This is an urgent undertaking as our faltering steps back into public space after lockdown measures leave us confronting the challenge of reconstituting it with a view towards a post-pandemic world.

How to rethink 'the public' in order to revive it

Having traced the contours of 'the public' as both an elusive or indeterminate concept and a flickering or evanescent realm which resists authoritative definitions but welcomes ambivalent exploration, any attempt at capturing how it can be exercised or brought about as both a civic identity and a field of activity inevitably requires the same humility. This urges an interpretive approach which favours open, tentative and flexible blueprints over rigid or tried and tested templates, so the last section of this chapter should be read as nothing more than an experiment in reformulating ideas of and approaches to 'the public', as a sense of self (identity) and a way of life (practice) that makes room (space) for citizenship in everyday life – even in socioeconomic and political conditions that discourage it. Drawing on such a conception of 'the public' as something we *are*, something we *do*, and something we *create*, it will be argued that an important step towards becoming citizens involves recognizing ourselves as such, acting accordingly, and encouraging types of action that sustain collective, associational life.

Becoming citizens

Any process of *becoming* inevitably involves developing into and being accepted as something or somebody else,[6] thereby also implying and requiring a change in how we might have been identifying or identified until that moment of transformation. In the context of social life in the public realm, the process of *becoming citizens* acknowledges the possibility that we may have hitherto been languishing in the doldrums of another existential condition that we would need to abandon. This earlier existential condition is no other than our socialization into a 'postmodern society' which not only 'engages its members primarily in their capacity as consumers' (Bauman 2000: 76), but also leads us to be 'socially defined, and self-defined' almost exclusively as such (Bauman 1998: 38). This complaint is hardly new or original,[7] but difficult to deny if we reflect on what possibilities and opportunities we currently have to be and act in public if our presence cannot be justified by the purchasing of goods. Social distancing entails a radicalization of this condition, with more consumption drifting to the home while an edgy self-monitoring (coupled with biosecurity measures) comes to define the experience of public space.

Such a realization reminds us that public spaces have been colonized, commodified, privatized and reconfigured to accommodate the enjoyment of consumption instead of participation in public. This is particularly illustrated by the physical changes that public spaces have undergone by becoming intensely securitized, walled, barbwired, surveilled and patrolled environments rather than open spaces. The assumption which is so deeply ingrained into our thinking about and participation in public spaces, such as they are today, is that the precondition for being 'public' is the ability to afford this as buyers of consumer goods rather than as citizens enjoying public space as a public good. To walk on highstreets, enter train stations, sit on benches, or gather in parks virtually requires buying something or preparing to be asked to leave by shopkeepers, waiters, customers, security guards, Transport Police officers or bobbies on the beat. To freely wander is to loiter, to assume that sitting in a public space is allowed is to be reminded that 'implied permission' to be there was not explicitly given by the authorities and can therefore be withdrawn. To assemble is to appear suspect, out of place and risk being subjected to police powers such as stop and account, or even stop and search depending on the situation and the demographic characteristics of the citizens in question (Butler 2015). All the above are often described as 'quality of life offences' by law enforcement agencies, suggesting a further remove in our understanding of who belongs and who does not belong in public, and what one can and cannot do in public, with the scales tilting favourably towards those who have the right to be in public because they have the purchasing power to do so.[8]

This might seem like a diversion from discussing processes of 'becoming citizens', yet public space is a key location where the transformation of the *homo civicus* into the *homo consumens* has taken place. By emphasizing this qualitative shift in citizenship we are not in any way claiming that the privatization and monitoring of public space is anything entirely new,[9] but to stress that the scale and spread of it is not just unprecedented, but has become the veritable 'zeitgeist of urban restructuring' and social life (Davis 1992: 223). The 'privatization of the architectural public realm' (Davis 1992: 226) has seeped into our civic conscience to the point where our ability to see ourselves as 'public' largely depends on our restricted access to physical environments where public life otherwise happens. This can easily make the architecture of participation which social media promises seem like a solution to exclusion from the public but we will caution in the coming chapters that conceiving of this problem as one of a sphere to which we do or do not have access obscures the political challenges posed by digital platforms (Marres 2012, 2017). This being the ideological, sociocultural and political context in which we are continually *de*-publicized, becoming *re*-publicized inevitably requires overcoming barriers to civic life which produce citizens who are denied the capacity to think and act as such. In an important sense, we argue that both advocates and critics of social media carry insights concerning the capacity of platforms to de-publicize and re-publicize in turn. The challenge for public sociology is to negotiate these parallel potentials and the messy contextual questions that determine which of them comes to the fore and to what extent. This involves understanding the architecture of the platforms themselves, as well as the business models of which they are part. But it also entails capturing an ethos of *publicness* which can sustain us in this analytical, methodological and most of all sociable endeavour. Given the stranglehold that the commodification of citizenship has on our intellectual habits and social life, this can admittedly seem like an inconsequential, starry-eyed proposition rather than a workable plan. No practical response to passive atomism, however, can exclude the repositioning of ourselves as citizens as a precondition to reanimating collective life. Lofty, idealistic or hopelessly abstract though this may sound, reclaiming citizenship as an attitude which we instil into our individual and public selves opens up the space for it to flourish. By educating ourselves into seeing citizenship as a form of 'sociable interaction' (Simmel 1949: 254), we can train ourselves to do the nimble footwork for it as an embedded and embodied feature or being (in) public. This involves not just 'the improvement of the methods and conditions of debate, discussion and persuasion' in a 'culture-debating' polity, as Dewey (1927: 208) and Habermas (1989: 159) respectively put it. It also entails direct involvement and active participation in public as a committed *demos* that aims at the (re)constitution of its *polis*. This is not sufficient to negotiate the politics of platforms we will encounter in subsequent chapters but it is necessary.

While reasoned argument is a vital ingredient of associational life, creating what Latour and Weibel (2005) call 'atmospheres of democracy' requires a practice of public life as an 'art or play form of association' (Simmel 1949: 254) where rational discourse gives way to the realm of the senses and emotions. This is not to discard reason in favour of emotiveness, or sacrifice thought to feeling, but to recognize that public participation is a visceral act which enlists the mind and the living body as team players in the making of citizenship. Becoming 'public', therefore, requires more than merely re-*thinking* 'the public' as a consequence of rational discourse at the service of political deliberation alone. Rather, becoming 'public' also involves re-*viving* public life as a lived experience in which we exercise our ability to be sociable as sensuous bodies, not just as thinking brains or talking heads. This realization is important given that *being public* means more than simply exchanging opinions and information. It involves being there, bearing witness to, participating in, and staying with the difficulties of associational life as a unique experience. Conceived this way, the process of *becoming citizens* depends on what Simmel (1997) calls processes of 'sociation' to highlight the importance of our ability to be social (soci-*able*) in order to (as)*sociate* with our fellow citizens as companions in the same social, cultural and political community rather than mere rational debaters of political ideas, positions and beliefs. Echoing Simmel then, becoming citizens requires that we acquire and practise social interaction as a skill for citizenship, out of which webs of social relations are spun to form a social fabric that is stitched together by vibrant social relationships rather than dry exercises in logic.

The power of Simmel's suggestion lies in the vocabulary he uses to inspire a vision of social life which democratizes citizenship by envisaging it as a festival of sociability rather than a gladiatorial arena of political contestation. The very word 'sociability' itself becomes immensely empowering as it reminds us of our ability to become social, and therefore 'public', in and through interactions with our fellow citizens. In Simmel's conceptual language, society (*Gesellschaft*) is social life that is lived, enabled by and held together through 'sociation' (*Vergesellschaftung*), not (just) rational decision making. Reviving associational life, therefore, only becomes possible by educating ourselves into sociability as the practice of associational life which empowers and affirms our sense of citizenship as active participants in meaningful interactions with our fellow citizens, by virtue of our ability to be social with all the pleasures of companionship and the dangers of conflict that such activity inevitably entails. In fact, Simmel (1904: 490) saw conflict as an integral part of social life, 'a form of socialization', which teaches us how to be social by learning how to counter and encounter each other in dialogue and finding common ground through disagreement, without encouraging factionalism or stifling dissent. Under current conditions, this might seem like an intractable challenge but it presents us with a horizon of possibility that can operate as what Taylor (1989) calls a 'moral source'.

For citizenship to flourish, however, it also needs to leave its mark as something that we do (practise) as a result of our commitment to our citizenly selves. This requires that we place citizenship-as-identity at the service of citizenship-as-practice by drawing on our intellectual attitude and thinking habits (*hexis*) towards public life to realize it as a civic practice (*praxis*) through exercising our skills in public. While these two processes are inseparable they involve different tasks. Becoming citizens as an identity primarily requires a (re)orientation of our sense of self as 'public' persons rather than private individuals, who also recognize that citizenship is not an existing 'thing' but a name we give to our capacity to realize it as desired goal in our daily social life. Practising citizenship, however, calls for making it happen as something to be founded, made and produced as a result of our public presence and the mark that this leaves on ourselves, those who we associate with, and the webs of relations that we establish. The shift from being or becoming citizens to practising citizenship, therefore, is one of emphasis where *being citizens* creates the conditions for citizenship to be experienced as a way of life, and *practising citizenship* amounts to living that life as a skill, a craft that is practised, exercised and which produces 'public' life as an outcome. While citizenship enables its practice, practising it brings it to life as a creative endeavour, and it is this emphasis on citizenship as an exercise in making public life that will dominate the following and penultimate section of this chapter.

Practising citizenship

Having perfunctorily sketched out how practising citizenship can be thought and brought about, this section will explore examples of what this might look like in practice by offering some illustrations of it as sketched by arresting passages from the work of Rebecca Solnit (2006), Jane Jacobs (1961), Stefano Harney and Fred Moten (2013). What connects the thinking of those authors about the practice of citizenship is the idea of making publics as a creative process. Being and acting as a public creates publics, not just as a collective body of people (a public) but also as an activity (public life) and a location (public space). What all four authors seem to point towards without using the word is a conception of citizens as *dēmiourgoi* (*demos* + *ergon*); people who constitute a 'public' (*demos*) but also work (*ergon*) towards making 'publics' like craftsmen (*dēmiourgoi*) of the public realm. The practice of citizenship therefore will be approached here as a process of sociocultural and political craftsmanship that we exercise daily as a 'bodily' and 'tangible' activity (Solnit 2006).

Starting with Rebecca Solnit, the practice of citizenship is seen as a synonym and a routine practice of democracy on foot. In her words:

> The exercise of democracy begins as exercise, as walking around, becoming familiar with the streets, comfortable with strangers, able to imagine your own body as powerful and expressive rather than a pawn. People who are at home in their civic space preserve the power to protest and revolt,

whereas those who have been sequestered into private space do not. (Solnit 2006)

This understanding and appreciation of active democratic citizenship as footwork brings to mind Jane Jacobs' (1961: 50, 68) famous description of city life as an 'intricate sidewalk ballet', where we flex our muscles as immersed choreographers or 'public characters' rather than aloof, distant, or '*blasé*' (Simmel 1969) observers of the frenzied metropolitan buzz. In defining 'the public character' Jacobs' (1961: 68) cast list includes:

> Anyone who is in frequent contact with a wide circle of people and who is sufficiently interested to make himself a public character. A public character need have no special talents or wisdom to fulfil his function-although he often does. He just needs to be present, and there need to be enough of his counterparts. His main qualification is that he *is* public, that he talks to lots of different people.

This attitude towards spontaneous, unrestricted, and unpoliced sociality that Jacobs longed and lived for, re-emerges in Harney and Moten's (2013: 110) powerful vision of 'the undercommons' as a form of subversive and transgressive practice of citizenship which is described as: 'what you do with other people. It's talking and walking around with other people, working, dancing, suffering, some irreducible convergence of all three' which is likened to a rehearsal; 'being in a kind of workshop, playing in a band, in a jam session'. This can help us understand the civic shock of lockdown, as well as the gravity of its economic consequences and the social suffering entailed by them. How can we revitalize the undercommons under conditions of social distancing? It seems essential we find a way to do so if we aspire towards a meaningful post-pandemic public life.

In Harney and Moten's mind, practising citizenship is like practising an instrument in a collective ensemble where harmony, sense, or sound only emerge if we 'learn to *see* more, to *hear* more, to *feel* more' as Susan Sontag (1982: 10) would have it. This idea of practising or exercising citizenship as a walk (Solnit), a ballet (Jacobs), or a rehearsal (Harney and Moten) returns us to the importance of understanding and practising citizenship, not purely as an intellectual or dianoetic function of democratic politics but as an embodied, lively, exciting and even carnivalesque performance. This is an important, hence frequently recurring, observation in this chapter, as it allows us to see beyond competing visions of 'the public' and citizenship that either dismiss it as an impossibility due to the crowd-like behaviour of large numbers of people in public,[10] or remain cautiously optimistic about its prospects but only if a 'percipient elite' among an otherwise 'brutish mass' of people is to be recruited to form a conscious body politic (Rothbard 1975: 28–29). Against such a simplistic dichotomy, the idea of practising citizenship as a peripatetic, choreographed or rehearsed activity teaches us to see the practice of citizenship in and as a process of routine, everyday participation in an embodied 'parliament' or 'assembly' of sense and sound, to lightly paraphrase David Oswell (2009: 12). Seen this way, the practice of citizenship as a democratic endeavour is one which re-*cognizes*, and literally re-thinks, democracy as 'figured through the modalities of speaking and listening within different parliaments or assemblies of mouths and ears (but also eyes that see the words sounded in the mouth of another or skin that feels the vibrations of an argument that rolls out across a room)' (Oswell 2009: 12). Theoretical effusions aside, this is a crucial comment which de-intellectualizes and re-publicizes (Fatsis 2018, 2019a) citizenship and public participation by reintroducing both as embodied, sensory endeavours that are open to anyone who *is* a citizen by virtue of their entanglement with everyday social life as an inhabitant and custodian of public space(s). Oswell's argument is also helpful in empowering us by making room for interpretations of citizenship as something than can be practised not only through acclamatory participation as assertive speakers (*rhétores*), but also through sensitive, silent but by no means less engaged presence as attentive listeners (*akoustés*). This is a useful reminder as it opens up the possibility of thinking about civic interaction through listening, as an unappreciated and often neglected quality of democratic participation and 'agency' (Back 2007, LaBelle 2018). The much-fêted theatre director Peter Brook (1996: 23–4) understood this very well when emphasizing the vital role that the 'quality of the attention' and 'concentration' plays in enabling what is happening on stage, so much so that the success of a play largely depends on the attentive listening that audiences bring with them. (Re)thinking the practice of citizenship in this manner allows us to see it as an activity that can take place in and through multiple forms and modes of 'being public' with the most important requirement being our ability to be (co-)present in public as walkers, talkers, listeners.

Approaching citizenship as the practice of sharing and making room for common space through being active and present within it brings us to our last suggestion of how to rethink 'the public' in order to revive it, which is no other than the suggestion that public life requires a space for it to take place. In the context of the commodification and transformation of many public spaces from places of encounter to 'non-places' (Augé 1995) for distraction, onward travel, business or consumption, this means rescuing public spaces from their neglect as a 'sites with no real place' (Foucault 1986: 24) to reclaiming them as a 'meaningful terrain[s] for sociation, culture, and community' (Bookchin 1974: 137). The final section of this chapter therefore will explore ideas, suggestions and examples of how public space(s) can be (re)made as a result of our ability to practice citizenship as an activity that is not just formed in public space but also forms public space too. This feels more challenging than ever in a world ravaged by COVID-19, but we must sustain this civic aspiration in order to rebuild towards a post-pandemic world.

(Re)making public space(s)

Having hitherto attempted to rethink 'the public' as a civic identity that is predicated on and validated by the practice of citizenship as an activity that is paved within public space, it now remains to show how such public activity can create the space(s) for it to flourish. Paradoxically, part of the problem is conceptual given that the process of making space involves planning, designing and constructing such a space according to our conception of it and our motivation for how it is to be used, for what and for whom. Building on the ways in which the identity and practice of citizenship are theorized here, public space is conceived as a physical location that (be)comes alive through the 'ensemble of associations' that happen within it (Taylor 1990: 98). In short, 'public space' is seen here as a territory which hosts various spheres of activity. The meaning and substance of public space, therefore, is acquired by the ways in which that space is used by those who occupy it with their physical presence, as well as fill it with their conversation and cultural, commercial and political interactions. Conceived this way, space becomes a public space when it functions as a hub of activity where citizens assemble to practise their citizenship, in ways that can be likened to what Elijah Anderson (2004) describes as a 'cosmopolitan canopy'.

According to Anderson (2004: 25) 'cosmopolitan canopies allow people of different backgrounds the chance to slow down and indulge themselves, observing, pondering, and in effect, doing their own folk ethnography, testing or substantiating stereotypes and prejudices or, rarely acknowledging something fundamentally new about the other'. As a result of such co-presence, 'strangers in the abstract can become somewhat more human and a social good is performed for those observing. As people become intimate through such shared experiences, certain barriers are prone to be broken' (Anderson 2004: 17). What is revealing in Anderson's conception and ethnography of cosmopolitan canopies is the power that physical proximity and interaction acquire to reduce social distance and increase opportunities for (as)sociation by creating the physical conditions for it. Following Anderson's sensitive ethnographic eye, public space becomes the by-product and the producer of social interactions by operating as a shelter for public life. This allows us to think and behave towards public space not as a receding horizon that we have only restricted access to, but as a space we can open up, draw out, spin, shape and twist into being in, by and through sociability. This is not to deny or downplay the challenges posed by the ever-growing disappearance of such spaces, but to alert us to opportunities for reclaiming public space through the attitude and activity we bring into them. Drawing on our argument that the very mental gearshift by which we become citizens and practise citizenship by moving through our physical environment also creates public space(s), we will draw on some illustrative examples that illustrate how reclaiming public space through the activities we engage in it, paves the way for producing such space(s).

In the context of 21st century city life, reclaiming public spaces as terrains for the practice of citizenship involves re-learning 'how to move politically' (Lepecki 2013: 13) and doing so in ways that involve going beyond the limits of what are considered morally, socially or legally acceptable ways of being in and using public space. To practise citizenship as civic performance on the move, in public space is to confront and navigate it as something akin to a forbidden zone due to the privatization, securitization and 'militarization of city life' (Davis 1992: 223) where 'public activity is sorted into strictly functional compartments, and circulation is internalized in corridors under the gaze of private police' (Davis 1992: 223). Walking on and moving through public spaces, therefore, becomes synonymous to trespassing on privatized, 'pseudo-public' property (Davis 1992: 226), while occupying or reclaiming public spaces inevitably becomes a subversive and transgressive act under conditions of over-policing and over-surveillance. Such privatization of the public realm, and its policing as property does not just distort the meaning and morphology of public space, as the physical location where a social body of citizens assembles to be(come) public, but also alters the political and social circumstances that can give birth to it as a lived experience, unless the new rules of participation in public spaces are broken. To practise citizenship in public spaces that are intensely regulated and controlled, therefore, amounts to a dissensual choreography (Lepecki 2013: 22) which creates the conditions for citizenship to emerge by inscribing (*graphein*) our presence in space (*chóros/χώρος*) as a dance (*chorós/χορός*). Such 'choreopolitics', or politics of space and bodily movement of the kind that Lepecki (2013) advocates, becomes difficult to perform without flouting the rules that regulate how public space is to be used, as well as what it can be used for and whom by. Our search for indicative examples of such activity, therefore, borrow from and burrow into (counter)cultural practices that disrupt existing uses of public spaces, thereby revealing how criminalized the use of public space has become and how it can be transformed as an arena for public social life.

The first example comes from hip-hop culture and the practice of the 'cipher' or 'cypher' which can be described as a 'circle of participants and onlookers that closes around battling rappers or dancers as they improvise for each other' (Chang 2009). A cipher can take place anywhere, but is usually performed in open-air spaces; be it roof-top terraces, public parks, neighbourhood corners, empty or unused parking lots as well as planned or unplanned events or festivals. Part of the excitement of the cipher derives from the energy and thrill of assembling to listen to or perform lyrical competitions, or 'rap battles', as well as from the spontaneity and infectious energy that the simple act of gathering, being together, listening to, and talking in, or 'spitting', rhymes involves. In many ways, the cipher retains something of the much-mythologized *agoras* of Classical Athens or, the lamentably less-revered, African dance rituals where citizens assemble to encounter each other as active members of their political community by engaging in dialogue or communicating via dance to perform citizenship in open public spaces. Describing one such cipher, UK grime music chronicler Dan Hancox (2015) gives an eloquent and evocative description which brings this situated form of citizenship to life:

> It's a mild spring evening, and about a thousand young Londoners have gathered on the uneven gravel and dirt of the Holywell Lane Car Park in Shoreditch, beer cans and spliffs in hand, going completely berserk to grime. This show has no tickets, no VIP, and no permit, just a borrowed sound system set up on the back of a truck parked under a railway overpass. The gates at the entrance have been swung shut, so scores of hyped-up fans are climbing over the 10-foot high wire fence to get in.

This evocative description of a cipher as an embodiment of what the practice of citizenship in public spaces can look like, echoes Franz Fanon's (1963: 19–20) account of the dance circle as a performative expression of citizenship and belonging under colonial rule:

> The dance circle is a permissive circle. It protects and empowers. At a fixed time and a fixed date men and women assemble in a given place, and under the solemn gaze of the tribe launch themselves into a seemingly disarticulated, but in fact extremely ritualized, pantomime where the exorcism, liberation, and expression of a community are grandiosely and spontaneously played out through shaking of the head, and back and forward thrusts of the body.

What both Fanon and Hancox describe, and the cipher or the dance circle embody, is the importance of using public space in the service of associational life as an activity that need not be detached, dispassionate and coolly rational. Rather, being in public amounts to a sensuous lived experience that is vital to politics as an art of sociation even in oppressive conditions that discourage such activity. In our contemporary times such unfavourable conditions are the result of the militarization of public space, while in colonial times such restrictions were the spatial expression of colonial subjugation. Both, however, are aimed at removing any form of action that is not targeted at consumption or slave labour which is not to flippantly equate postmodern securitocracy with colonial plantocracy but to show a similarity in how subversive and transgressive the use of public space can be when it is designed out of social life.

A second example of using public space for the benefit of citizenship can be drawn from skateboarders and graffiti writers who transform public spaces from hyper-regulated environments into arenas for playfulness, sociability, as well as creative and political expression. By gliding through and spray painting on public space, skateboarders and graffiti writers challenge existing uses and meanings of urban life, while also reclaiming and re-appropriating public space to show how it can be re-conceived and experienced as a malleable surface that can serve our expressive, participatory, public needs instead of posing as a fortified stronghold which prioritizes the movement of capital over the movement of people. As Borden (2002: 195) puts it, skateboarders don't just navigate public space on wheels but 'carv[e]' it out by: '[R]ethinking the suburban drive as ocean surf, taking over schoolyards and drained swimming pools, and, in the purpose-built skateparks, producing a super-architectural space in which body, skateboard and terrain were brought together and recomposed in an extraordinary encounter.' (Borden 2002: 179)

In so doing, skateboarders radically disrupt and give new meaning to the 'form and political mechanics of urban life' by emphasizing 'pleasure rather than work, use values rather than exchange values' and 'activity rather than passivity' as 'potential components of the future, as yet unknown city' (Borden 2002: 179). In a similar vein, graffiti writers make their public presence felt by occupying public space on their own terms through visual interventions that rewrite the script of what messages can and do circulate in public, in what form, expressing whose viewpoint, what standards or values and serving whose interests. In making their public interventions through drawings that are scribbled, scratched, stencilled or sprayed illicitly on walls and other surfaces in a public place, graffiti writers, like skateboarders, remind us how citizens' voices are drowned out in a sea of traffic, storefront, and CCTV signs, corporate ads, company logos, and a host of other visual reminders of how hyper-consumerist and over-securitized our experience and aesthetics of urban life has become. As Ferrell (1993: 176) argues:

> Graffiti writing breaks the hegemonic hold of corporate/ governmental style over the urban environment and the situations of daily life. As a form of aesthetic sabotage, it interrupts the pleasant, efficient uniformity of 'planned' urban space and predictable urban living. For the writers, graffiti disrupts the lived experience of mass culture, the passivity of mediated consumption.

Such refashioning of public space allows us to see and act towards it as something we can shape, and empowers us to do so by redeeming public space as our own. A similar sentiment informs our last three example of (re)making public space(s): the Reclaim the Streets (RTS) party protests of the 1990s; the parading brass bands, or second lines, of New Orleans; and the more recent Grenfell Silent Walk protests.

The RTS party protests were founded in the early 1990s as both a form of protest and a type of party with the aim of reclaiming the streets 'FOR walking, cycling and cheap, or free, public transport, and AGAINST cars, roads and the system that pushes them' (Jordan 2009: 2807). Armed with such an aim, participants in RTS collectives were initially involved in interventions that had an ecological focus and articulated a critique of the motorization of public space, by painting cycle lanes on the roads at night and picketing car fairs. In addition to such objectives, however, RTS parties gradually grew into what their name describes by organizing illegal, or rather unlicensed, street parties that were aimed towards reclaiming 'the right to uncolonized space – for homes, for trees, for gathering, [and] for dancing' (Klein 2000: 312). More than a movement with a fixed manifesto, settled hierarchies, or authoritative action plans RTS became a rallying cry and a broad international movement against global capitalism and its deleterious effects on the ecosystem and urban culture, but positively carnivalesque in spirit. It is therefore that spirit of rescuing urban life from marketization that RTS serves as an excellent case study of how to reclaim public space as an arena for celebrating citizenship as a pleasure-seeking endeavour.

Similarly New Orleans brass band, or second line, parades are part of a rich musical and civic tradition of 'takin' it to the streets' by marching through them as a joyous, creative and publicly-situated form of citizenship. With their roots in the early 19th century, the parading brass bands of New Orleans accompany various Social Aid and Pleasure Clubs which were founded in the Black communities of New Orleans as a way of pooling resources and providing financial assistance for their members in the form of medical insurance, funeral costs, disaster relief and other difficulties. But as their name suggests, Social Aid and Pleasure Clubs also offered 'pleasure' in the form of street parades which snake through the neighbourhoods where club members live. On any Sunday afternoon from September to June, second lines dance their way through the city performing not just their allegiance to their respective club, but acting out citizenship in a live(d), grounded manner.[11]

In a more soundless, yet no less powerful way, the Grenfell Silent Walk protests are held on the 14th day of every month to commemorate 14 June 2017, when a fire engulfed the Grenfell tower block in West London resulting in the death of 72 people while hundreds of others were left displaced and traumatized.[12] The aim of these silent walks is both commemorative and political, if the two can ever be separated in the context of this tragedy. The silent marchers gather to walk together in order to remember those who lost their lives in the fire, while also challenging the Kensington and Chelsea London Borough Council and the Kensington and the Chelsea Tenant Management Organisation which was responsible for the borough's council housing. The silent marchers' presence, therefore, becomes an embodiment of citizenship as a tangible, felt intervention in public space which is also a protest against a political environment that creates social injustice through negligence towards its most disadvantaged citizens. By paying tributes to the victims of the fire and protesting against injustice, these silent walks are a powerful embodiment of how the physical occupation of urban public spaces can serve both as a location for political protest and a source of community cohesion, thereby revitalizing our sense of belonging as citizens (*polites*) in the political community (*polis*) we reside in and can be a vital part of.

All these examples demonstrate how to (re)make public space(s) as places where 'the public' can live their social lives by occupying and stamping them with their presence, rather than simply traversing them on the way to the commercial marketplace or avoid them altogether as forbidden zones where citizens are not allowed to tread for fear of being accused of trespass. But they also remind us of the importance of reinventing and repurposing public space as a platform for citizenship as a result of the mindset and the activity we bring into the spaces we walk on and occupy. This is an important qualification as it encourages us to (re)define 'the public' not merely as a euphemism for 'the people' or a long lost civic Eden, but as an ecosystem or an associational infrastructure which is composed of a sense of self (identity) and a way of life (practice) that makes room (space) for citizenship in everyday life. The difference between those competing visions of and narratives on 'the public' is that what we espouse in this chapter encourages us to see public life not as something that pre-exists as an essence but an activity that is brought about through what we are, what we do and the place where we make it all happen. In doing so, 'the public' then is demystified and can become something we associate as, something we do with others and something that is collectively created and imprinted on our physical environment as a relationship which is renewed daily rather than a far-flung telos or an unachievable chimera. Our effort to redefine 'the public' as an identity, an activity we engage in, and a space that we create as a result has been aimed at offering a more empowering vision for thinking about and acting towards the public, without quotation marks that denote something that it eternally discussed as an abstraction; preferring instead to revive our public selves and public deeds as a lived experience that can be moulded into our social reality. We saw this as a challenge when we began this project, only to see it mutate into something else entirely as a consequence of the COVID-19 crisis.

In the context of current technological developments that have ushered in an era of social media, much of this is complicated further by the question of how digital technology can be used by publics in order to be(come) and remain 'public'. Or indeed the sociopolitical implications of our dependency on digital platforms during lockdown and social distancing. Navigating the Scylla of democratization of connectivity that social media affords and the Charybdis of social isolation and fragmentation that they encourage, thinking about the role of technology as a platform for public life inevitably leaves us rowing in choppy waters. Yet this is the challenge that is taken up in the next two chapters, which examine the uneasy but not always extractive or doomed relationship between human values and the devices through which they are often embedded into our social lives. The thick and multimodal ethos of publicness we have introduced is our guide to this endeavour, challenging us to explore how platforms can be used to *produce* the public while negotiating the many threats they pose to it.

The History of Platforms

To understand the emergence of digital platforms it can be helpful to look back through the history of the media in order to understand how new media technologies have always been embedded within a broader apparatus of technical developments. The materialist phenomenology of Couldry and Hepp (2018) conceives of a sequence of *media systems*, underwritten by technological advances with an array of interdependent effects. The broadcast media system emerged with electrification, the capacity of media to operate through electronic transmission (Couldry and Hepp 2018: loc 1299–1375). Numerous media emerged from this, ranging from the telegraph, through to telephony and broadcast media, with their own particular dynamics and effects. However, the capacities of the media system as a whole were defined by simultaneity in terms of public broadcast and personal communication. Exploiting these possibilities facilitated the growth of enormously influential media organizations, producing connectivity through shared patterns of experience grounded in their production cycles and control over the relatively unified attention space within a media system where broadcast capacity was only accessible to a few.

Under these conditions there was a relative scarcity of representations of *publics* in their own terms, ensuring the social visibility of those which did pass through the many filters in operation. Professional expertise meant representations of lives tended to be presented in appealing and engaging ways, filtered by professionals based on an expectation of what will win the attention of a general audience. Furthermore, the commercial imperative to ensure an audience means norms, genres and expectations will be shaped by the past experiences of these professionals and lessons learned from them. While more differentiation entered into the system in its later stages, as the number of television channels expanded and the audience for print media was increasingly segmented, the media system facilitated by electrification appears remarkably closed, particularly in terms of the representation of publics within it, in comparison to what has emerged with digitalization over the past three decades (Carrigan 2016, 2018). However, as Wu (2010: 214) points out, the fragmentation of audiences is the norm and their unification is the exception. In this sense, we are returned to 'the more scattered pattern' of attention which characterized audiences prior to the era when broadcast and print media were dominated by a small number of channels.

It should be stressed this apparent heterogeneity includes a centralization of power for content producers and content distributors, as opposed to being a free market utopia in which a thousand flowers bloom. The 'triple revolution' of mobile computing, the internet and social networks has consolidated into a new media system, with radical implications for the representation of human lives (Rainie and Wellman 2012). Two and a half billion Facebook users, two billion YouTube users and a billion Instagram users appear to speak for themselves (Statista 2020). However, these headline figures entail blind spots which we cannot ignore: some of these users will be much more active than others, many will have multiple accounts, much of the activity will be oriented towards commerce rather than everyday life, and large swathes of the remaining population do not participate on any of these platforms for a whole range of reasons. Furthermore, only half the world is connected to the internet, with current penetration rates of less than 60 per cent in Asia and Africa (Internet World Stats 2019).

There are obvious parallels to the speed with which these developments have shaped the world. As Urry (2013: 37–38) observes, a cluster of new systems emerged in Britain in a short period around 1840, encompassing the first railway system, national post system, commercial electrical telegram and scheduled ocean steamship. To draw this parallel doesn't mean we should treat breathless invocations of the 'fourth industrial revolution' uncritically, but it does suggest that the changes we see around us might later come to be regarded as of epochal significance. If mobility were the defining capacity of the aforementioned technologies, as Urry (2013: 38) observes, it would surely be monitoring which is central to the innovations we see around us. There is a *reflexive capacity* to digital infrastructure, in the sense of producing knowledge that is potentially action guiding in the course of its mundane operations, which is of immense sociological significance (Thrift 2005). The concept of a *platform* can help us understand this capacity and how it is being presented by those who are utilizing it for commercial ends. All signs from the COVID-19 crisis point towards the platform economy growing at an accelerating rate, given increasing reliance on them for delivery, communication and entertainment. During this time *physical distancing* has not meant *social distancing,* enabling connectivity and isolation to co-exist for those working from home. However, the limited nature of this experience draws our attention to the class dimensions of the platform economy, expressed in the contrast between those comfortably working from home and those undertaking the platformized labour which makes that comfort possible. To suggest we focus on platforms does not entail a preoccupation with the 'virtual' but rather a commitment to understanding how digital infrastructures facilitate complex processes which traverse the boundaries of the unhelpful distinction between the 'online' and the 'offline'.

The rise of the (digital) platform

What is a platform? The term is ubiquitous within literature on social media, including the present text. It often substitutes for what might have previously been termed a 'network', recognizing there is more to social media than the social networks it facilitates and the social networking services that were dominant among its earlier instantiations. It further signifies the knowingness of the speaker, implicitly acknowledging seismic changes that have led critics like Srnicek (2017) to speak of 'platform capitalism'. It is also a term embraced by corporations themselves, incorporating a diverse range of organizations (from old-school social networks to the face-to-face provision of services within the so-called 'sharing economy') into a common conceptual space. This is a space within which critique has thrived, as can be seen in the 'platform co-operativism' advocated by Scholz (2016) or the 'protocol communism' suggested by Rushkoff (2016). But business bullshit has proliferated even more readily, with the notion of a 'platform' being a reliable means through which upwardly mobile entrepreneurs can frame their operations as part of this wave of the future. Much as perhaps social scientists can adopt the language of platforms in order to place their work at the (perceived) cutting edge of sociotechnical change. It is a term which facilitates an epochal cut, marginalizing continuities in order to facilitate a rhetorical opposition between the 'old' and the 'new' (Crow 2005, Carrigan 2018). The exact interests being served by making such a cut might vary considerably but the capacity of the 'platform' concept to perform this discursive work, as well as the temptation inherent in it, suggest we ought to be cautious when one speaks too unreflectively of platforms.

One of the earliest advocates of its sociological use observes how it has drawn on a specific computational meaning, as a 'programmable infrastructure upon which other software can be built and run' that in turn relied on an older sense of a platform as 'an architecture from which to speak or act, like a train platform or a political stage' (Gillespie 2010). Among the earliest technical uses were Microsoft's description of Windows as a platform in the mid-1990s and their one time rival Netscape's public statement of a cross-platform strategy for the web browser (Plantin et al 2018: 296). However, the technical sense of programmability came to be replaced by the foregrounding of human action in more recent uses which focus on digital media of the form we examine later in this chapter (Gillespie 2018). It is an ambiguous term and there are subtle variations in how different groups talk about and understand platforms (Gorwa 2019: 856). To a certain extent this reflects the over-determined character of the word itself in which computational, figurative, architectural and political meanings come together to produce a resonant term which simultaneously trades off multiple meanings (Gillespie 2010: 349–350). This is entrenched by the intellectual politics implied by the use of the term within the academy, as what has been called platform studies intersects in antagonistic and complex ways with existing fields of study[1] (Apperley and Parikka 2018, Plantin et al 2018). This compounds the difficulties created by the self-interested embrace of the term by firms operating these platforms. The terminology of 'platform' is put to profoundly ideological uses by firms which have a vested interest in presenting themselves as neutral mediators of activity undertaken by others: letting new forms of social interaction happen while stepping back as mere facilitators (Gillespie 2010). In doing so, it becomes easier to stave off legislative intervention, even if firms like Facebook, Google and Twitter seem increasingly to accept that this rhetorical strategy cannot be sustained in the face of their increasing centrality to social life. The role of the 'platform' concept in fighting a rear-guard action against regulation might lead one to conclude the term is more trouble than it is worth. However, we wish to persist with it for three reasons:

- It enables us to connect corporations and their services in important ways. Ensuring we distinguish between the platform and the firm operating it enables us to consider the relationship between emerging sociotechnical forms and the business models emerging *with* them, inviting questions of how the former is shaped by the latter and vice versa. It draws attention to the possible ascendency of these sociotechnical forms and their associated business models, as well as their implications for how we conceive of capital accumulation (Zuboff 2019).

- It ensures we recognize that sociotechnical innovation *is* taking place, even if firms have a vested interest in overstating the extent of their innovation and the implications likely to flow from it. Cloud computing, machine learning, widespread broadband, high speed mobile internet and the proliferation of network devices enable new forms of coordination and cooperation across time and space (McAfee and Brynjolfsson 2017). The platform model is an *expression* of these developments even as its meaning is rendered murky by the business interests tied up in their growth.
- It helps us see the connections between different forms of platforms. Social media platforms like Twitter, Facebook and Instagram are the focus of our book because of their significance for the production, circulation and application of knowledge. But we want to stress the characteristics they share with cloud platforms (Amazon Web Services, Microsoft Azure), service platforms (Uber, TaskRabbit), subscription platforms (Spotify, Comixology) and sales platforms (Amazon, eBay). In this sense our argument about public sociology and social media platforms could be one element in a broader argument about sociology as a discipline and platforms in general.

To stress the connection between different forms of platforms does not imply their *similarity*. It follows from our first point that differences in service, business model and the relationship between them need to be respected. For this reason we are only going to touch on the platform model in its broadest sense here before turning to the *business model* of social media platforms later in this chapter and the *business climate* it creates for other firms in the subsequent chapter. However, what they do share is a common basis in the aforementioned infrastructure of digitalized social life, ranging from what Delic and Walker (2008) call 'emerging computational mega-structures' down to the personal devices which obliterate the distinction between online and offline (Carrigan 2018). Platforms are made possible by a cluster of technical innovations which have rapidly become a familiar feature of everyday life. For example it would be difficult to imagine how most platforms could operate without smart phones, mobile internet and cloud computing. However, a focus on the technology shouldn't obscure the significance of the coordinated interaction which the technology facilitates. Platforms in this sense are technical infrastructures which create opportunities for interaction that would otherwise be absent: 'digital infrastructures that enable two or more groups to interact' as Srnicek (2017: loc 596) puts it in his influential account. Exactly what form this interaction might take varies considerably; for example, the interactions facilitated through Instagram and through Uber have little in common. However, there are common features which make it meaningful for us to speak of a platform in each case, in spite of the differences between them. Srnicek (2017) suggests three key characteristics of platforms:

1. Platforms act as intermediaries between different users, facilitating the production and exploitation of digital data from the ensuing interactions. Platforms in this sense have an epistemic privilege, as well as a commercial priority, over the activity taking place through their affordances. While they can facilitate activity by eternal actors, in some cases building a business model on precisely this, it is the platform itself which is necessarily best placed to generate data from this activity and deploy it to commercial effect.
2. Platforms are reliant on network effects, with their commercial value and user-value depending on how many people are using the platform and how regularly they are doing so. This produces a 'winner-takes-all' or 'winner-takes-most' dynamic where the dominant platform within a given category will enjoy an ever-growing competitive advantage over the others.
3. Platforms are prone to using cross-subsidization to draw more users into the network, deploying pricing structures which enable free services at the point of contact with the user because of the gains which can be made elsewhere. It is only by drawing ever more users into the network that a platform has any hope of being the winner within its category.

These three features of their business models don't exhaust the sociological significance of platforms. In many cases platforms act as what Giddens (1991) would call 'disembedding mechanisms'. A service platform like Uber inserts itself as an intermediary into an existing social relationship between drivers and riders (itself embedded within a network of relationships with a proximate licensing authority, a dispatch firm, potential owners of the taxi, and so on). It relies on network dynamics and access to cheap capital to scale this model with the intention of squeezing out the assembly of previous relations which *facilitated* but only contingently *mediated* the relationship.[2] The only occasion on which a rider encountered the taxi dispatch firm was if they phoned to book ahead, even while it lurked in the background as the condition for the interaction. In contrast the entirety of the interaction is mediated through Uber, substituting the scaffolding of local relations for distributed ones with a platform: this includes the development of trust relations which are inflected through the platform's system of reciprocal rating rather than emerging intersubjectively with the driver one has on a particular occasion.[3] Uber's explicitly antagonistic approach to municipal governance becomes more sinister in this light with the platform coming to appear as a machinery for obliterating contextual embedding (Stone 2017). It is a striking example of a social practice 'being removed from the immediacies of context, with the relations they involve typically being stretched over large tracts of time and space' such that '[l]ocal experiences and events are shaped by processes taking place on the other side of the world, and vice versa' (Stones 2012). While the enforced deceleration of COVID-19 has disrupted the business model of platforms predicated on an ever-growing appetite for mobility by consumers (for example Airbnb) it has fuelled demand for platforms which facilitate immobility, by enabling in the home what would formerly have required a journey outside of it. For this reason, we expect the present crisis will accelerate the process of disembedding, by expanding the pool of social action which typically depends on the mediation of a platform.

This is a brief sketch of a much more complex issue which only applies to some platforms and doesn't engage with the additional complexity entailed by platforms *creating* new activity in the process. There are many conceptual and empirical issues which we cannot do justice to here[4] but hopefully we have illustrated the potential sociological significance of platforms. The tendency for *functional replication* within the digital economy compounds this effect by ensuring multiple competitors within any area seen as being viable. We stress 'seen' here because so many of these start-ups fail and there is increasingly prominent discussion within tech circles of the limitations inherent in the 'Uber for X' model which was dominant for a period of time.[5] But, nonetheless, the potential disembedding effects are likely to be more pronounced, at least in the short term, if multiple start-ups are trying to insert themselves into existing social relationships in the manner described previously. The failure rate of platform start-ups raises the question of longer-term consequences though. It might be that one firm survives the waves which engulf the others, as many of the venture capitalists are betting when spreading investments across a dizzying array of firms in the expectation that one or two real successes will mitigate the potential for many losses. But what happens if the category itself collapses, after years of being propped up in an otherwise sclerotic investment climate by cheap capital and heightened expectations of return? The longer-term implications of the uncertainty at the heart of the platform economy are unpredictable but potentially severe. However, this macro-instability is belied by the micro-control which platforms are able to exercise. Lazega (2015, 2017, 2018) draws attention to their *parameterizing* capacity to establish the horizon of interaction taking place through their systems, as well as what this means for social power (Kornberger et al 2017). This a theme we explore at length in a later chapter, with a view to understanding the significance of publics, public knowledge and public sociology within a landscape where governance is largely imposed by feat in an asymmetric relation where one party has a 'gods eye view',[6] as Lazega (2015) analyses, with the other party restricted to a reactive relationship (Tufekci 2014a).

The exercise of machine learning by platforms only entrenches this asymmetry (Alpaydin 2016). This technology is used across the full range of front-end and back-end services we associate with the platform ecosystem: online search, social media filtering, linguistic translation, email spam filtering, content moderation, voice dictation, chaotic storage, route planning, fraud detection and content recommendation are only a few examples of what has become ubiquitous within platform firms. The techniques which are jointly categorized as machine learning are a key means through which transactional data, produced as a by-product of interaction with a digitalized system,[7] can be leveraged for commercial gain. For example by serving appropriate adverts, presenting appropriate products or establishing optimal pricing for a particular user. They seek to exploit existing data on user behaviour to infer preferences which will govern future activity. There are many methodological, sociological and political challenges raised by machine learning, including the inequalities it gives rise to and its capacity to frequently fail even in its own (narrowly commercial) terms.[8] But what success it is liable to achieve will tend to accumulate over time through the growth of the datasets and past trajectories of machinic interaction with them. This cumulative advantage creates an oligopolic tendency because there are few players with the computational or human resources to fully take advantage of these opportunities.[9] This creates the possibility for firms like Google, Microsoft and Facebook to exercise an immense influence in an economy in which machine learning is likely to become ubiquitous, particularly if we consider the geo-strategic implications of the machine learning 'arms race' currently underway between the US, EU and China with a view to its significance for economic growth and for cyberwar/defence capacity. But for present purposes the salient fact is that platforms are well suited to such operations because of the proliferation of data within their remit, their privileged relation to it and their expertise with which to exploit it. This commercial imperative for **machinic expansion** is explored towards the end of the chapter in order to understand what, following Seymour (2019), we call the **social media machine** lurking beneath the highly modulated user experience which establishes the parameters for the interaction taking place on the platform (Lazega 2017, Carrigan 2018).

A brief history of social media platforms

There is a change of register involved in the switch from 'platforms' to 'media'. It also presents us with a definitional puzzle because *all* media are social by definition, in so far as they mediate between people. From a theoretical perspective this raises the question of what we mean by 'social', with the potential of a detour into a dispute which has plagued sociology, as the self-appointed science of social life, since its inception (Latour 2005). We recognize the significance of the question of what the 'social' in social media means in these terms (Fuchs 2012, Seymour 2019). But our intention is to take a different route, looking to 'social media' as a category which emerged in a particular context and was made to serve specific purposes. To render this legible entails going further back than 'social media' itself in order to understand the contextual shocks which precipitated its social articulation. This is how the infamous investor Peter Thiel, who has played a significant role in the development of the context which gave birth to platform capitalism, narrates the story of the 'dot-com' mania which gripped the financial world at the turn of the century:

> Dot-com mania was intense but short – 18 months of insanity from September 1998 to March 2000. It was a Silicon Valley gold rush: there was money everywhere, and no shortage of exuberant, often sketchy people to chase it. Every week, dozens of new startups competed to throw the most lavish launch party. (Landing parties were much more rare.) Paper millionaires would rack up thousand-dollar dinner bills and try to pay with shares of their startup's stock – sometimes it even worked. Legions of people decamped from their well-paying jobs to found or join startups. One 40-something grad student that I knew was running six different companies in 1999. (Usually, it's considered weird to be a 40-year-old graduate

student. Usually, it's considered insane to start a half-dozen companies at once. But in the late '90s, people could believe that was a winning combination.) Everybody should have known that the mania was unsustainable; the most 'successful' companies seemed to embrace a sort of anti-business model where they lost money as they grew. But it's hard to blame people for dancing when the music was playing; irrationality was rational given that appending '.com' to your name could double your value overnight. (Thiel and Masters 2014: loc 165)

After this gold rush came what some described as 'nuclear winter' in Silicon Valley. High profile firms vanished, much of the investment dried up and the seemingly fertility of the ecosystem near immediately gave way to an arid climate in which little could grow. However, as Cohen (2018: loc 2910) observes, 'Silicon Valley's nuclear winter provided a clear path to dominance for a group of clever, well-connected, already wealthy entrepreneurs'. While the investment climate was austere, the underlying context provided for those with sufficient capital to support nascent enterprises, as internet access grew precipitously over these years. Furthermore, hardware was growing cheaper and more powerful while internet speeds continued to increase. With fewer competitors and a greater demand for viable growth strategies from straitened investments, the environment was one conducive to real business growth for those corporations able to survive the initial winter. For new entrants, 'there was a chance for great success quickly, provided that you arrived on the scene with a new service that was interesting, reliable, and scalable' (Cohen 2018: loc 2908–2965).

The nascent idea of 'web 2.0' should be seen against this background, as a designation enthusiastically seized on by firms emerging from this desolation in order to demarcate their offering from what had come before. In many cases, these initiatives were begun by new entrants to the Valley but underlying their growth were the same old figures, flush with capital and the impulse to mentor the next generation as they sought to get in at the ground floor of what promised to be a second gold rush. For example Peter Thiel was famously an early investor, providing $500,000 at a crucial stage in the platform's early growth. Underlying so many of the start-ups emerging was what has since been dubbed the 'PayPal Mafia': an influential cluster of alumni from the digital payments start-up, moving onto new start-ups after PayPal was sold to eBay. What later became 'social media' emerged through a seasonal change within Silicon Valley, as investment once more rushed in and a second gold rush began, making many new fortunes and consolidating existing ones in the process.

It can be useful to distinguish between the successive waves of start-ups which have come to define 'social media' as a category. Even though we tend to think of Facebook, Twitter and YouTube as being the most established firms in their current social media landscape, they edged out predecessors who failed for a multitude of reasons. It can be jarring to consider how ascendent these firms once seemed. For example, a *Guardian* article from 2007 despaired as to whether MySpace would ever lose its monopoly. Following its purchase by News International for $580 million in 2005, Keegan (2007) worried that MySpace 'could eventually extend Murdoch's influence in ways that would make his grip on satellite television seem parochial'. The reality is that Facebook overtook MySpace in 2008 and the latter service began rapidly losing users in the ensuing years. Friendster and Google's Orkut launched in a similar period of time, enjoying some success[10] but falling into decline as Facebook rose to ascendency. If these firms intimated what social media *could* be, it was the generation of Facebook (2004), YouTube (2005), Twitter (2006) and LinkedIn (2009) which began to actually realize these possibilities. In this sense Friendster (2002) and MySpace (2003) could be seen as only *slightly* too early, almost arriving at a moment when society, culture and technology were ready for social media.

Instagram (2010), Pinterest (2010), Snapchat (2011) and Vine (2012) began to develop new categories of social media driven by the social and technological changes which earlier platforms had brought into being. They leveraged the expansion of mobile internet to make possible forms of sharing which, given the data-intensive character of images and short form video, would have been restricted to desktop internet access only a few years before. Pinterest and curation services[11] like it profited from the over-abundance of sharing driven by the emergence of this second generation and the mass adoption of the first generation: helping people create order from the ensuing chaos, with their collections of eclectic items from different social media platforms then being shareable *through* social media, contributing in turn to the cacophony encountered by all users. In many ways services like WhatsApp (2010), WeChat (2011), Telegram (2013) and Signal (2014) represent a further generation of social media platforms even if their restriction within existing networks pushes against the boundaries of how the term is conventionally understood. Miller et al (2016) helpfully describe these as 'private-facing social media'. As they put it, 'These tend to be used to form smaller, more private groups than QQ or Facebook, often around 20 people or less' in which 'all members can post equally' because 'these are groups rather than the networks of any one person' (Miller et al 2016: 347). They suggest social media can be understood in terms of two scales: from the most private to the most public, as well as from the smallest group to the largest group. In this sense we can see private-facing social media as a (partial) retreat from the publicness and scale inherent in other platforms, as well as facilitating more durable and sustained back channels in circumstances where they (often) already existed.[12]

This helps illustrate what we might think of as the *intergenerational dynamics* of social media, in the dual sense of the interaction of generations on social media (for example, children moving towards private-facing social media once their parents are part of their online Facebook networks) and interactions between different generations of platforms. For example, Snapchat was expressly motivated by a sense that the enforced visibility of Facebook was unhelpful and unwelcome, creating a need for a more ephemeral alternative. The truth of this insight could be seen in Facebook's initial attempts to buy the company for $3 billion dollars, at an extremely early stage of its development, before aggressively attempting to replicate its functionality when this was rebuffed (Gallagher 2018). This is something Facebook enacted with much more success in Instagram which they acquired for $1 billion 18 months after its launch, granting it a great deal of autonomy as it grew to a level of popularity only surpassed by Facebook itself, before beginning to integrate it into their overarching corporate strategy. The same was true of WhatsApp, bought by Facebook for $16 billion in 2014, with both now incorporating into an overarching vision of the firm's place in the social media landscape. If these are a case of the first wave of social media giants consuming their potential rivals arising from the second and third waves, the ill-fated Google Plus shows how an earlier generation of tech firms were threatened by the rise of social media. The likelihood that a new layer of social infrastructure would mediate the web left firms who had seen themselves as disruptors newly anxious about the possibility of being in turn disrupted.

It is important to acknowledge that this account focuses on the American firms which have emerged from Silicon Valley. As Miller et al (2016: loc 507) observe, the history of social media likely began in South Korea with the success of Cyworld from 1991 onwards. However, it has been subsequently supplanted by Facebook and the language barriers which divide the internet, discussed in a later chapter, coupled with the extremely specific sociopolitical context of Chinese social media means that the most popular platforms (such as WeChat,

Sina Weibo and Tencent QQ) cannot easily be incorporated into this account (McGregor 2010, Strittmatter 2018). However, the move we are making for constraints of space and analytical simplicity will be decreasingly tenable over time, as two distinct spheres of social media look increasingly likely to collide. The political struggle over the future of TikTok's American operations illustrates how contentious this meeting has the possibility of being, with the data infrastructures and machine learning expertise of social media platforms increasingly framed in terms of geo-strategic threats and opportunities.

There are other platforms which defy easy categorization. For example, Borrow My Doggy is a platform which connects those seeking dog walkers with willing walkers who would like to occasionally borrow a dog. It's oddly reminiscent of a dating platform in its mechanics, with profile pictures and contact routines, but utterly specific in its scope. In fact we might ask whether dating platforms themselves should be included here, as they *are* social media in an important sense. This is something we decided against simply because their social scientific uses are limited, even if they might are fascinating objects of research in their own right.[13] They also involve a different machinery to the one which is our object of concern here, with their specific purpose leaving follower counts and popularity largely irrelevant (though the launch of Facebook's dating service suggests we might see this interaction incorporated into the machinery of social media in the future). The existence of over 200 dating platforms listed in Wikipedia's (2019) helpful compilation point to the diversity of forms this can take, even if our focus remains on the mass commercial social media platforms which tend to be associated with the term itself.

Platform and agency

The foundation of our argument is that we treat social media as *platforms* rather than *tools*. If social media were akin to a hammer, it would be a remarkably strange one which calls to you 'why not drop what you're doing and take me to find some nails?' every time you enter the room,[14] generating data on your behaviour which it would seek to use to make this siren song ever more effective. Not all the social media platforms fit this analogy,[15] but the ones which have the capacity for *generating publicness* which interests us here do. To treat social media as a platform means we consider how the architecture of a service constraints and enables the action taking place using it. This contrasts with what Van Dijck and Poell (2018) describe as a *social media as tools* approach which regards these services as neutral instruments that enhance or detract from activity but remain fundamentally independent of it. The core insight of what is often called platform studies[16] is that, as Plantin et al (2018: 297) remark of platforms, 'their affordances support innovation and creativity – supplying a base for video games or new media forms – yet simultaneously constrain participation and channel it into modes that profit the platform's creators'. Not only do they mediate interaction in the manner we have already seen but they do so in order to encourage certain *kinds* of interactions. Their operating principles are intended to produce outcomes which further the intentions of the firm operating the platform, even if the multiple and (sometimes) contradictory imperatives which a commercial operation is subject to mean there isn't a one-to-one relationship between a feature of the platform and a strategic objective. But it means we need to analyse the characteristics of the platform in terms of design, implementation and operation within a commercial firm.

In this sense, agency isn't only found *on* the platform in the activity of its users, it is crucial to understanding why the platform is the way that it is. This isn't just a matter of setting the platform up but rather its continuous operation as the service is modulated in real time through the data generated by user activity (Marres 2018). It means that we need to analyse characteristics of the platform as emergent from the activity of agents within the firm: data scientists, engineers, managers etc. But to recognize their role in this way doesn't imply they *determine* the characteristics of the platform because the agency of users, as well as the epistemic horizons of data science,[17] injects an unpredictability into these endeavours which in turn invites further rounds of interaction as platforms adjust to users who are themselves adjusting to the platform. In a sense, it can be seen in terms of structure and agency, described by Archer (1995) as the 'vexatious fact of society': to paraphrase Marx's famous opening passage in *The Eighteenth Brumaire of Louis Bonaparte*, we make history but do so in circumstances not of our choosing. But to leave matters here would understate the asymmetry at the heart of the platform, in which one party has the capacity to determine the conditions of social interaction, even if they can't determine *action* itself (Carrigan 2018, Marres 2018).

This is social structuring of a distinctive sort much more approximating structuralist visions even while the engineers of the structure can't ultimately control what people do within the conditions they have crafted. It emphasizes how the technical operations of a platform have an immense sociological significance if we wish to take the platform seriously as a *context* of social interaction. At times, these operations may be sweeping in their consequences, producing user complaints and protest. Facebook's Beacon update was the most high profile example of this but these user uprisings have been a persistence feature of mass commercial social media platforms. But more often they pass unnoticed as the architecture of the platform is transformed around users who habitually make their way through it. In this sense user experience of platforms has little relationship to the underlying reality of its architecture, with epistemic constraints shielding the platform from immediate scrutiny and the machinery of the corporation shielding it from more reflective analysis. Davies (2020: 16) argues that platforms[18] 'drive a wedge between the "front stage" and the "back stage" of social and political life' by setting up an extractive relation between them in which 'existing relationships built around mutuality and trust' are exploited for profit.

In no way are these operations divorced from the social though, as if they took place in a parallel fiefdom of the firm's own making. Much as interventions reconfigure the context for platformized interaction, these interventions take place in a socioeconomic context. These are technical undertakings but they remain business strategies. Underlying these techniques is a concern to bring about demonstrable improvement in metrics for user growth, engagement and retention which find their way into formal reporting with significant consequences for the firms. For example, when Facebook's monthly and daily active user growth failed to match expectations it was widely reported as a substantial crisis for the company with significant implications for its valuation. This reporting links the technical agency which the firm exercises over the platform with the business environment in which they seek to build a viable business through the operation of that platform. These commercial concerns are not the only consideration at work in determining the character, operation and mechanics of the platform, as we shall explore at length in later chapters (Gillespie 2015, 2018). But they remain the primary consideration for the simple fact that a firm which loses the confidence of its investors will have its long-term future placed in doubt, particularly for the great majority of platform firms which have yet to hit profitability.

It follows from this analysis that we should treat the characteristics of social media as *made* rather than given. Consider for example the 'real time' character of platforms: the sometimes overwhelming sense of simultaneity which so many users have experienced as they lose themselves into the apparent infinity of a feed. This can be particularly intoxicating when it comes to watching events unfold at a distance: seeing a scandal erupt around the world, fallout from a terrorist attack or international condemnation of political brutality live streamed in real time. Such experiences easily lend themselves to naturalization with the temporal excess appearing as an inevitable expression of the sheer quantity of people using the platform: how could it be otherwise when we have all come together to communicate in the way? However, as Weltevrede et al (2014) make clear, this is not a feature of platforms which can explain their social effects but rather something which itself needs to be subject to social explanation (Carmi 2019). In an earlier period of technical development the achievement of 'real time' involved processing being undertaken at a speed sufficient to eliminate perceived delays: an appearance of frictionless temporality is achieved through increasing the speed of operations (Weltevrede et al 2014: 128). With contemporary social media there is a more variegated production of real time, with empirically distinguishable paces being produced by different platforms as a consequence of 'the interplay of content, its storing and algorithmic processing, interfaces, search and rank algorithms, queries, user activities but also time and date' (Weltevrede et al 2014: 141).

The point is not that we should dismiss the experience of real-timeness but rather that we must inquire as to how that 'front-end' experience is produced in 'back-end' architectures, as well as the interests served by such an undertaking. The same is true of other salient features of social media. boyd (2014) offers an extremely useful account of the *persistence, visibility, spreadability* and *searchability* which social media affords communication that is itself explicable in these terms. Each of these characteristics shapes the front-end experience of social media but does so in a way that reflects back-end imperatives. For example, the ease with which content can be shared (spreadability) makes it possible for popular content to be discovered (to 'go viral') and ensures that user generated content which has the capacity to generate engagement will find a sufficient audience to realize this promise.

Once we sustain this line of inquiry we are left aware of a vast affective machinery which remains obscure if we persist with seeing social media platforms as tools or services. Seymour's (2019) concept of the *Twittering Machine* points towards the implications of this for how we engage with what he terms 'the social industry', drawing a parallel to the Frankfurt School's conception of the culture industry. His point is that behind the 'string of calamities – addiction, depression, "fake news", trolls, online mobs, alt-right subcultures' which social media confront us with is an affective machinery attuned towards 'exploiting and magnifying problems that are already socially pervasive' (Seymour 2019: 41). It's possible this machinery could get more aggressive over time. For example, the video sharing service TikTok, with over a billion users, eschews the familiar centrality of existing friendship networks and holds out the promise of instant visibility with an opaque algorithm which can immediately catapult a user's short video into global infamy (Hern 2019). The familiar concern of aspiring influencers to 'stand out' gets supercharged under these conditions but this still confronts us with the prior social questions of *why* young people are aspiring towards influence in the first place (Johnson, Carrigan and Brock 2019).

However there's a risk we fail to grasp the rich life world enacted through platforms, instead prioritizing the systemic features which shape its unfolding. The point is we need both perspectives: system/lifeworld, structure/agency, individual/society (Archer 1995). The challenge is how we relate them when platforms mediate interaction. Under these conditions the problem of *structure and agency* presupposes the problem of *platform and agency*. This means we have to understand how platforms change over time, as well as what this means for the social contexts they operate within and across. For example, is Facebook a walled garden which gradually substitutes for the internet as its consolidation into habit constricts the horizons of its users? This seems to be a likely outcome of projects like Facebook's Free Basics and Alphabet's Project Loon, offering new forms of low cost internet connectivity for selected website and services in the majority world, even if the firms would deny this characterization of their intentions. The capacity of Facebook Instant Article and Google Amp to offer lightning fast access[19] to external content within their own restricted interface is a further move in this direction. The operations of platforms are not fixed and we need a dynamic ontology capable of grappling with their ever-fluctuating boundaries (Bacevic 2019a). The thick representation of the platformized lifeworld serves a descriptive purpose but it risks hypostasing one moment in its development, at the cost of a deeper explanatory account of the relationship between structure/agency and platform/agency.

We should be cautious about too rapidly embracing the metaphor of a 'walled garden' because it implies these platforms are (expanding) containers for online activity. This obscures how much of their activity already takes place *beyond* what we tend to think of as the core services. Firstly, it doesn't help us recognize the growing collaboration between platforms. Facebook's planned integration of its original offering with WhatsApp and Instagram is the most striking example of this. YouTube has already been incorporated into Google's identity management architecture and their previous attempts to forcefully migrate users to the (now defunct) Google Plus network reflected a similar ambition. Microsoft supports integration between its acquisition LinkedIn and other services, encouraging users to combine them in order to bring their professional network into Microsoft apps and external services. There's nothing inherently malign about these initiatives but what Van Dijck (2013) describes as the 'vertical integration' of platforms is more complex than a view of interlocking containers would tend to suggest. Secondly, it detracts attention from the role platforms play as the shadow infrastructure of what they have helped constitute as the 'social web'. As Gerlitz and Helmond (2013) explain, Facebook's 'Like' button draws an ever expanding array of websites into the architecture of the platform by providing the ubiquitous button. By making it easier to signal endorsement and share through Facebook it promises traffic for the website but incorporates it into the platform as a consequence. There are now more than 8 million websites with the Like button, 2 million with the tracking pixel and 900,000 with the share button. This makes it possible for Facebook to track users and non-users alike across increasingly vast swathes of the web. The same is true of other platforms, even if the scale of their operations may dwarf in comparison to Facebook's. But the external availability of sharing buttons is common across the range of social media platforms while the interoperability of logs in can be found between external platforms (such as Twitter and the blogging platform Medium founded by Twitter's co-founder Ev Williams) and platforms within the same operating group (LinkedIn accounts being used to log into the Slideshare service it owns). In this sense we can see how 'platforms are *designed* to be extended and elaborated from outside, by other actors, provided that those actors follow certain rules' (Plantin et al 2018: 298). As we shall see in the next chapter, those rules change regularly and are often self-serving but they are nonetheless *rules*, which invites us to consider how we should conceptualize their apparently shifting borders, as well as how this machinery might develop in the longer term.

The ideology of social media

From the outset, the rise of social media has been framed as a matter of *participation*. This is why social platforms are so significant for public sociology, even if we must be critical of how the firms involved frame their participatory capacities. What was originally called web 2.0 was defined against the static web which preceded it. This involved, as Beer and Burrows (2007) put it in an early paper, 'dynamic matrices of information through which people observe others, expand the network, make new 'friends', edit and update content, blog, remix, post, respond, share files, exhibit, tag and so on'. This involved a significant change in the relationship between the production and consumption of content, such that 'users are involved in processes of production and consumption as they generate and browse online content, as they tag and blog, post and share'. The term itself was popularized through the web 2.0 conferences organized by O'Reilly Media but this merely condensed and profited from something which was emerging throughout Silicon Valley, as the sector's nuclear winter gave way to new opportunities. Internet access was rising, speeds were increasing, costs were falling and a crowded start-up scene had been largely wiped out by the crash (Cohen 2018: loc 2910–2924). Under these circumstances web 2.0 became a unifying brand for a distinct class of entrepreneurs, investors and consultants in a resurgent Silicon Valley. It highlighted a new commercial proposition and heralded a new age of digital capitalism, with the destruction of only a few years hence now framed as classically creative. This periodization ignored the many interactive technologies which predated web 2.0 such as email, usenet, internet relay chat and web forums. But only through such an occlusion could a new class of platforms be established as offering something distinctive and unprecedented (Marres 2017: 50).

Thus the *ideology of social media* was born. We mean this in Žižek's (1989) sense of structuring the *experience* of social reality rather than being a veil of lies which can be lifted to reveal the truth. It accentuates *real* features of social media but isolates them in the imagination, obscuring their interconnection as part of a systematic whole. It presents us with a partial rather than false view of social media, conducive to circulation because it coheres so neatly with prevailing currents in Anglo-American capitalism. Proto-Hayekian themes were rife in O'Reilly's (2009) later reflection on the role of web 2.0 in facilitating collective intelligence, the wisdom of crowds, flexible development and continuous iteration. This draws on the much longer standing marriage of countercultural thought and cyber-utopianism identified by Turner (2006): technology was framed as the means to the leave behind the stultifying bureaucracy which the 1960s counterculture rebelled against. It helped create a sense that living freely, living passionately and living openly could be best accomplished through technology, ideally *within* the technology sector itself (Turner 2006: loc 3838–3846). This radical impulse intermingled with the nascent market populism of the 1990s to produce a techno-optimism which equated *free markets* with *free information*, seeing the network form as an all-purpose mechanism for freedom and innovation (Frank 1997, 2000, 2012, 2016). The ideology of social media condensed this cultural trajectory, even if it remains one element of a broader story. As Marwick (2013: 21–22) summarizes, the claims made about social media:

> ... promised the democratization of celebrity and entertainment, new forms of activism, and the potential for open, transparent information of all kinds. Web 2.0 celebrated the adoption of social technologies as a precursor to a better, freer society, and framed the collection and sharing of information as the bedrock of revolution. Any institution that prevented people from accessing information and using cultural products as raw materials for creativity became an obstacle to overcome, through collective action if necessary.

This sense of insurgency was rife in the early days of social media firms. As Losse (2012: 37) observes, 'The hacker's capacity to surprise – or in Silicon Valley parlance, *disrupt* – is fetishized in the valley as a source of power and profit for tech companies, Facebook among them, which considers its stated ability to "move fast and break things" a core company value'. The embrace of this cultural heritage could be seen in the ubiquity of self-styled hackathons at Facebook, the company's self-chosen address at Hacker Way and the general ethos which Zuckerberg sought to cultivate within his rapidly growing firm. This sense of insurgency came to seem more sinister with the benefit of hindsight, as these firms went from upstarts to titans of global capitalism (boyd 2017). But it is still avowedly *social* in its intention: we provide a means for people to come together, letting us do what comes naturally to us but in a more pervasive and profound way. It is, as Couldry (2014) puts it, a story of 'what "we" do naturally, when we have the chance to keep in touch with each other, as of course we want to do'. His concern is that 'we must be wary when our most important moments of "coming together" *seem* to be captured in what people happen to do on platforms whose economic value is based on generating *just such* an idea of natural collectivity' (Couldry 2014: 885, emphasis in original). It encourages us to see the platform as a neutral stage *on* which action happens, as opposed to an infrastructure *through* which action happens.

Social media platforms present themselves as providing new enablements for and eliminating old constraints on 'natural collectivity': their business model simultaneously relies on monetizing the crowd which they have encouraged to gather, profiling behaviour in a manner susceptible to interference and allowing the growing data mining industry to do further work to this end (Zuboff 2019). The enticing sociability seen to characterize 'us' stands in sharp contrast to the interventions we are susceptible to in virtue of our participation in (digitalized) social life: we stand exposed, fragmented and scrutinized before a diffuse and inscrutable power (Lazega 2015). But we are potentially so enthralled by the sociability of the process that we are unlikely to look across to those other actors standing *besides* and hovering *above* the stage we perceive ourselves as acting on. This sense of a stage is integral to platforms presenting themselves as neutral facilitators of action (Gillespie 2010). Even when the language of platform is not explicitly invoked, it lurks in the background of claims about neutrality made by social media firms. For example Facebook's arguments that it is not a publisher imply it is a platform even when it does not use the term[20]: it claims to merely facilitate the exchange of material by parties who are external to it, as opposed to operating as a publisher in relation to their undertakings. In drawing attention to the social and cultural activity which they make possible, platforms frame themselves as intermediaries: the people are what matter and we are merely providing the conditions for them. This is crucial to their strategic approach to regulatory intervention, as Gillespie (2010, 2018) observes but it also represents their corporate branding and distinctive offering to the world. In this sense the early participatory promise made by web 2.0 has condensed into something more commercially weighty as rapidly growing platforms have sought to define themselves to the world. But the reality is more *demotic* than *democratic,* to use Turner's (2010) distinction concerning reality television, foregrounding ordinary people but doing so in controlled and often self-serving ways. Burgess and Green's (2018: 122) observation that 'the inclusiveness and openness of the YouTube promise that "anyone" can participate is also fundamental to its distinctive commercial value proposition' holds beyond the video sharing platform, even if the expression of it varies between services.

What we're calling the ideology of social media needs to be seen as integral to the business model of social platforms. The promise of cultural democratization is an important aspect of this, as is the political potential which cyber-utopians like Shirky (2007, 2009) saw in these platforms. What Seymour (2019: loc 2884) describes as 'the insertion of the platform brands into a captivating story of a global youth uprising' contributes to their prestige and allure. These events were seized on, including by commentators who had no vested interest in the commercial success of social platforms, as the material expression of the promise that social media could bring the world together. In this sense the mission statements and philosophical speculation that have emerged from figures like Facebook founder Mark Zuckerberg[21] should be taken seriously as organic philosophy native to Silicon Valley, shaping action within a firm that he still exercises enormous control over and shaping opinion across the wider tech sector and beyond. These pronouncements represent a real mission with its own distinctive intellectual sensibility, even if it inevitably intermingles with business strategy and commercial imperatives. We are only beginning to see the peculiarity of the sector represented in popular culture, through shows like *Start and Catch Fire* and *Silicon Valley*. It seems likely it will continue to grow in coming years given the influence this socio-culturally idiosyncratic region is having over the US and the wider world. Losse (2012) and Martínez (2016) engagingly convey what a strange place it is to work in first-person accounts, with Marwick (2013) providing an ethnographic counterpart to their personal reflections. However, it should be stressed that the longer-term ramifications of COVID-19 might displace the centrality of Silicon Valley as a geographical region,[22] even if the firms associated with it continue their growth.

The reality of online participation

Approaching user generated content in these terms helps us recognize the strange duality which characterizes social platforms. For example YouTube's strategy was predicated on making mass broadcasting possible at the same time as the firm recognized how peripheral much of the ensuing content would be to their core business. Internal emails released in a lawsuit suggest that YouTube's expectations of user generated content did not match the significance accorded to it in their rhetoric. The point is not that they didn't *value* this content but rather they recognized from the outset that the capacity of personal videos to *generate traffic* was likely to be limited (Taplin 2017: 102). Seen in this light, 'user generated content' operates ideologically, helping produce a sense of mission for staff and excitement for users, while simultaneously framing infringement as an unintended by-product of platforms with a primary focus on facilitating the circulation of material generated by ordinary people (Gillespie 2010).

The rhetorical embrace of user generated content has been uniform but the role this content has played in the actual growth of each platform is a more complicated matter. It likely varied between platforms, with the aforementioned evidence for instance suggesting that YouTube early on recognized the importance of pirated material for ensuring their own popularity. Stressing the importance of user generated content in this way allowed YouTube to claim it was a different enterprise to a music sharing platform like Napster (Cohen 2018: 2965). Burgess and Green's (2009) early study found that the most popular content on the platform was split in a roughly equal fashion between what they term 'vernacular producers' (amateurs) and commercial producers. But if we consider how the former vastly outnumber the latter, it suggests what tends to be called a long tail distribution: the vast majority of the content produced by vernacular producers achieves little visibility (Anderson 2006). Research on other platforms has similarly found what Rogers (2013: loc 769) describes as a 'tiny ratio of editors to users', often described in terms of a 'power law' (Marres 2017: 148). The YouTube study hasn't been replicated since because changes to the platform and its API make it difficult to operationalize in a comparable way. However, Burgess and Green's (2018) later work found a convergence of vernacular and professional logics over time, partly as a consequence of the platform seeking to encourage the professionalization of amateur producers.

This raises an important question: what interest does a platform have in generating its own cohort of stars? The star system is a corollary of the aforementioned power law distribution. Under these conditions, as Dean (2010) points out, there are inherent inequalities in who is able to stand out on the platform. While 'user generated content' has been central to the self-presentation of social media platforms, evidence suggests they have been aware from the outset of celebrity content and high profile films being the most important engines driving their traffic, even to the point of the deliberate engineering of a star system into the platforms themselves (Taplin 2017: 102, Van Dijck 2013). Even if the so-called '1% rule', suggesting that only 1 per cent of the users of a website produce content in an active way, might have fallen away we are still someway short of the ubiquitous networked creativity predicted by commentators like Shirky (2007, 2009). These platforms are still dominated by a mass of people who are stuck on the margins of the attention economy, a significant number of whom we might suspect as having their cultural production driven by an aspiration to join the burgeoning ranks of micro-celebrities (Marwick 2013, Johnson, Carrigan and Brock 2019). It is certainly the case that digital media has made cultural production *accessible*, relying on devices which are widely available and requiring little specialized knowledge, producing artefacts which by their nature can be reproduced in a potentially endless way without any increase in cost or decrease in quality (as opposed, say, to the risks entailed in passing a photographic album or self-published book around the entirety of one's social circle). The mobility of phones and tablets, as well as the rise of locative social media, ties representations to particular places in which everyday life is enacted, while the audio and visual capacities of phones and tablets allow it to be documented in rich multimedia.

Under the previous media system, difficulties were encountered in sharing material whereas now the challenge is ensuring a *potential* audience, as cultural scarcity gives way to cultural abundance. Social media platforms have 'immense power over what speech is possible' under these conditions 'and their decisions are opaque and not subject to external review' (Zuckerman 2017). Their influence is encountered throughout the cultural lifecycle, encompassing the production, circulation and reception of material. Producers are reliant on them for access to these platforms, increasingly casting social media corporations in the role of media enterprises, in spite of their continued protestations to the contrary. Platforms provide access to audiences, facilitating the discovery of material online through the sharing functionality made available to their users within the networks which the platform has facilitated. Furthermore, they profoundly shape the reception of this material by constituting the environment within which these cultural encounters happen. What are often claimed to be small tweaks, optimizations undertaken for narrowly technical reasons, might have significant consequences for cultural producers in terms of production, circulation or reception. They constitute a constantly evolving architecture within which everyday forms of cultural production take place (Tufekci 2017).

The motif of participation has been integral to social media, as it was to the earlier concept of web 2.0 (Beer and Burrows 2007, Marres 2017). However, the elimination of formal constraints on access has been mitigated by the informal constraints which users find themselves subject to, not least of all the challenge of 'being heard above the din' and all the behaviours this gives rise to (Beer 2013). While the transition from print and broadcast media to digital media can easily be cast in terms of closed/open, homogenous/heterogeneous and professional/amateur, the reality of this transition is rather more complex: we are presented with a sequence of predicaments which take different forms depending on the nature of our practice. But the simplistic narratives which have been self-servingly propagated by social media firms hinder our negotiation with these predicaments, veiling them in Pickering's (2010) sense of rendering them unrepresentable. In the coming chapters we clear away some further conceptual detritus surrounding social media, much of it specific to academics and higher education, before turning to the specific predicaments facing public sociology and how we might reconstruct public sociology in order to better meet them.

Between Publics and Platforms

In recent years, the term 'platform' has become ubiquitous, taken up by both business gurus and critical social scientists in a way liable to leave many suspicious of what appears to be a passing fad. It is a slippery term, trading off a range of connotations which are not always apparent to speakers, helping social media firms shield themselves from their responsibilities as gatekeepers of our media ecosystem at the same time as being used to analyse the business model and hold the firms behind the platforms to account. But it is nonetheless a useful word because it identifies a significant change in how digital technology is being deployed within social life, underscoring a turn towards an approach which has rapidly become ubiquitous.

The utopian ambitions which defined the internet as it grew revolved heavily around **virtuality**, the possibility of escape from the mundane constraints of the physical world and the promise of a better world which could be built beyond them. As John Perry Barlow ([1996] 2019) put it in his *A Declaration of the Independence of Cyberspace*, these pioneers saw themselves as building a world where 'all may enter without privilege or prejudice accorded by race, economic power, military force, or station of birth' and where 'anywhere may express his or her beliefs, no matter how singular, without fear of being coerced into silence or conformity'. The fact it was published from Davos, at the World Economic Forum where Barlow was an invitee alongside other 'digerati', detracts slightly from the epochal character of his declaration and his frustration at the 'self-congratulatory arrogance of my hosts' could easily be levelled at the man himself (Barlow 2006). But it nonetheless captured an ethos which was pervasive, with its resonant condemnation of 'weary giants of flesh and steel' who failed to understand this brave new world which they sought to regulate. He was far from the only prophet of an internet age. Figures such as Stewart Brand, with his often repeated yet little contextualized soundbite that 'information wants to be free', reflected the ethos which was emerging among digital pioneers while also giving it further shape. What they shared was a commitment to Barlow's 'civilization of the Mind in Cyberspace': the promised land which could be built from the capacity of digital technology to undermine the role of gatekeepers, strip out intermediaries and free individuals from the constraints of material existence.

As the second decade of the 21st century draws to a close, the reality of the internet has become something else entirely. Far from a virtual world existing 'out there' beyond society, we instead confront a social order undergoing profound disruption because virtuality is now woven into every aspect of it. For all the hyperbole which accompanies the terminology of 'post truth' and 'fake news', few would disagree that social media has contributed to social and political upheaval, even if there remains widespread disagreement about the character and extent of that contribution. Firms like Uber and Airbnb, leaders in the so-called 'sharing economy', roll through municipalities like juggernauts, explicitly rejecting constraints on their activities and fighting to ensure maximal freedom for these operations. Google and Amazon compete for their voice assistants to take a central place in as many households as possible, in the process ensuring their platforms are woven into the everyday fabric of domestic life. These are just the highest profile example of a process through which the infrastructure of social life is being reconfigured around the operation of a small number of firms with soaring market capitalizations and opaque corporate strategies.

The platforms they operate are sociotechnical systems which enable users to interact within specific parameters, with the data generated by every facet of this activity existing as a proprietary resource to be drawn on by the firm in question. This might be innocuous, used for little more than improving the user experience or tweaking the platform to encourage more frequent use. But it might also be profoundly sinister, as the Snowden and Cambridge Analytica revelations made clear, constituting a shadowy apparatus of surveillance and control which resists oversight and analysis (Greenwald 2014, Harding 2014). Increasing tracts of social life are now being conducted through platforms, with complex implications for power and inequality which we are only beginning to understand at the level of either empirical research or social and political theory. What had once been a dream of disintermediation, the removal of gatekeepers from social life, finds itself transformed into a project to insert distant and opaque intermediaries into every facet of existence.

This makes a confrontation with platforms unavoidable for public sociology, as their implications for *publics* and *publicness* mean our familiar coordinates for these undertakings can no longer be taken for granted. The implicit social ontology of public sociology is being eroded by platformization. The approach we adopt is concerned with social media platforms but these are just a subset of a much broader category, raising a dizzying array of social and political questions which have barely begun to be addressed (Srnicek 2017, Gorwa 2019). This focus leaves our project more tractable than would otherwise be the case, as it narrows our engagement to the role of platforms in the (re)organization of (public) sociologists and the (re)organization of their publics to which they address their activity. But there is a much broader issue lurking in the background concerning the changing character of the public in an increasingly platformized society. As we have seen, 'public' is a nebulous term used in what Mahony and Stephansen (2016) helpfully identify as three overlapping senses: *normatively*, *epistemically* and *ontologically*. In each sense we can see how platforms change what we mean, as well as what is at stake in what we mean.

Firstly, the public is a locus of concerns about how political life should unfold, as a matter of how individuals and groups contribute to public affairs or are impeded in doing so. These concerns tends to rest on the distinction between the public sphere and the private sphere, as well as the changing relationship between them (Papacharissi 2010). It was once claimed that platforms would empower the public to exercise a profound influence over politics outside the boundaries of mediating institutions.[1] But these claims have given way in recent years to ones concerning the fragmentation of social life into a series of echo chambers which render publics untenable, even if the empirical basis for this remains far from conclusively established (Pariser 2011, Margetts 2017a. These are compounded by concerns that what was once called the 'sharing economy' in fact undermines secure employment and fragments communities (Scholz 2016, Stone 2017). Furthermore, the political power of Big Tech is increasingly framed as a political threat in its own right with extensive regulation and anti-trust action on the political agenda for both left and right (Foer 2018, Pasquale 2018, Mason 2019). Democracy is seen to be under threat and platforms are widely considered to be playing at least some role in this (Bartlett 2018, Runciman 2018).

Secondly, the public is an object of knowledge, susceptible to measurement and intervention, capable of being represented through the familiar repertoires of social research (Mahony and Stephansen 2016: 587). In this sense publics and social research have always been bound together, at least in terms of their social representation and the effects which follow from it. But so too has the critique of this relationship and the implications which it has for social life (Marres 2017. While much social research has always been carried out by commercial agencies, the opacity inherent to platforms entrenches the privacy likely to follow from this: the data isn't accessible to external agencies and they would lack the analytical expertise necessary to work with it in the same way even if it was. Furthermore, as Marres (2017) points out, publics don't know they are being enrolled in research in more than the generic terms inherent to rising public concern about issue like surveillance. Whereas older forms of social research treated publics as objects in order to learn how to engage with them as publics, platforms relate to publics in a way that entrenches their objectness (Tufekci 2014a). Can a public still be a public when it is reduced to a collection of data points contained within a proprietary data infrastructure?

Thirdly, the public is something which comes into being under certain conditions, exceeding positivistic attempts to represent it through quantitative methods. This invokes a thicker sense of public in which people assembling together can bring about effects which they could not as individuals, even if this is nothing more than the sheer fact of their assembly (Butler 2015). To participate in this way can be transformative for those involved, leaving them returning to the private sphere indelibly marked by these experiences (Carrigan 2016). But it can also lead to movements being characterized by a striking fragility, coming together in loud and noisy ways but without the capacity to adapt to changing conditions or articulate durable agendas (Tufekci 2014b, Brock and Carrigan 2015, Couldry 2015). The empirical and theoretical questions posed by this are immensely complex (Gerbaudo 2012). But it's sufficient for our purposes to stress that this third sense of publics is a locus of concerns and hopes, with the same tendency towards oscillation between optimism and pessimism as found with the normative sense of 'public'.

The understandable framing of the pandemic as an epidemiological challenge risks entrenching the second sense of public, as objects of knowledge and intervention through which transmission can be controlled until such point as it can be stopped. COVID-19 has involved the evisceration of public life in the sense we introduced in the first chapter: removing the workplace as meeting site for a significant proportion of the population, injecting significant risk into working life for those who cannot work from home, calling into question the sustainability of 'third spaces' between home and work, and so on. For this reason we urgently need to recover a multi-dimensional sense of the public in the face of an epochal crisis of public health, political economy, civic life and governance.

Platforms and their publics

Platforms always imply a relationship to a public, in the thinnest sense of a group of users who are assembled and (knowingly) engaged. Even if a platform fails entirely to attract a user base, its trajectory to that point has been marked by the aspiration to encourage its use. This is what platforms have been designed to facilitate, even if for contingent reasons they've failed in practice. A social media platform filled with virtual tumble weeds is still a social media platform. But the important question is *what relationship* is created with *which publics*? How does this relationship contribute to or diminish their status as a public? How is this dynamic managed by the organization responsible for the (re)production of the platform? The most obvious sense in which platforms build a relationship with their users is through the behavioural data generated by their use. Even if this wasn't the initial intention behind the functionality, the fact of their use being digitally mediated means that the platform producer has an enormous array of data about *who* is using the platform, *how* they are using it, for *how long* and with *what frequency*. There are rich insights made possible by this data, produced in real time in an unobtrusive manner as a by-product of their existing activity (Savage and Burrows 2007). The fact that there are all manner of epistemological, methodological and ethical problems with the form often taken by 'big data' driven research, most powerfully summarized by boyd and Crawford (2012), shouldn't lead us to deny the novel features of such data or the insights that can be generated from it (Carrigan 2018). But it should give us pause in the face of boosters who claim it can provide us with the reality of human behaviour, cutting through the thickets of interpretation and showing us 'who we are when we think no one is looking', as a book by the dating service OKCupid's lead data scientist once memorably put it (Rudder 2014).

User data can provide rich insights into the behaviour of users, with their practical significance being underscored by the privileged relationship the platform provider has to this data. By default only *they* have access to it. In fact they are the only actors who can even know the parameters within which the data is being generated. This makes it easier to leverage the data for analysis and intervention because influence is always liable to be more effective in an interaction characterized by epistemic asymmetries, where one party is known to the other but not vice versa. As Gerlitz and Helmond (2013: 1360) put it, 'Being social online means being traced and contributing to value creation for multiple actors'. This is the sense in which Couldry and Van Dijck (2015) talk about 'social media' as an *appropriation* rather than a description of the social. It is a project 'to move social traffic onto a networked infrastructure where it becomes traceable, calculable, and so manipulable for profit' (Couldry and Van Dijck 2015: 3). It is a machinery which gradually consumes social life, spewing out *representations* of sociality which are at risk of coming to substitute for the substance it has eviscerated (Carrigan 2018). But if we see a platform like Facebook as an engagement machine, it leaves us with the question of what this machine runs on: a fuel described by Davies (2018: loc 4127) as the 'existing commitments and care that we have for each other, in addition to the more egocentric urges to show off', that is *lay normativity* in the sense invoked by Sayer (2011), meaning those human concerns defining the horizon of our engagements with the world (Archer 2000, 2007, 2012). There are a number of forms which this dependence takes for social media firms. While these are often empirically overlapping, it's useful to distinguish analytically between the specific modes through which platforms relate to users.

- Platforms depend on *existing* social relations, approaching users as **connected actors**. This can be seen most explicitly in their harvesting of existing networks, through email contact lists or the social graph from other platforms, in order to ensure users form the connections which will lead them to experience the platform as worthwhile. Their capacity to catalyse new relations, as analysed by Bucher (2013) provides new 'fuel' for the machine. The balance between the two categories varies between platforms. Facebook and Snapchat have a network structure which tends to depend on a thick web of existing interpersonal relationships. Twitter and YouTube can be productive of such a web for sustained users but their functionality in no way depends on it. In fact the latter's networking capacities are relatively opaque to casual users and only come to significance for those who are highly engaged with the platform (Burgess and Green 2018). However, what they share in common is a reliance on turning social connections into data as a means of monetization, as well as leveraging personal connections into user retention[2] by creating an engagingly personal experience.[3] It's for this reason that Facebook began to panic in 2016 about a decline in personalized sharing, as opposed to sharing links to outside content (Hoffmann 2016). The tension here is between what Van Dijck (2013) calls (human) *connection* and (automated) *connectivity*: the capacity to nurture *connection* was among the participatory promises of web 2.0 but the development of social media has revolved around *connectivity*.

- Platforms depend on encouraging us to join, approaching users as **deliberating consumers**. Through the success of their marketing, they seek to recruit a cross section of a broader target population who can be encouraged to become a regular use of the platform, downloading the apps required for use and embedding these into regular habits. There are many activities involved in this which operate *below* deliberation but the extent to which platforms seek to exercise an influence over consumers as deliberating agents shouldn't be underestimated. This has been particularly pronounced in recent years as the backlash against tech firms has led to international cross-platform advertising campaigns which seek to reframe social media platforms and address growing concerns among users about issues such as privacy.

- Platforms depend on *ensuring we return*, approaching users as **manipulable actors**. These are the machinic tendencies of social media we described in Chapter 2. Each platform is under immense pressure to demonstrate a growing cohort of engaged users, with significant penalties likely to accrue if investors lose confidence in their capacity to do this (Lanier 2018). The filtering of content is the crucial mechanism through which engagement can be encouraged, with past data leveraged in order to present users with content which is likely to attract their attention and provoke a reaction. Even Twitter and Instagram, which initially framed their sequential feeds as integral to their services, moved towards algorithmic filtering in order to increase engagement and improve the user experience. Even when it takes the form of behavioural prompting to encourage the renewal and maintenance of friendships, as Bucher (2013: 487) considers, it nonetheless involves a data-driven relationship with users which sits in tension with approaching them as deliberating consumers.

- Platforms depend on the generation of content, approaching users as **creative producers**. This has been part of the offering of social media firms from the outset, promising a means to 'broadcast yourself' as YouTube's early slogan promised. But it has mutated into a broader sense that social media offers the opportunity to achieve fame, even if this has now grown beyond the claims made by the platforms themselves (Abidin 2018). It trades off the sense of social media as a stage *on* which one can perform for the world, operating a back-end calculus in which engaging content can be crowdsourced and widely disseminated in order to keep users coming back to the platform and engaging heavily while they are there. The 'us' which comes together on social media has to be managed in order to integrate this creative work into the firm's ambitions for the platform by encouraging some forms of creative production and discouraging others, in the manner discussed in the previous chapter (Scholz 2016: 87).

- Platforms depend on the ordering of their environment, approaching users as **evaluative agents**. The endless outpouring from users would be overwhelming were it not for the fact they are also a source of what Brutton (2013) describes as 'salience': reacting, classifying and evaluating what they encounter on the platform. Consider Facebook's transition from a chronological newsfeed to an algorithmic newsfeed in 2009. It sought to 'impose a subtle sense of order on the babbling chaos of the growing network' by prioritizing posts which had already proved to be popular. This algorithmic filtering grew as networks expanded and content proliferated in order to ensure users encountered material they would find engaging from an ever expanding torrent that could not be assumed to be so (Abramson 2019: 271). In this sense algorithmic filtering is necessary to cope with the platform's success, as a rapidly expanding user base spends more time on the platform risk overwhelming each other with content (Carrigan 2017a). However, it is reliant on the evaluations of users (through what they click on, how long they spend on it, how they react to it and what they choose to share to others) as well as tacitly assuming those evaluative capacities in the ambition to serve people *relevant* content.[4] Even a mechanism as seemingly reductive as the 'Like' button needs to be recognized as an affective shorthand which seeks to routinize a social reaction[5] (Gerlitz and Helmond 2013). For all its algorithmic complexity, social media filtering is fuelled by salience: a property which users are only able to generate because they are evaluative agents able to draw distinctions and act on them (Taylor 1985, Archer 2000, Sayer 2011).
- Platforms depend on the vested interests of those building businesses through them, approaching users as **enterprising strategists**. Marwick (2013) suggests that social media has

been designed to draw ever more people into this category, inviting them to approach their online activity through the prism of brand identity. This reflects a pervasive culture within Silicon Valley which is captured pithily in LinkedIn founder Reed Hoffman's (2012) book *The Startup of You* (written with by Ben Casnocha). As Marwick (2013: 10) puts it, 'Social media has brought the attention economy into the everyday lives and relationships of millions of people worldwide, and popularized attention-getting techniques like self-branding and lifestreaming'. These developments can be seen in the growth of influencer culture, itself an increasingly familiar feature of media commentary provoked by the growing armies of viral celebrities and YouTube stars (Abidin 2018). This relational mode is the inverse of relating to users as creative producers, holding out the prospect that cultural work through platforms can be a means of building a career in a context where economic prospects for many are increasingly uncertain (Johnson, Carrigan and Brock 2019). The obscene irony is that platforms have been complicit in destroying the conditions under which the vast majority of artists, musicians and authors are able to build sustainable careers (Taplin 2017).

To recognize six relational modes complicates judgements which are predicated on the recognition of one (or two) to the exclusion of others. For the partisans of web 2.0 what matters are the opportunities for creative production which social media platforms open up (Shirky 2007, 2009). For the media ecologist what stands out are connected yet manipulable actors who are changing within a transformed media environment (Vaidhyanathan 2018). For the sociologically inclined media theorist what stands out are the role of social connections in the machinery of the platform (Van Dijck 2013). There is a risk of straw man in these characterizations. It is not our suggestion that analysts of platforms have heretofore only dealt with one or two of these relational modes, as opposed to inevitably foregrounding one or two at the expense of others. However, we do suggest there has been a tendency, within social science and popular culture, to avoid dealing with the multiplicity as a multiplicity[6] and to fail to disentangle these relations on an analytical level. There are a whole range of ways in which platforms relate to their users. It is essential we grapple with this multiplicity if we want to understand publics in an era of ubiquitous platforms because the effects which platforms have on publics are multilayered, tangled and overlapping.

However, from the perspective of users, it appears as if social media platforms pay little attention to their views when it comes to changes on the platform. New features are introduced, old functionality is removed, the interface is tweaked. Sometimes these new features pick up and implement innovations which users have spontaneously brought to the platform, as was the case with the retweet on Twitter that originated with a user convention (Bilton 2013). Often these changes pass unnoticed, helped by being rolled out gradually across different sections of the user base. If there is protest, it inevitably seems to be short lived, as continued use of the platform means indignation fades as the novelty melts into the background of everyday life. If the unpopularity looks set to continue, Facebook are adept at changing course and removing the offending feature, as Facebook did with the Beacon system that broadcasted purchases to followers (Galloway 2017: 101–102).

The really interesting question is how they make this evaluation, leveraging the data available to them about their users to infer which objections are liable to stick and which are not. The predictive capacities of these platforms seem inarguable, at least when operating at the level of the aggregate user base. But the epistemic culture they give rise to exceeds their analytical capacities, expressing a belief that the platform knows users better than they know themselves. This is a sentiment we have seen endlessly repeated by senior figures in tech firms. This is why it is a mistake to assume that platforms don't care about their users because protests are ignored. Instead this is a sign *of* their concern, refusing to take these protests at face value when there is a deeper reality accessible through the platform itself. That at least is what they believe.

In this sense there is a fundamental asymmetry in the relation between platforms and users. Platforms *know* across the front *and* back end, operating through a panoramic perspective on what their users do in real time as expressed through the data generated by their use. There is a fundamental rejection of *interpretation* built into the knowledge architecture of platforms, expressing itself in a reliance on behavioural traces as the means through which to know the truth of their users (Andrejevic 2013, Couldry 2014). But platforms are simultaneously reliant on the *thinking, feeling, caring, making* and *doing* capacities of their users to keep the social media machine running. This is the aporia of social media: platforms produce *known* users as their product but their machinery for doing so is reliant on *knowing* users.[7] Platforms negate human agency while remaining utterly dependent on it. They are committed to rendering it machine readable, atomizing it and trading off it (Carrigan 2019, Zuboff 2019). But they also need to ensure users are willing to return, avoiding their reflective judgements about privacy concerns or time wasting taking precedence over the embodied habits which have accumulated over years of use. This is the terrain on which public formation is now taking shape, pulled in one direction by platforms while pushing them in another, as well as being the field in which political challenges to the growing hegemony of platform firms will be fought (Mason 2019). This is the context which public sociology needs to adapt to, with a resurgent mission and revised modus operandi. But understanding what form this might take involves an encounter with one further piece of the puzzle: the individuals, networks and organization which mediate between publics and platforms.

Caught between publics and platforms

Thus far we have encountered a sparse ontology in which platforms exist in relation to users. To leave matters here would present us with a misleading image of the salient relations existing solely between the infrastructure and those who use it. This would obscure the labour involved in the production and maintenance of the platform; able to fall so easily into the background because the character of digital labour (disaggregation of tasks, distributed workflows, digitally coordinated, and so on) renders it largely invisible when it comes to the user-facing product (Scholz 2016). But it would also miss the many firms which have grown up within the platform ecosystem, building businesses which work on one or more platforms through mediating the relationships which users have with them. For example Gerlitz and Lury (2014: 175) draw attention to the 'data-aggregating services' which 'organize and re-present the personal user data generated by individuals in different social media platforms'. The main focus of their analysis is Klout[8] but they also cite Tweetstats, TwentyFeet, TweetReach, Twittercounter, Crowdbooster, Kred and PeerIndex among others. In some cases these produce a composite score intended to measure and compare influence.[9] In others they present existing user data in new and useful ways, such as LikeJournal which repurposed Facebook likes as something akin to a social bookmarking system. Others offer visualizations of the network connections found on platforms or the patterns of interaction taking place through them. Finally, they cite services which facilitate the curation of social media, enabling users to pull together materials and present them in a manner which tells a story (Gerlitz and Lury 2014: 175–177). This last category clearly reaches beyond their own analytical concern for data (re)presentation and self-evaluation, pointing to a broader range of services which have grown enormously since their publication. Pinterest, Flipboard and Scoop. It are the most successful of a diverse range of services which facilitate curation: inventorying material and providing a qualitative organization which enhances engagement with it (Rosenbaum 2011). Couldry (2012: loc 1534–1732) astutely identifies how this imperative precedes digital media but acquires a new urgency with the abundance that digitalization brings.

There are many electronic precursors to these filtering services such as 'filter blogs', selecting and commenting on material, as well as the much broader category of portals which dominated the early years of the consumer facing web (Rettberg 2008: 13–17, Carlson 2015). But what these newer services have in common is rendering this function an everyday activity, even if their scope ranges from knowledge management in organizations through to individuals mediating their consumption through the production of pinboards. The demand for this functionality can be seen by its incorporation into Twitter through the introduction of Moments (compiling tweets with commentary into a shareable story) and Bookmarks (saving tweets in a private list). In fact one could make the argument that this imperative is inherent to the social media machine. Much of its use involves highlighting material in a claim for attention to it, even as the growth of this activity leads to an escalating threshold on what is necessary to win the attention of others (Carrigan 2016).

Each of these categories reflects a challenge which users face in their relation to the platform. **Influence measuring services** help users understand their standing on a platform relative to others, **data representation services** realize a latent utility of user data by freeing it from the confines of the platform and **curation services** help users cope with the abundance of the platforms by selecting and organizing material found on them in helpful and shareable ways. This is far from an exhaustive list of challenges users face or of services oriented around these challenges. In fact the character of the Application Programming Interfaces (APIs) on which these services rest make it difficult to characterize these services in conclusive ways: the potentially open ended character of add-ons means that there is always the possibility of novel contributions, while the instability of APIs means it is always likely that these contributions will be rendered untenable by later changing in the platform. Gerlitz (2016: 28–29) draws attention to the 'extensive sets of rules and strategy plans' determining which enactments of these opportunities 'are supported by the platform and which are not'.

The interpretive freedom inherent in the API is constrained in unpredictable and opaque ways by a platform firm modulating its business strategy within a rapidly changing environment. This can raise near constant development challenges for firms operating services which intersect with multiple platforms in a range of ways, such as post scheduling and analytic services like Buffer and Hootsuite. This in turn encourages a thriving sphere of online exchange in which developers, marketers and consultants converse around impending and expected API changes and what this means for their respective operations. In an important sense the practical challenges following from dependence on platforms helps constitute this as a distinct sphere of technological, intellectual and commercial activity.

The pace of change found within this sphere is why it is useful to focus on the relation between platforms and users, in order to understand how firms seek to operate within this landscape to address a problem which users experience or present them with an opportunity that would be impossible within the existing confines of the platform. In an important sense this is crucial to the business model of the platform itself, as the distributed ingenuity of these intermediaries means they will inevitably hit on possibilities which sufficient numbers of users value to make their incorporation into the platform itself worthwhile (Plantin et al 2018: 298). McAfee and Brynjolfsson (2017) frame this in terms of the *crowd* and the *core* in an explicitly Hayekian peroration to the capacity of the former to outstrip the latter in terms of creativity. This dynamic is very common in the development of mobile operating systems and it can often have catastrophic consequences for firms which have built a niche for themselves in this way. For example the social media blocking software Freedom was simultaneously rendered near useless[10] by an update of iOS which also introduced comparable functionality through the Screen Time system. There is no evidence Apple's decision to disallow this functionality from a recent iOS update had anything to do with the firm. In fact one could assume the firm is barely on Apple's radar beyond the testing their software goes through to gain access to the App Store. But the fact this decision coincided with the introduction of Screen Time is emblematic nonetheless, revealing the vulnerability which firms operating at the intersection of the platform and their users face.

Publishers as intermediaries

The other type of intermediary we want to draw attention to is somewhat different. It might seem counter-intuitive to describe online publishers, such as BuzzFeed and the Huffington Post, as intermediaries in this sense. Would it be meaningful to talk about as the *Guardian* as an intermediary between the printing press and their readers? It would not because the readers have no independent relationship with the press, itself owned and operated by the company from which they purchase their newspaper. However, when it comes to social media platforms, users have an existing relationship with the platform which transcends the one they have with the publisher. It is tempting to cast this in terms of *passivity* and *activity* such that old media involved silent consumption in the private sphere and new media meets people in a public sphere where they are already participating. As Marres (2017) explains, the reality is more ambiguous. It is not just that many of these nascent publishers rely directly or indirectly on unpaid labour, as do the platforms themselves (Fuchs 2012). 'From audience to participant' overestimates participation in new media and underestimates it in old media:[11] ignoring the ratio of active participants to lurkers in the former and ignoring active engagement found in the latter, even if its habitual confinement to private life meant it was not immediately visible (Marres 2017: 148–149). Once we leave behind the old/new and audience/participant distinctions it becomes easier to identify the role that publisher intermediaries play in organizing the relationships between platforms and their users. They attract attention, inculcate habits and drive trends even as they depend on activity which takes place elsewhere on the platform. They rely on winning audiences through the platforms on which they operate, with the larger publishers now having a presence across a dizzying array of platforms, in the process contributing to the organization of attention and interaction on these platforms.

In the early years of platforms the Huffington Post was the most prominent example of a publisher operating as an intermediary in this sense. It was co-founded by later BuzzFeed founder Jonah Peretti and the early seeds of the latter's approach can be seen in HuffPost's operations. Within six months of operation it had surpassed the traffic of the *Wall Street Journal*, the *New York Times* and the *Washington Post* (Abramson 2019: 23). It used Google Trends data to drive editorial decisions, it normalized the repackaging of external content as new features, used search engine optimization to ensure these adaptations appeared above the originals in Google searches and developed expertise in choosing titles which ensured their version would be more likely to be clicked on (Abramson 2019: 25–29). But its operations were still fundamentally human, unlike the era of data science driven content production which Peretti's BuzzFeed inaugurated.

With sufficient funding and expertise these intermediaries function as laboratories of optimization, working at the most granular level to adapt their material to the environment in which it has to thrive. For every item posted on Upworthy staff would write 25 different headlines which would all be published before software identified which was generating the most click throughs on social media (Foer 2018: 138). Porntube sites algorithmically select thumbnails through real time testing of which choices maximize engagement (Ronson 2019). What's striking about platform intermediaries, at least ones flush with venture capital, is how comprehensive the analytics apparatus they construct tends to be. It penetrates all aspects of the firm and aggressively pushes activity in the direction of maximizing virality. For example, BuzzFeed sends out score cards to staff based on the popularity of their material and awards virtual badges to each day's winners. Those who regularly achieve arch-viral posts with at least a million views are inducted into a sequence of clubs with ever more rarified names. While the cultural trappings are clearly tongue in cheek, it points to the pleasure which the company encourages staff to find in virality and the pressures which those who fail in this respect quickly find themselves subject to (Abramson 2019: 116–117). A thriving industry has emerged which develops systems that can be sold to publishers who don't have the resources to undertake such projects in house (Christin 2015). There is an obvious competitive dynamic at work with optimization by one publisher inevitably encouraging it in others who seek to keep up, as what's perceived to be best practice shifts rapidly within an uncertain landscape.

However, optimization in this sense implies the rules of the game are well known. Within known conditions it is possible to modulate the creation, curation and communication of material in order to increase the likelihood it will be opened, engaged with and shared. But the conditions are changing because the rules of the game are far from fixed. The arms race this generates resembles the early incorporation of search engine optimization into business practice: 'a thicket of rumor, folklore, sophisticated technical activities, and behavior classified as "spam" – some of it nebulously illegal and some of it sanctioned by its adoption into corporate culture' (Brunton 2013: 144). Google rapidly became so prized as a source of traffic that constant adaptation to its shifting incentives becomes the norm, compounded by the thick layer of bullshit that inevitably emerges under these conditions.[12] Facebook has been no less mercurial but for different reasons. If shifts in Google's algorithm have predominately been micro-gestures of a frequently technical sort[13] rather than editorial policy, Facebook's shifts have reflected corporate strategy at the highest level as the firm has sought to steer itself through a politics of platforms that has only become more difficult with the firm's growth (Gillespie 2010).

The transition from prioritizing friends in the news feed to prioritizing (trusted) publishers and back again has been an immensely difficult journey for firms whose viability depends on their successful negotiation of these changes. It's no surprise that 'the Facebook gods' figure in both the corporate planning and folk wisdom found within them (Abramson 2019: 310). For example Upworthy, committed to uplifting viral content, suffered a drop in traffic from 87 million to 20 million within a couple of years. The rationale for Facebook's decision in this case was perfectly plausible, with click throughs to optimized headlines rarely being matched by reads or shares in a way that would suggest people found value in the content (Sanders 2017). But the capacity for such a precipitous drop defines the strategic horizons of intermediaries, rewarding those who can adapt with agility to changes in platform incentives and punishing those who remain set in their ways. The platforms constitute the landscape in which these intermediaries operate, leaving it constantly reshaped by the shifting fortunes and whims of platform firms. What it is tempting to think of as 'old media' are equally caught up in this dynamic, as Caplan and boyd (2018) document, even if their operations spill beyond the boundaries of the category of the intermediary we have introduced here. But they are entangled in the same dynamics in which their business is vulnerable to fluctuations within the platform ecosystem. The declining revenue of print publications during the pandemic means they might dispense with physical copies sooner than expected, leaving them more closely resembling their digitally native competitors.

The dominant assumption in digital publishing has long been that information wants to be free (Doctorow 2014). To publish material without restriction ensures it will circulate widely, creating the largest possible audience which can in turn be monetized through the sale of advertising. That at least is the theory and it underwrites what has been the dominant approach to advertising across social media (Auletta 2018). Advertising revenue relies on a relationship with readers as individuals, in effect selling the attention which has been won to a third party who hopes it can be leveraged towards persuading them to take some action extrinsic to their reasons for visiting this site. However, in recent years the titans of digital publishing such as Huffington Post, BuzzFeed, VICE and Vox have all begun to move away from this model, introducing a range of membership options which seek to monetize the commitment that their audience has to their publishing operation. These have become pronounced during the COVID-19 crisis, as firms have leaned into new funding models in an unstable economic environment.

This pattern reflects the unstable or declining advertising revenues across the industry and the difficulty digital publishing operations face in securing their future, in spite of their audience size and capacity to manage it across platforms. However, it also represents a move from individual to collective, shifting from the persuadability of the individual to the commitment of the collective. It differs in this sense from the introduction of a paywall which simply eliminates the assumption that the material should be free to access while leaving the rest of the model in place. Not only are membership perks a supplement to the existing content rather than a replacement for it, they are perks in the sense of being benefits attached to a role rather than being the substance of that role itself. The role itself is one of supporter, performing appreciation of the site through the act of sponsorship. We use the terminology of performance because these initiatives open up a new role which can be occupied, as well as *being seen* to be occupied, solely through participation in it. There's no way to be a *Guardian* member, with the identity work and social connotations that entails, without signing up to this scheme in order to financially support the *Guardian*. There's a shift in how publishers orientate themselves towards publics, as well as the competitive pressures they face operating within the horizons of the social platforms.

The same mechanism can be seen at work, usually in a smaller scale way, through platforms like Substack and Patreon. The former is a subscription newsletter service, making it easy to make newsletters available to those who pay a certain amount each month. The latter is a crowdfunding platform, building on earlier projects such as Flattr which paved the way for online patronage before being superseded by their newer arrival. It is interesting to note that Flattr was initially a more granular service, allowing a monthly subscription to the firm to be distributed across websites which had installed Flattr buttons in order to allow users to flatter content they valued. But the success of Patreon has gone hand-in-hand with a wider normalization of the model of subscription to individual content producers, offering a monthly donation which comes with certain perks correlating with the size of the donation. It's important to note this switches the focus of support from the content to the content producer.

As an example of what this looks like in practice, one of us uses Patreon to subscribe to the writings of the theorist and commentator Richard Seymour, donating $3 per month as one of his 335 patrons at the time of writing. This provides us with regular blog posts which are emailed directly immediately after they are published. There is little instrumental gain here, as the posts are soon available for free on Seymour's site and there is an extensive back catalogue of articles which are freely available in the same way. In fact Seymour is an interesting example because his categories of support suggest how it is possible to use a platform like this without taking it entirely seriously. Whereas those who donate $3 per month are promised that 'Any doom you experience while using this product will be entirely coincidental', those donating $5 per month are cautioned that 'Your doom will be slow and painful'. The categories continue in this vein, up to and including 'Achingly poignant utopian yearnings' for $20 per month and 'For a darkness of the Left. Give in to the sultry siege of melancholy' for $50 or more per month.

The cautiously cynical distance expressed through this facetiousness is less visible elsewhere on the platform, as we might expect those willing to financially support a content producer to take that person seriously and the vested interest they in turn have in taking neo-patrons seriously. We urgently need empirical and theoretical work to understand this vested interest as a social relation. For example it remains to be established what role the Patreon account of a figure like Jordan Peterson has played in the rise to prominence of this alt-liberal superstar but the financial resources it has facilitated, coupled with the direct connection to an ever expanding base of super fans, has certainly been a factor. However, to focus on a figure like Peterson seems somewhat unfair, as one can find an astonishing range of content producers soliciting donations through Patreon, even if there appear to be the same 'long tail' dynamics we find elsewhere online in which a small minority of content producers monopolize the vast majority of donations. Nonetheless, Peterson surely represents the potential horizon of academic engagement with the platform, even if this might appear to be a negative example for us. There's a model of neo-patronage which could be viable for academics here, even if the capacity to take advantage of this opportunity is unevenly distributed; for example, neo-patronage requires a large and engaged fan base.

Even if it remains individuals who subscribe in this way, these platforms are not defined by individualism in the same manner as online advertising. They draw together people with converging commitments, reflecting their evaluative capacities in having found the same initiative worthwhile, formalizing this (albeit loosely) into a sustained relationship of financial support. In turn the initiatives in question enter into a relationship of accountability and engagement with these nascent communities, with significant implications for what they do and how they account for it. There is nothing inherently progressive about this tendency, as can be seen in the many reactionary figures and movements which crowdfunding models have already helped to inculcate.[14] But it does suggest a changing role for the public within the landscape of social media, as the strategic challenge of the present landscape gives rise to a range of still nascent communal forms, with the capacity to influence how ideas circulate and groups form through the affordances of social media.

The divided soul of the platform

There is a puzzle at the heart of digital platforms. On the one hand, platforms assume the agency of their users and relate to them as thinking, feeling, wanting subjects who can create, collaborate and connect. On the other hand, this agency is computationally dissolved into a series of statistical artefacts which are used to facilitate behavioural intervention aimed squarely at their much invoked 'lizard brains'. This tension isn't just a matter of corporate culture, business model or technological design. It cuts across them all, with a fundamental division between engineers and engineered running through the heart of platforms. This is what Marres (2018: 435) describes as 'a research-centric apparatus, in that their design directly reflects the epistemic needs of the data scientists whose analytic operations are key to their commercial model: to target information to groups of friends, to track shares and likes in the aggregate'. The architecture of platforms is built around knowledge production, with an empirical register which is predicated on the influenceability of users: behavioural traces are generated through their activity on the platform which facilitate real time analysis and intervention, as well as the detection of trends and strategic responses to them (Lanier 2018, Williams 2018). As she goes on to write,

> social media present an environment in two halves, where, on the one side, we find users with 'influence-able' and 'target-able' opinions, tastes, and preferences, while, on the other side, we have authoritative data analysts who

> 'know' the population's fine-grained and ever-changeable preferences and tastes. Scientists – the proponents of knowledge – haven't been by-standers but active participants in the crafting of a media architecture designed to enable the influencing of users' actions. (Marres 2018: 437)

But this fundamental divide finds itself inverted when it comes to the self-presentation of the platform at the level of corporate branding, narrative strategy and organizational rhetoric.[15] Even if the influenceability of users, enacted through behavioural intervention, remains crucial to the growth strategy of the platform it remains peripheral to its marketing. These are techniques which are used to hook people into the platform, nudging them into returning more often and staying for longer. But they are not part of the story that the platform tells about itself, to users, investors and those within the company itself. These stories are something else entirely. On one level these tend towards being a simple narrative concerned, as Pasquale (2016: 309) puts it, with 'the incentives created by reducing transactions costs and creating more opportunities for individuals and firms to compete to provide services'. But these technocratic accounts are just the thin end of a much thicker story about the Great Disruptive Project in which these platforms are engaged, one liable to be transformative for society at large:

> According to some thought leaders in Silicon Valley, global platforms for labor and services will provide extraordinary opportunities for workers. A 'peer economy' of platform-arranged production will break down old hierarchies. Gig workers will be able to knit Etsy scarves in the morning, drive Uber cars in the afternoon, and write Facebook comments at night, flexibly shifting between jobs and leisure at will. (Pasquale 2016: 312–313)

It is a narrative which speaks to people's concerns and commitments, offering a vision of a brighter future in which technological innovation unites individual freedom and economic progress in a rising tide which lifts all boats. It promises to empower people in spite of the machinery which lurks back stage to quantify, analyse and modulate that empowerment (Williamson 2018). It would be easy to reject these claims outright, seeing them as nothing more than self-interested fabrications contrived to legitimate a (digital) boot beginning to stamp on a human face for eternity. It's important to take seriously the possibility of a **digital authoritarianism**: the unprecedented surveillance apparatus rapidly being constructed in China and the digital savvy security industry in which it is increasingly enmeshed should give us all cause for concern (Strittmatter 2018, Robinson 2018). It seems plausible to argue that something akin to techno-fascism is as feasible in the future as post-capitalism or digital socialism (Mason 2016, 2019, Morozov 2019).

In fact at the time of writing, it is increasingly difficult to see how neoliberal capitalism could emerge from COVID-19 in its previous form, raising the prospect of what comes next. If the next mode of governance is coalescing under these conditions, it would be a mistake to see 'the digital' as a specialized element within it. However, we shouldn't allow claims about disruption to obscure the interests and agendas at work here, obliterating continuities in the breathless invocation of the transformation which is underway (Carrigan 2018). For example, the impending threat of mass redundancy driven by automation, the much heralded 'rise of the robots', only makes sense against a background of de-skilling and precarity which has reduced labour to its most machine-like components (Srnicek and Williams 2015, Lanchester 2015). It would be self-defeating to deny the significance of technological advances like machine vision, cloud computing and miniaturized sensors (Ford 2015, Kaplan 2015). But these don't bring about socioeconomic change in themselves even if we can't explain such change without reference to them.

The same is true of the platform economy more broadly, leaving us with the challenge of disentangling the claims made about human agency from the self-branding of platform firms, as well as the broader intellectual tradition from which they have drawn (Turner 2006, Dean 2010). A strategy of detournment can be adopted here in order to rescue the participatory promise of social media from its embedding within the ideology of social media (Keucheyan 2012: loc 4454). In fact this promise can be used to critique the existing reality of platform governance and point to future possibilities (Gorwa 2019). Can we make platforms public? If so, what role can public sociology play in this? This is a theme we will return to later in the book but our intention at this stage is simply to consider what follows from representations of platformized agency being representations, as well as the vested interest which platforms themselves have in this. This infrastructure 'tells about society', to use Becker's (2007) phrase, in a manner profoundly at odds with the mainstream of the sociological tradition: it's hostile to hermeneutics, behaviourist in its orientation and reductive in its treatment of meaning. To have platformized sociality come to stand for sociality as such furthers the interests of platforms in turning social life into data which can be monetized (Van Dijck 2013, Couldry and Van Dijck 2015). This feels particularly urgent after months of reliance on video conferencing platforms to keep in touch with friends and family. It doesn't mean sociality is exhausted by the platform but it does mean we'll struggle to understand its changing character if we fail to account for the platform's (subtle) role in these changes. in touch with friends and family.

To illustrate this point, consider the public assemblies that social media has helped to facilitate. The protests of the Arab Spring, the SlutWalk movement, the Occupy Movement, #MeToo and #BlackLivesMatter were all claimed in varying degrees to be reliant on the affordances of social media. What was the role of social platforms in what Gerbaudo (2012) calls the 'choreography' of these protests? These noisy, energetic and colourful gatherings are imbued with visibility, through the spectacle of the assembly itself and the countless images of it which circulate through social media. Couldry (2015) cautions us to recognize our bias towards the *visible* when analysing the implications of platforms and how this might render non-empirical and/or longer-term effects opaque. This includes the role of platforms in mediating access to the visible: constraining and enabling the gathering in ways which are not immediately observable, as well as controlling access to the evidence through which we catalogue that viability and its mediation beyond the site of the event itself (Couldry 2015: 609). Their interventions to moderate, guide and delete tend to drop out of datasets leaving us with the methodological challenge of accounting for what is not manifested empirically within the horizon of the platform (Gillespie 2015). The issue this raises is a broader conundrum for knowledge production in which the affordances of 'big data' go hand-in-hand with the constraints of the platforms which control access to such data[16] (Kitchin 2014, Margetts 2017a). Naive accounts of data science render this mediation obscure by reducing the horizons of the real to what registers empirically within the confines of a particular platform, suggesting the ascendency of data science might involve a radical contraction in the explanatory and critical horizons of the social sciences (Carrigan 2019).[17]

For these reasons, we insist on the irreducibility of the infrastructure for understanding platformized social life. As Gillespie (2015: 1) puts it, 'For some reason, it remains tempting to study social dynamics on platforms while ignoring the platforms themselves, treating them as simply there, irrelevant, or designed in the only way imaginable'. To understand the public consequences of social media it is necessary to account for what we do *through* them. These are not stages *on* which we act but infrastructures *through* which we act, constraining and enabling our actions in shifting and complex ways, reflecting the fluctuating interests and concerns of the firms running them within a rapidly changing landscape. We need to render the ensuing challenges representable by clearing away the conceptual detritus which the ideology of social media brings with it, as well as providing a strategic orientation for the problems social media poses for us. This requires a platform literate public sociology, able to grasp the role of platforms in shaping and representing social life.

This isn't just a matter of knowing what platforms are in order to ensure we can use them. What Couldry (2015: 621) describes as the 'necessarily inflationary and simplifying language' surrounding platforms isn't just a problem 'out there'. It can be found 'in here' providing a 'default map onto a simplified social' which mystifies how we might use them in relation to what we imagine as the wider world beyond the boundaries of the ivory tower. Their relative novelty for professional practice means that we will inevitably draw on the conceptual elements available to us to make sense of them, even if we might reject their implications on an intellectual level. But we draw on the tropes of social media ideology in making sense of what we can and might do with these platforms, inclining us towards them in a certain way while foregrounding the prospects and backgrounding the problems. Orthodox and influential framings inevitably rush in to fill the discursive void unless we carefully scrutinize and reject them. This extends to the contemporary 'techlash' in which utopian expectations are replaced with dystopian fears without examining the underlying assumptions about what social media are. This is why common assumptions about social media, as well as the institutional reasons for them, figure so heavily in the ensuing chapters. If this seems an overly negative project at points then please bear with us because our intentions are wholly positive. But we need to dispense with some conceptual baggage before we can begin to rebuild public sociology in a way that is adequate to the transformed sociotechnical environment which we all increasingly confront (Carrigan 2016, 2019).

4

Sociology and its Platforms

For many readers, the phrase 'sociology and its platforms' will immediately bring to mind images of blogs, Facebook pages and Twitter feeds through which sociologists engage with audiences beyond the traditional venues of conferences and scholarly journals. However, the thrust of our argument ha s been that we misunderstand such contemporary activity unless we consider it alongside the analogue platforms through which sociology has sought a relationship with a public. A platform in this sense is a position from which to communicate, facilitated by a material infrastructure,[1] more or less able to draw attention and rendering some modes of reception more likely than others.[2] For example, this monograph provides us with a position from which to speak, materialized through the codex book and its related apparatus of production and distribution. It encourages a monological mode of reception in which communicating about *it* or back to *us* as authors requires switching to another technology, with its capacity to draw attention being reliant on the publisher's leveraging interest in the topic and the authors within a difficult marketplace for scholarly monographs (Thompson 2005: 79).

There are many limitations to the codex book, which we'll explore as part of the broader category of 'legacy scholarship'. However, we want to be clear that we're not advocating its wholesale rejection, as evidenced by the fact we've chosen such as technology to deliver our argument. Rather than dismissing the 'old' and valorizing the 'new', we're trying to retrieve the technological aspect of publishing as an object of scholarly reflexivity. To get beyond the narrowly textual in order to understand the materiality through which it is delivered, as well as what this means for scholarship. To talk of sociology and its platforms in this sense is therefore a broader endeavour than the aforementioned focus on the digital would allow. It involves recognizing that sociology has *always* relied on platforms for sociologists to communicate, even if these depend on a legacy infrastructure of scholarly publishing (monographs, edited books, journals and so on) so familiar as to fade into the background for most of us. These platforms were oriented towards a small community of fellow specialists affiliated with a university and reliant on it to secure their access to them (Daniels and Thistlethwaite 2016: 7–10). To publish in a highly regarded journal within one's field was a reliable means to draw the attention of the relevant group of scholars, encouraging their response through the same platforms in a manner which, at its best, kept a conversation going which contributed to the development of knowledge within that domain. The orthodox conception of scholarship can in this sense be seen as the institutionalization of these legacy platforms, inflecting intellectual exchange through their constraints and enablements, as well as the norms and expectations which these have generated over time (Thompson 1995: 13). The most familiar units of scholarly exchange, such as the journal article or the book chapter, reflect the material constraints which have been associated with these platforms, much as the 'size, location, length and format of a conference are influenced by the considerations of bringing together a group of people to one location and making best use of their time, within certain financial restrictions' (Weller 2011: loc 146).

An inclination towards communication between experts has been built into the orthodox conception of scholarship from the outset, encompassing *what* scholars communicate, *how* they communicate and *why* they communicate. These institutions were never hegemonic and there have always been exceptions,[3] such as the purchase by Du Bois of a printing press or the multifaceted publishing operations of the early founders of British Sociology (Daniels and Thistlewaite 2016: 21, Scott and Bromley 2013). But these legacy platforms are sticky and continue to draw us back, not least of all because the career structure of academic life has been designed around their ubiquity. However, the legacy platforms of scholarship are being transformed by digital technology, with no aspect of the industry underlying it being untouched by these changes (Thompson 2005). This provides us with a timely opportunity to reflect on what it means to 'make public'; the assumptions and expectations sedimented into the conception of publishing we are socialized within graduate school and beyond (Agger 2007). The manner in which the COVID-19 crisis disrupts the routine operations of the university only underscores the need to be reflexive about our taken for granted practices. At the time of writing, it's difficult to be clear about *how* scholarship will be changed by this crisis but it seems clear that it *will* change, as a result of us all overnight becoming what Weller (2011) calls 'Digital Scholars' with universities switching to a digital-by-default mode of operation in which the explanatory burden is increasingly placed on face-to-face activities to explain their existence.

Social media is an important part of this landscape even if it far from exhausts what is meant by digital scholarship (Weller 2011). It would have once seemed implausible to suggest social media would become an integral part of scholarly life, with its potential significance only coming to be recognized in recent years and still disputed in many circles (Carrigan 2019). There remains uncertainty about the number of academics using social media, with 30 per cent being a robust estimate for higher education in the UK (Carrigan 2019: 14–15). To focus on uptake by individuals, with its associated methodological difficulties,[4] risks obscuring a broader picture in which social media has been taken up by universities, funders, publishers, departments, projects and networks to a remarkable extent (Stuart et al 2019). It is this institutional buy in, coupled with the likely growth of academic users over time, which suggests that social media is here to stay within higher education. Even more so after academics came to depend on it during the COVID-19 crisis, as a means to sustain scholarly communities in the absence of face-to-face events.

This has been a source of excitement for many because these platforms differ so markedly from those utilized in legacy scholarship. A number of books have advised on how social media can be incorporated into scholarly practice (Weller 2011, Badgett 2016, Carrigan 2016, Daniels and Thistlethwaite 2016, Reed 2016, Mollett et al 2017, Stein and Daniels 2017). Training sessions are offered in countless universities, with the slide decks often made available online. Funding bodies support social media in the name of research impact and online engagement increasingly figures in debates about professional development.[5] These platforms are coming to be institutionalized within the academy, though this varies across national systems in a way which requires detailed empirical examination. Even if it is not unambiguously part of scholarly communication in a particular context, it seems increasingly likely that it will be at some point in the future. If we are correct that the mandated digital scholarship of the COVID-19 crisis is a turning point in scholarly practice, these platforms can no longer be treated as a peripheral or emerging feature of academic life.

For those striving to ensure a public role for sociology this can seem like a remarkable opportunity. These platforms are easy to learn, free to use and outside of institutional control (Weller 2011: loc 227). They make it possible to publish in real time, combining heterogenous elements in order to facilitate new ways of what Becker (2007) calls 'telling about society': representing social life with an immediacy and force that is inconceivable with the legacy platforms of scholarly communication (Back and Puwar 2012). The potential audiences involved are vast and the possibilities for dialogue can feel overwhelming. Popular blogs like Sociological Images have brought sociological ideas to millions of readers in uniquely engaging and thoughtful ways (Wade and Sharp 2013). Sociological thinkers like Zeynep Tufekci have hundreds of thousands of Twitter followers who follow their thinking on emerging issues far in advance of any formal publications. It can feel as if social media *must* have a crucial role to play in what Hartmann (2017: 4) describes as 'a new golden age of sociological engagement, visibility, and influence'. However, we urge caution in the face of these apparent opportunities. This not because we doubt that social media *can* be used effectively for public sociology, or related movements in cognate disciplines such as public anthropology, public geographies and the public humanities.[6] In fact, the book as a whole is intended as a theoretical framework for exploring how we can do precisely that. It is simply a recognition of the ambiguous character of social media and the position it offers us from which to communicate. These ambiguities have been more pronounced than ever during the pandemic, which has shaped our approach to writing in the final stages of this project.

Reasons for caution

There are three **vectors of ambiguity** we will explore in the coming chapters. These issues complicate the tendency to frame social media as *inherently* positive or negative, necessitating that we move beyond the simplistic dichotomies which too often accompany thinking on emerging technologies. Instead, we focus on how the institutions of scholarship, including the conception of publicness at the heart of public sociology and parallel movements in other disciplines, encourage a particular orientation towards the enablements and constraints of digital platforms. These assumptions and their corresponding limitations are summarized in Table 4.1. It is one which we fear leaves users simultaneously unprepared for some of the difficulties to be found in these online environments and the strategies necessary to ensure the successful uptake of the opportunities on offer.

Table 4.1: The assumptions made about social platforms and their corresponding limitations

Assumption	Complicating factor
Social media platforms are **dissemination engines** which enable us to reach a vast audience	Building an audience
This capacity for dissemination means that social media platforms can help us **escape the ivory tower**	Negotiating filtering mechanisms
Getting our research 'out there' will **ameliorate social problems** by ensuring that people have the knowledge they need	Thriving in the acoustics of social media

The vastness of social media's user base figures heavily in how we think and talk about it.[7] In terms of Facebook's operations, the 2.5 billion users of the core platform, 1 billion users of Instagram and 1 billion users of WhatsApp go much of the way to conveying their sociological significance. The total user base looms large in how we imagine platforms and how their success is evaluated. The temptation is to imagine them as **dissemination engines** through which it becomes possible to reach a vast and undifferentiated audience.[8] Consider for example the countless elements of grey literature (training materials, blog posts, podcasts, slide decks etc) which proclaim the power of social media for getting your research 'out there' without specifying *who* it will be disseminated to, *how* they will be reached or *why* they will care (Carrigan 2019: 93–120). The user base of any platform is profoundly segmented, tangled into networks in a path dependent manner which exercises a powerful influence over how content circulates across the platform (Beer 2013). The algorithmic sorting on which most platforms depend compounds this even further by using *past engagement* as a basis to make inferences about your *present interest* (Carrigan 2018). This also empowers gatekeepers and 'influencers' who can plausibly claim[9] to offer a path through this hyper-segmentation in order to ensure the successful pursuit of visibility for an item (Abidin 2018).

This leaves (strategically-oriented) users with a time consuming activity of **building an audience** which will inevitably reflect the existing segmentation of the platform, with the implication that followers will likely be much less heterogenous than a naive account would tend to imagine. The imperative of building an audience too easily substitutes for the strategic goals which rendered that audience desirable in the first place. Furthermore, an update will only be seen by a fraction of these followers, with the rate of engagement as low as 1 per cent or less. The promise of being able to communicate directly to a vast audience has been central to individuals, networks and organizations investing time and energy in building a social media presence. But platforms which rely on the sale of advertising have a vested interest in depressing rates of organic engagement (visibility won through activity rather than paid advertising) over time in order to incline people towards purchasing paid advertising (McNamee 2019: loc 1147–1161). The capacity of social media platforms for dissemination is a much more complex issue than it initially seems, even if the business model we encountered in the previous chapters has led firms to suggest otherwise through their valorization of participatory culture.

The traditional sense of publishing has tended to see it as a matter of 'making public':[10] ensuring that published items are, in principle, accessible to many individuals across a range of potential contexts (Thompson 1995: 30–31). This fails to grasp the struggle for recognition which occurs when there is a rapid escalation in the number of outputs within a category, as can be seen in a market like books (Thompson 2010: 328–240). But it remains a plausible outlook because we still ascribe significance to a scholarly output being 'out there' even if it's failing to reach an intended audience. Unfortunately, social media radically intensifies this competition for attention with thousands of items of content uploaded every second (Internet Live Stats 2019). This is rendered tractable by filtering it through networks and algorithms in the manner described previously (Carrigan 2017a).

These **filtering mechanisms** determine who gets heard and who doesn't but their primary imperative is to increase user engagement, ensuring people are encountering content which generates a reaction in them and keeps them returning to the platform (Vaidhyanathan 2018). The simple fact of something being 'out there' becomes decreasingly salient and what matters is instead the likelihood of it being *discovered* (Zuckerman 2017). To be discovered on social media involves the successful negotiation of filtering mechanisms, with all spheres of cultural production increasingly drawn into the centralized incentive structure of these platforms (Taplin 2017, Foer 2018).[11] Not only does publishing in the traditional sense do nothing to ensure engagement with what has been published, the realization of the competitive struggle to be heard means we must begin to adapt to the constraints of these filtering mechanisms or risk being locked within insular networks. Far from **escaping the ivory tower**, social media has an uncertain capacity[12] to enable us to reach audiences outside the academy. It also risks leaving us ensnared within what Seymour (2019) calls the *Twittering Machine*, displacing our original motivations with the machinic imperative to spend ever greater periods of our time writing and reading, in the hope we will one day find what we are looking for (Eyal 2014, Schüll 2014, Gilroy-Ware 2017).

To get our research 'out there' seems like the inevitable preliminary to exercising a public influence. It might not be sufficient but is surely a necessary step, with research dissemination acting as a first step for research impact. Framing the issue in this way sensitizes us to constraints on this circulation, such as the arcane language and journal paywalls which are imagined to impede our audience.[13] If only we could eliminate those constraints then our research would flow freely, ensuring that those who need our knowledge would receive it! In this way our research could help **ameliorate social problems**, or so we hope in those moments when we feel optimistic about what we are doing. To the extent we perceive social media as dissemination engines, these platforms will promise to help us escape the ivory tower and ensure our research makes a difference in this way. However, a dissemination-centric orientation to social media obscures the politics of circulation inherent in each platform (Beer 2013). Building an audience in an information environment governed by filtering mechanisms means that circulation is not a linear process in which the removal of constraints on our communication will mean our message travels further.

What Margetts (2017a) calls the 'acoustics of social media' are much more complicated than that such that there's no inherent relationship between how clearly things are expressed, how free they are to access and how far they circulate. Carmi (2019) highlights the selectivity involved in listening, identifying how the experience of immediacy (by users) is dependent on its backstage operation (by moderators) in an orchestrated sociality. It is a complex environment with a managed cacophony which we fail to grasp if we approach it in terms of a Euclidian geometry in which material diffuses (or fails to) through time and space in a more or less linear way (Marres 2012: 182). What we publish online doesn't circulate in a straightforward way, diffusing outwards from our original act of making it public. It's a messy and convoluted process, particularly given its increasing reliance on the opaque machinery of social platforms.

There is a risk of a straw man in the argument we are making. How many people *really* believe that social media could prove so useful in the pursuit of a public role? It is our contention that these assumptions can be found throughout a voluminous grey literature (the webpages, blog posts, videocasts and podcasts promoting the use of social media) but we do not claim to have undertaken an exhaustive content analysis. Certain motifs are recurrent across it ('getting your research out there', 'raising your profile', 'facilitating dialogue') which embody these assumptions in partial form. To get a sense of what we mean, search for 'getting your research out there' and 'social media' with a focus on library websites or blog posts with a pedagogical intent. These motifs also figure in the motivations which academics have for using social media and reflect ideas in circulation about what these platforms can be used for (Jordan 2017, Jordan and Weller 2018). They have certainly been prominent when we have discussed social media in teaching and training sessions with academics conducted over almost a decade, predominantly in the UK but occasionally to international audiences as well.

Even though we have suggested a logical relationship between these assumptions, such that adopting one will *incline* one towards adopting another,[14] they will often appear in isolation. This is less about what platform users *say* as much as what they *do*, as well as the implicit assumptions which inform these practices. In some cases we encounter 'specific representations of what each platform "is", and how it works', as Comunello et al (2016: 528) put it in an analogous investigation of how activists perceive digital platforms[15]. However, we suggest these remain exceptions and most academics approach social media in partial and piecemeal ways, informed by assumptions which are 'in the air' or transmitted through peer networks.[16] We are not suggesting these are uniformly held nor denying the many exceptions to them but simply reconstructing an account of *misconceptions* and the relationships between them. We are suggesting these are intuitions about how platforms can be used for academics, ones which we have attempted to explicate into a coherent whole to illustrate a **platform imaginary**: a conception of what platforms are which facilitates their use by academics through making sense of them[17] (Bucher 2017). It is grounded in the ideology of social media we encountered in Chapters 2 and 3, namely that neutral platforms facilitate the coming together of everybody, but we argue that these assumptions about social media find support in a scholarly orientation which predates them to a significant degree. If we intend to cultivate a nuanced view of social media and its opportunities for public scholarship then it's necessary to consider our attachment to *outputs*, *expertise* and *knowledge*. These were the anchors of legacy scholarship, emerging in relation to analogue platforms and carrying conceptual baggage which obscures our path forward.

Rethinking sociological practice for platforms

Decentring outputs

In his appendix to *The Sociological Imagination*, C. Wright Mills (2000) offered advice on what he termed 'intellectual craftsmanship'. It describes scholarship in terms of everyday activities through which reflection on the life we are leading facilitate systematic analysis of the world we are leading it in. He advises readers to keep a file in which you 'try to get together what you are doing intellectually and what you are experiencing as a person' (Mills 2000: 196). This involves 'fringe thoughts' which occur in everyday life, overheard conversations or even dreams. The file *is* the intellectual production through which publication comes to be possible. These books, chapters and papers depend on the contents of the file but they emerge *through* it, standing as crowning moments in a process of making sense of the world which precedes our outputs and will continue after they are 'out there'. The vision of scholarship offered by Mills is one in which formal outputs are grounded in engagement with the world, as expressions of our commitment to understanding it. He is far from the only sociologist to explore these backstage aspects of sociological labour. Abbott (2014) and Becker (1986) have comparable levels of insight but the one offered by Mills surely the most poetic and his vision the most powerful (Gane and Back 2012). It has influenced our approach because of its sensitivity to what we will later term **technological reflexivity**, as well as its centrality to knowledge production, reflecting the American sociologist's own proclivities as an amateur designer and builder (Treviño 2013).

It is an outlook which has obvious ramifications for how sociologists use digital media, with a platform like Twitter being a powerful conduit for fringe thoughts to be shared in real time and blogging being a powerful means to keep a file which can be shared with others. These are just two examples of the many ways in which digital platforms can be incorporated into scholarly workflows (Carrigan 2019: 71–92). They offer the opportunity to 'keep one's inner world awake' in the manner advocated by Mills but with a social inclination[18] that was unthinkable with legacy platforms. Intellectual fragments and observational snippets can be shared in real time in a manner that encourages other people to do the same. Carrigan (2019) describes this as 'continuous publishing' and Little (2012) refers to it as becoming an 'open source philosopher'. It is still unusual to embrace this approach for the research lifecycle as a whole but the direction of travel in research culture is towards increasing openness (Cohen 2018). It's crucial we recognize that the freedom to improvise in public and share provisional ideas is more easily realized by those who already enjoy prestige, who are also less likely to be the targets of gendered and racialized harassment on platforms where these pathologies are rife (McMillan Cottom 2015). Furthermore, there are parts of the research process where this might be inappropriate or obviously unethical, such as fieldwork which is in process. Daniels and Thistlewaite (2016: 75) also make the important observation that open data might involve researchers and participants being drawn into political disputes.

However, these constraints reinforce the point that social platforms engender a publicness to the research *process*, as opposed to being a characteristic restricted to our outputs: publications which manifest our scholarship. Outputs become less central when more of the research process is undertaken in public. We can see a proliferation of outputs, with content produced and circulated through digital platforms (tweets, blogs, podcasts, videos, slides) joining the familiar outputs of legacy platforms as the record of our intellectual engagement. There are many questions this raises about how the two categories might be joined together and what this means for how we conceive of publication (Carrigan 2019: 24–46). If we dislodge outputs from their pride of place in how we imagine our work then a more radical transformation comes into view. As Healy (2017: 771) puts it, 'these technologies enable a distinctive field of public conversation, exchange, and engagement' which has 'some of the quality of informal correspondence, but they are not hidden in private letters'. To engage in this field imbues our exchanges with a visibility which qualifies as publicness in the orthodox sense of being in principle accessible to dispersed others, even if the valence of this has been transformed by an explosion in the quantity of material it is true of (Thompson 1995, Carrigan 2018). This is a state which Healy (2017: 775) describes as being 'slightly in public' and which is the new normal for scholars using social media. Under these conditions 'successfully engaging with the public means doing it somewhat unsuccessfully very regularly' –building the foundations of interest in our work through regularly doing it in a proto-public manner rather than plotting a dissemination strategy for each 'output' that remains isolated from the rest of our work. Even many who don't approach it in such an instrumental manner are prone to seeing the potential implications for publicness solely in terms of announcing traditional publications, as opposed to embracing the incipient publicity which now characterizes knowledge production for those heavily engaged with social media. This doesn't mean abandoning scholarly outputs but rather recognizing them as moments in a trajectory of engagement which itself is an object of interest and publicity.

The fact that we have stopped searching for dissemination engines doesn't mean we have stopped caring whether anyone reads our work. But it means that we have a new relationship with them in which the boundary between reader and writer is blurred as part of a much more dialogical relationship (Stewart 2018). This interactivity isn't something we can avoid if we are seeking a public role in the manner discussed in this book. In fact it might be decreasingly possible for *any* academics to avoid it, as academic life comes to be comprehensively platformized such that the same tendencies we identify 'out there' are simultaneously taking place 'in here': we'll see in future chapters how digital platforms increasingly organize academic life, even before the pandemic provoked a radical pivot to online teaching and remote working (Bacevic 2019a, Robertson 2019). If the output remains in its present position as the crowning expression of scholarship then this will feel like the labour of scholarship has been supplemented by the burden of publicity, with the risk we feel negatively about it and approach it in an instrumental way. It inclines us towards a view where there is a *research phase* and then a *publicity phase* (Healy 2017: 775). However, if we dislodge the output from its pride of place then publishing and the dialogues which surround it comes to seem like two sides of the same coin, with writing enriched by the conversation which surrounds it. Once we take a step back from the significance we attach to our publications then a more sociable scholarship becomes possible (Pausé and Russell 2016). However, this enrichment necessitates coming to terms with the assumptions we bring to those conversations, as well as how they might hinder our capacity to enjoy them and the capacity of others to enjoy talking to us.

Decentring expertise

If scholarship is a matter of sustained learning at a high level[19] then *expertise* is inherent to it. It doesn't necessarily mean the scholar is at the forefront of knowledge production in their field, though we should remember the awarding of a PhD is predicated on an original contribution to knowledge. But it does entail the mastery of a particular domain of knowledge in a manner which renders the scholar an outlier in the population at large. As Stein and Daniels (2017: 8) write,

> Academics tend to subscribe to the model of scholar-as-expert because we see ourselves as holders of privileged

insight. After all, we spend a good chunk of our professional lives training for the day when we can call ourselves experts. When we speak in public, we use the mantle of academic authority we've worked long years to display.

To suggest we should decentre expertise doesn't entail a denial of this insight. It merely insists on careful reflection as to the privilege we believe should follow from it. We implicitly make a claim to status when we write, expecting potential readers to respond to our insight with their attention (Mills 2000: 218). The non–citation rates found within the humanities and social sciences suggest that this cannot be taken as a given within our own fields, even if the reasons for it remain uncertain (Remler 2014). The low readership and dismal citation prospects which many perceive in journal publishing are often cited as a reason for enthusiasm about social media. A recurrent comparison is made in the grey literature between the blog post which is read thousands of times and the journal article which is read by numbers so few as to feel negligible. But this rhetorically effective contrast belies the reality that few blog posts receive such attention and even those which do will have been skimmed by many distracted readers (Carrigan 2016, Williams 2018). Far from resolving the problem of audience, social media radicalizes it by expanding the range and quantity of material in circulation, leaving each individual with the challenge of being heard above the din (Beer 2012). It helps address problems of visibility in legacy publication systems but in the process it draws us into the competition dynamics of platforms, as we struggle to develop a following which might translate into a readership for our books, papers and chapters.

It can be difficult to reliably accumulate an audience online and uncertain how they will respond once they are assembled. In a prescient essay Bacevic (2017a) cautions against the expectation of a 'benevolent reception of scientific knowledge' within a public sphere which 'resembles less a (however cacophonous) town hall meeting than a series of disparate village tribunals'. This fragmentation means that we cannot assume that our sense of factfulness,[20] itself relative to disciplinary conventions which are themselves partial,[21] carries the weight we assume when our interventions are received in the public sphere. Even those who advocate co-production and dialogicity have the tendency to 'let in through the back door the implicit assumption of the normative force of our arguments' (Bacevic 2017a). It is difficult to avoid this when so much of our professional socialization inculcates an orientation towards the world in which our descriptions *of* it have a privileged relationship *to* it[22] (French 2012, Bacevic 2019b, 2019c). Furthermore, as Woodcock (2017: loc 2698) puts it, 'Researchers often attribute a level of importance to their own research that is not shared by others, assuming that because they spend so much time on it others will want to know all about it too'. We tend to assume that our descriptions are important as well as epistemically privileged. They relate to a patch of social life over which we have a specialized right to speak and our claims about it ought to be recognized as socially important. When we interact with fellow expertises, we jointly operate within the confines of this assumption but it provokes challenges when we encounter much more heterogeneous audiences through social media. This is crucial when expertise and factfulness are in crisis, in the manner we explore later in the book.

It's necessary to reflect seriously on this because social media radically increases the likelihood that people directly or indirectly implicated in our knowledge claims will talk back to us. Furthermore, these conversations are likely to tread on the patch which we had been socialized into believing was our specialized domain. The fact they are likely to do so in a way which treats our pronouncements as equivalent to their own, reflecting the participation architecture of platforms and the culture which has emerged within them, only compounds the (potential) jarring of our professional dispositions. It can be disorientating to discover that 'the public' might be disinterested in or even actively hostile to what we are doing. However, if we can ask the question 'why should people listen to us?' then these reactions are easier to negotiate because they are a contingent feature we happen to encounter rather than the breakdown of what we felt was a necessary relationship to the world. It's a practical challenge which we negotiate on a case-by-case basis rather than being an unsettling reversal of how we were trained to see ourselves within graduate school.

It also makes it easier to see how, as Cohen (2018: 121, emphasis in original) puts it, social media has 'multiplied our capacities to get other people's ideas *in here*, and that's not an opportunity we can afford to forego'. There are immense opportunities for co-production facilitated by social media and our suggestion is that the scholarly disposition leaves us ill equipped to realize them. To enjoy these opportunities it's necessary to move beyond what Hynes (2016: 806) characterizes as the 'heroic image of the public sociologist exchanging knowledge with the public on whom his existence and moral purpose depend' in order to embrace a more limited orientation as conversational partners, even if ones characterized by certain asymmetries which need to be negotiated in the context of the relationship. This involves turning our back on a comforting image of our exceptional status while recognizing how it carried with it a certain insecurity about our professional status and place in the world (Mills 2000, Healy 2017: 779). In other words, it forces us to step out of our comfort zones, at least if we want to take advantage of the dialogical encounters which social media inevitably facilitates, even if we make little attempt to reach beyond our existing academic networks.

There needs to be an openness to the encounter, even if any particular encounter might not prove fruitful. This will be difficult to achieve if we carry a sense of epistemic superiority into our interactions, particularly if we fail to acknowledge it in our own sense of what we are doing and why. Social media increasingly forces us all to confront what Burawoy (2017: 282) describes as 'the underlying dilemma of ethnography – that we are part of the world we study' with the ensuing challenge of how we make sense of our relationship to those people we study. It used to be these people were reliably 'out there'. In a remarkable intervention Stan Cohen (1979) presented a piece of fiction which one might now classify as post-horror. In fact it has more than a little in common with Jordan Peele's film *Us* (2019) as an exploration of the uncanny intrusion of the repressed and excluded into spaces where they were expected to be absent. In the story, research participants inexplicably appear around the campus, leading to the unsettling realization that they are seeking revenge. The story ends with Cohen's narrator desperately bundling up his most treasured books before fleeing the burning campus as gun fire echoes in the distance. It is a parable about the distance which sociologists feel from their participants and the security they derive from this. The erosion of the institutional and territorial boundaries which underwrote this distance make the story feel remarkably prescient. The point can be extended much further than research participants. How do we prepare ourselves for the possibility that those we assumed were 'out there' might be found 'in here' (Papacharissi 2010: 69)? Can we ensure these encounters are fruitful rather than frightening? What might have to change at the level of academic culture and professional self-conception? The orthodox conception of expertise tends to get in the way of facing these questions, or at least doing so in the spirit which is necessary to answer them successfully.

In fact the distinction itself breaks down because social media allows us to undertake activities 'in here' which would have formerly required us to be 'out there', enabling us to participate in the public sphere from the privacy of our homes and offices[23] (Papacharissi 2010). It doesn't obliterate the difference between inside and outside but it does transform where this boundary is drawn and how familiar it feels to us. Bacevic (2019a) analyses this in relation to the Steven Salaita and George Ciccariello-Maher cases, where online academic speech in a seemingly private capacity was subject to public sanction. A tacit mapping in which we do our work 'in here' before engaging 'out there' can't do justice to the complexity of the landscape we confront where what we understand as *private* activities routinely have *public* consequences and vice versa (Marres 2012). Firstly, it leads us to downplay work done 'within' the ivory tower that might nonetheless have public ramifications. For example, Housley (2018: 435) suggests how ethnomethodological work could help inform the future development of social media platforms. Kennedy and Moss (2015) consider how digital social scientists could contribute to making data mining tools and expertise more accessible. These are initiatives that would lead organically from existing research agendas that have public significance without requiring a public orientation.[24] Secondly, it can lead us to assume a dissemination model in which work undertaken 'in here' then has to be publicized 'out there', with the rigour of the former underwriting the legitimacy of the latter. As we shall see this replicates an assumption at the heart of the public sociology literature from Burawoy (2005) onwards. The practical negotiation of the interface between the university and wider society is a potent site for existing assumptions about knowledge production and social life to be restaged (Bacevic 2017b). We need to be wary of restating old certainties, as if the comfort of repetition can substitute for analysis of changing conditions. Thirdly, it can encourage us to imagine public life as a preconstituted sphere which we leave the ivory tower to enter, bringing our epistemic armour with us. This reflects the tendency we encountered in Chapter 1 to see publicness as a sphere we enter into rather than something we co-create through our actions. Politics exists in the movement between public and private, as well as the shifting boundary between them (Papacharissi 2010: 23). If we see it as something we only enter into when we leave the imagined ivory tower then we will fail to be reflexive about our engagements 'out there' while the politics of our engagements 'in here' will remain obscure (Bacevic 2019c).

What is significant is our distance or proximity in relation to latent and realized publics rather than whether we are inside or outside boundaries of the university which themselves are undergoing change. The decentring of expertise is not sufficient for recalibrating these relationships as the landscape changes but it is necessary if we hope to equip ourselves to perform this task successfully. It can be easier to see this point if we look towards another profession undergoing similar changes. Boczkowski and Papacharissi (2018: 4) make the argument that journalism's confrontation with social media erodes the capacity to adjudicate on what constitutes news, even as it facilitates opportunities for transformed connections such that old functions can be carried out through new means. It's a threat if journalism remains unchanged but an opportunity if there's a willingness to reconfigure established practice for a new environment. As they go on to write,

> Social media enable journalists to have a connection to the public that can be employed so as to transform ambience into higher degrees of vigilance and relevance. It is through these heightened states of vigilance and relevance that journalism can rebuild networks of trust; give voice to diverse stories; reconnect publics that feel displaced, misunderstood, and insecure; and restore the fractured sociocultural fabric connecting diverse publics together.

The *Guardian* journalist Jon Henley (2018) makes a similar point in a more allegorical mode. Whereas once the public were satisfied for journalists to fling down their wares from the balcony of the *Guardian* offices once a day, or at least lacked the recourse to any alternative, they now wait outside the office doors hungrily and (potentially) angrily. It would be easy to feel defensive and worried by this, retreating behind the battlements with a view to escaping what appears to be a braying mob. But if it can be embraced as an opportunity, the apparent mob is revealed as a collection of people, with stories and insights which can enrich journalism if only journalistic practice can adapt to take advantage of it. At least some of them will be. It's an unfortunate reality of social media that with the crowd will come the likelihood of toxicity, with the burden of it falling in profoundly uneven ways (McMillan Cottom 2015). However, rather than ossifying these difficulties and presenting them as an unfortunate expression of the epistemic chaos which the platform generates (determinism) or social maladies for which the platform is a neutral conduit (voluntarism) decentring expertise enables us to approach them as agents relating to other agents in circumstances which none of us have chosen but which we can fallibly contribute to remaking. It helps us confront these as questions of strategy and tactics, rather than diffuse qualities of the platformized environment about which we can do little in a practical sense. This in turn raises the question of the knowledge we imagine ourselves to bring to those endeavours and the role we conceive for it in this landscape.

Decentring knowledge

In a thoughtful essay Richard French (2012), a current academic and ex-politician, reflects on the misconceptions about politics which are common among academics and how they undermine their ambition to exercise an influence over policy. He is concerned by the 'partial, shallow and etiolated vision of politics' affirmed by many academics that 'compromises their potential contribution to the improvement of public life'. In failing to grasp how competition, publicity and uncertainty characterize the working lives of elected representatives, it becomes feasible to expect 'that important improvements in policy making would ensue if only policy makers would attend to the knowledge which researchers of all sorts produce and possess'. While he is concerned with the explicit forms this takes, such as evidence based policy, he suggests it is 'so well-entrenched in the socialisation associated with doctoral education that it exists in varying forms in every empirically oriented discipline and research laboratory'. It frames policy in epistemic terms as relating to states of the world which researchers study and hence 'what meets the epistemological standards of the various empirical disciplines merits privileged status in policy making' (French 2012: 532–535). In its crudest form this amounts to the assumption that problems could be fixed if only those in charge would listen to us. In its more sophisticated variants it assumes that specific blockages (excessive jargon, commercial paywall, hostility to expertise) preclude otherwise viable expert-led solutions. In doing so, as French (2012: 533) puts it, civic judgement is replaced with academic judgement. This is a decidedly unpolitical understanding of politics that excludes the contestation, struggle and uncertainty that are constitutive features of the political sphere (Crick 1962, Mouffe 2000).

French's (2012) observations bring into focus a broader question which Bacevic (2019b, 2019c) analyses as the relationship between *knowledge* and *action*. Bacevic (2019c) unpicks this question through a detailed study of the critique of neoliberalism within higher education, drawing attention to the paradox we encounter in 'the "proliferation" of critique alongside the proliferation of neoliberalism in knowledge production'. Her diagnosis concerns the 'politically soothing, yet epistemically limited assumption that knowledge automatically translates into action' which has its origins in a belief in performativity and the prevalent style of critique as unmasking (Bacevic 2019b: 389). She suggests this 'gnossification' is a contemporary instance of Bourdieu's scholastic fallacy: 'assuming that power relations – including those that impact the production of knowledge – are equal to knowledge about power relations and that, further, the latter is an efficient way of changing the former' (Bacevic 2019b: 387). This 'excessive confidence in the powers of language' leaves academics with the tendency to 'regard an academic commentary as a political act or the critique of texts as a feat of resistance, and experience revolutions in the order of words as radical revolutions in the order of things' (Bourdieu 2000: 2). This primes academics to be pushed and pulled by the behavioural levers of the social media machine, leading them to give much more weight to the intellectual content of online exchange than is warranted by its consequences. It carries the further risk that their default response to the experience of difficulty will be to dive further in rather than pull out and critically reflect, imagining agreement as something further down the line rather than a near impossibility given the character of the platform. However, what moving further in and retreating backwards mean are not straightforward once we have begun to decentre expertise in a refusal to be fixated on the ivory tower and its imagined boundaries. The seemingly mundane question of how academics use social platforms indexes diffuse yet important issues about the boundaries of the university, the social role of knowledge and its relationship to the public sphere (Bacevic 2019a). In a sector where tacit knowledge can often be undervalued, it's important to try and recover the assumptions which are made here and which inevitably guide our practice. All the more so when it comes to a sociotechnical apparatus which is distinctively different from the familiar platforms through which academics have sought to make things public.

The public tends to be seen as distant from the private, both in a *spatial* sense (we have to travel 'out there' to participate in it) and a *normative* sense (we should be guided by imperatives appropriate to it). It is a matter of the individual and invisible opposed to the impersonal and the seen (Papacharissi 2010: 23). Marres (2012) explains how the tendency has been for the public to be purged of the material dimension,[25] including the vested interests which motivate people as private actors. In seeking to ensure the public sphere remains free of private interests, the hope is that deliberation about the public good becomes possible and individual concerns give way to collective ones. In making 'the passage from the private to the public' it is expected that we leave the sphere of dependency 'behind' in order to 'appear as self-standing actors within established public spheres': this has been conceived historically as the domain of the speaking male citizen (Butler 2015: 43–45). It is a place for the free exchange of speech acts in pursuit of the public good, obscuring the question of *who* speaks and who forcibly remains offstage.

It should be stressed that this is a normative ideal rather than an empirical reality but the baggage brought by the former has a significant impact on the latter. As Marres (2012: 153) puts it, 'Conversation has been the privileged genre of public action since time immemorial – at least since Socrates engaged in dialogue in the streets of Athens'. This habit of 'projecting the general and abstract metaphor of debate' onto everything is a practical problem as well as a conceptual one because it obscures the complexity of these emerging spaces and limits our responses to them, in much the same manner as insisting on a Euclidean geometry through which our publications circulate or fail to (Marres 2012: 151). It encourages us to view social media in terms of its capacity to facilitate rational discussion oriented towards agreement, denying the role of affectivity or framing it as external to the telos of these platforms, reflecting the messy humanity of the users rather than the architecture of the service (Papacharissi 2015). This can often include a sense of consensus as the intended conclusion of dialogue with all the problems this creates under the epistemic conditions lazily summarized as 'post truth' (Papacharissi 2010: 78, Davies 2018). It can also incline us to see online publishing as 'as a kind of community or a place people go and spend time reading around in depth' when the empirical data makes clear this isn't true of even the most popular blogs or websites (Healy 2017: 775). It's a powerful trope which carries a great deal of conceptual, normative and political baggage. Yet it has frequently figured in research on the impact of the internet, as well as recurring in everyday discussions of it (Papacharissi 2015: 26).

If this is just another forum for debate, the novelty of digital platforms becomes little more than an occasion to perform the scholastic prejudices which academics are inclined to bring to such exchanges as a consequence of their professional socialization. This sits uneasily with the quotidian reality of debate where everybody 'knows that they can get nowhere and peter out, they can cause people to become even more confused than they were at the outset and that they can lead to the hardening of opinion and the formation of increasingly rigid and impenetrable fronts between different parties' (Guess 2019). But this naivety, wilful or otherwise, concerning the power of discussion to resolve conflict becomes positively destructive when it encounters social media platforms in which contention is rewarded with visibility, frustration generates spectacle and value is reduced to popularity (Van Dijck 2013, Vaidhyanathan 2018). To approach what Seymour (2019) calls the *Twittering Machine* with a naive idealization of debate can be a markedly dangerous undertaking. The conditions which facilitate fruitful dialogue tend to be lacking,[26] the architecture of platforms tends to compound misunderstandings[27] and the affective machinery called into life under these circumstances is the raison d'être for platforms seeking to provoke users into staying for longer, returning more often and taking more action while they are there (Lanier 2018). The widespread reliance on social platforms during the COVID-19 pandemic, as a substitute for face-to-face interaction during lockdown and as a supplement for it during social distancing, make it more urgent than ever that we develop a literacy about the architecture of these platforms and the business imperatives underlying the engineering decisions. Our fear is that the scholastic orientation of academics leaves them primed to see this as a stage on which to perform in public, encouraged by universities seeking to capitalize on the profile of their staff at a time when their own social role is undergoing renegotiation.

What does this mean for public sociology?

Sociology's 'founding father' Émile Durkheim (1982: 163), as conventional historiography has it, wrote in his notorious conclusion to the Rules of Sociological Method that 'the time has come for sociology to renounce worldly successes, so to speak, and take on the esoteric character which befits all science'; an unusually sceptical, insecure and introspective prelude to such a new discipline, finding sociology already 'embroiled in partisan struggles' which can threaten the new discipline's 'dignity', 'authority' and 'popularity'. In his 1904 essay on 'Objectivity in Social Science and Social Policy', Weber (1994: 51) observed how the emerging discipline of sociology was characterized by dissension, rather than by agreement, decrying 'the continuous changes and bitter conflict about the apparently most elementary problems of our discipline, its methods, the formulation and validity of its concepts'. This lack of consensus about the discipline's methodological and conceptual tools was picked up by Michels (1932: 123–4) who, writing on intellectuals for the *Encyclopedia of the Social Sciences*, saw sociology as 'largely demoralised' and undergoing 'an intense spiritual self-criticism'. Robert Merton (1975: 22) returned to this theme, commenting that 'Sociology has typically been in an unstable state, alternating between planes of extravagant optimism and extravagant pessimism', thus justifying in part Holton's (1987: 503) observation that '[i]n the midst of these pervasive perceptions of crisis it is not surprising to find social thought to be diagnosed as crisis ridden'; a diagnosis that inspired Raymond Boudon (1980) to write a whole book on the matter, entitled *The Crisis in Sociology*.

It is inevitable that a discipline so prone to a sense of crisis would remain uncertain about its public standing. The visibility and prestige enjoyed by other disciplines (for example, economics and behavioural science) can only intensify this tendency but it runs deeper than these disciplinary rivalries. Boyns and Fletcher (2007: 120) offer anecdotes of common misconceptions of what sociologists do by the public, the confusion and conflation of sociology with 'psychology, social philosophy, social work, criminology, social activism, urban studies, public administration, journalism, and perhaps, most disquieting of all, with socialism'. This, in Boyns and Fletcher's (2007: 120) view, reveals a deeper problem than the recognition of sociologists by the layperson, leading to the suspicion that 'as a discipline, we do not, ourselves, seem to know who we are', resulting in a bricolage of frustrating terms: 'are we scientists or activists, positivists or postmodernists, philosophers or theorists, teachers or researchers, qualitative or quantitative, micro or macro?' This uncertain disciplinary identity has led some to suggest that a public role is rendered difficult by this underlying tension or that core ideas must firm be reformulated (Hashemi 2016). For example, Turner (2006: 276) rejects Burawoy's idealism by insisting that only 'intellectually coherent disciplines can speak with a unity and power', not 'fragmented ones like sociology'. However, for others, it has appeared to that public sociology offers us the opportunity to secure the legitimacy and reputation of the discipline in the face of external threats (Cohen 2018).[28] We share Hartmann's (2017) optimism that public sociology can unify rather than being undermined by a lack of unification, helping orientate the discipline and its practitioners as they negotiate the difficult changes which are the subject of the later chapters of this book. In this sense, revisiting the public sociology debate can be a way of reflecting on the prospects and promises of the discipline more broadly.

Unfortunately, there is an ambiguity at the heart of public sociology which we must urgently address. As we will see in the next chapter, it is defined by a division between *public intellectualism* (traditional public sociology) and *scholar activism* (organic public sociology). This sits uneasily within a schematization of the discipline in which *professional sociology* underwrites the *epistemic legitimacy* of public sociology (Burawoy 2011). The prioritization of knowledge produced through orthodox means[29] squeezes out meaningful opportunities for co-production in scholar activism and creates a slide towards what Arribas Lozano (2018) identifies as a 'dissemination model' of public sociology. This tendency to conceive of its practice in terms of the 'unidirectional flow of knowledge from the academic expert to extra-academic audience' is compounded by the strategic considerations involved in Burawoy's project of institutionalization, particularly the impulse to please everyone involved in the discussion, as well as the propensity for an ambiguous term to fall into a vernacular usage (Lozano 2018: 102). The lack of clarity surrounding what 'public sociology' is makes it difficult to examine the assumptions which guide it in practice. While it is far from uniform, we believe Lozano (2018) is correct to diagnose a narrow conception of public sociology that primarily revolves around the dissemination model, even when this includes the participation of specified publics. It is a tendency inherent to the project, in its current formulation, as opposed to a failure of it. Public sociology in this sense has been indelibly shaped by the character of sociology as a disciplinary field in the United States where professional sociology dominates the disciplinary imagination. The vision of public sociology as resistance to professional sociology universalzed an orientation which is itself provincial, projecting it outwards from the United States to national contexts with extremely different disciplinary cultures (Arribas Lozano 2018).

To help illustrate this point, we can turn to a reflection by Gans (2016) on the mainstreaming of public sociology that explicitly frames its success or failure in terms of dissemination. He suggests that sociologists are necessary for public sociology but the public are the sufficient condition 'for until it accepts the sociology we present, it cannot become public sociology'. These remarks are confined to what he describes as 'the primary variety' of public sociology, namely 'any sociological writing or other product created by sociologists that obtains the attention of some of the publics that make up the general public' (Gans 2016). In doing so he recognizes that books and articles have been supplemented by new forms of media, such as podcasts or blog posts, which might achieve a much wider circulation than sociological writing. He advocates a 'clear and parsimonious language, with as little technical vocabulary as possible' in order to 'help the public understand the product' and to 'enable the presenters, who are generally not sociologists, to communicate it to their publics'. This reflects his assumption that presenters 'offer sociologists the only access to the non-student public' and 'the process by which sociology turns public must begin by attracting the attention of the presenters' who then ensure sociology can be presented to a public. These include teachers, journalists, editors, columnists, book reviewers, film makers and trade presses. It is a conception of public sociology which sees sociologists as operating at an intractable distance from publics, unavoidably relying on mediators in order to facilitate engagement, the success or failure of which is primarily judged in terms of the reach of sociological outputs outside the professional community of the academy. It involves a linear trajectory in which research moves (or fails to) from 'in here' to passive audiences 'out there' with the success or failure of this movement being amenable to audience analysis because these are known rather than knowing publics (Kennedy and Moss 2015).

This is Lozano's (2018) dissemination model explicated with great clarity. It conveys much of what we shall argue is the vernacular understanding of public sociology within the discipline, at least beyond the specialized literature, with the term conveying public engagement by sociologists often through the unacknowledged lens of the 'public intellectual'. Even with sophisticated accounts of what public sociology *is* alongside them, what public sociologists *do* (or aspire to) can often be another matter. The rhetoric of public sociology can be an occasion to restage the performance of the intellectual in spite of the decline of the conditions which facilitated it (Baert 2015). There is a tendency for public sociology to slide from dialogicity in theory to dissemination in practice, encouraged by the apparatus of legacy scholarship. The influence of sociology's traditional platforms exercises a constraining influence over aspirations towards engagement, with the weight of books and papers pressing down on those with the ambition that sociology might be a companion to action. However, a parallel tendency can be found in sociology's emerging platforms grounded in the ideology of social media propounded by platform firms and the aforementioned tendencies regarding outputs, expertise and knowledge. In this sense, we are arguing that the platform imaginary we elaborated earlier, in which we rely on dissemination engines to escape the ivory tower and ameliorate social problems, should be understood as over-determined. There are three distinct trends pushing our practice in this direction and it's essential to overcome them because a bigger change is underway and we need to grasp it, if sociology is going to realize the promise of its platforms. The coordinates in which a Gansian public intellectual operates are rapidly breaking down such that this model will in the future cease to be action guiding, as well as already being somewhat untenable for scholars who deviate from the traditional image of the public intellectual with the consequences that entails in platformized environments where misogyny and racism are endemic (McMillan Cottom 2015).

Social media provides us with an opportunity to move beyond the dissemination model in which, as Gans (2016) puts it, publics have the last word but sociologists have the first. These platforms encourage us to adopt a more collaborative orientation for which, we agree with

Lozano (2018: 105), 'the position of the professional scholar needs to be decentred'. But it also means the position of outputs and the position of audiences need to be decentred as well. For these are corollaries of the professional scholar when *he* (we use this pronoun deliberately) descends from the ivory tower to turn outwards, promulgating knowledge commodities to external audiences who are more or less able to receive them. In a later chapter, we argue that the epistemic conditions emerging in social media platforms, as well as the broader social and cultural trends they reflect, mean this model is becoming untenable. It will be necessary to leave it behind for the public face of the discipline to survive. In fact perhaps for the discipline as a whole. But first we need to look more closely at the current practice of public sociology and consider how social media can and is taken up as part of it. This will enable us to move beyond it in subsequent chapters as a contribution to what Hartmann (2017: 4) describes as the project of building a '"next generation" framework for sociological engagement'. If this chapter seemed unduly negative in its preoccupation with the view we must move away from, it is because it was necessary to clear away the conceptual detritus littering the field before we could move on to develop something more positive.

5

The Past, Present and Future of Public Sociology

For many sociologists, public sociology and Michael Burawoy are indelibly associated, as if it were a project he initiated with his presidential address to the American Sociological Association in the early years of the 20th century. Though understandable when one figure has played such a crucial role in popularizing the term, such mental associations betray a complex history which precedes his formulation. In tracing the origins of the term 'public sociology', one is immediately confronted with a penumbra of problems; historical, epistemological, philosophical, ethical and political alike. Historical because there is no adequate historiography of the term, philosophical because it is an immensely difficult term to accurately pinpoint without the risk of sounding arbitrary or selective, ethical because the term's parentage is uncertain, with Gans (1989), Seidman (1998), Agger (2007) and Burawoy (2005) all aspiring to the role of the putative father, and lastly, political because, as Becker (2003: 661) notes, 'what things are called always reflects relations of power', with aspirations to legitimation, recognition, influence, and authority.

This concatenation of dilemmas makes it difficult to establish any authoritative definition of the term 'public sociology', or provide any accurate depiction of where it resides in the relevant literature and public usage. Rather than an attempt to describe 'public sociology' as an ineluctable fact of the discipline's history, we approach it for these reasons as an ongoing, and often confusing intellectual debate. We are much more interested in the debates which now tend to be signposted using the terminology of public sociology than we are in the term itself. In this way we hope to remain grounded in the existing literature while moving beyond it to engage with the field of practice often named using this term but which inevitably extends far beyond the naming power it is able to exercise. It also means that the thrust of our argument is relevant for other disciplines making a public turn (public anthropology, public criminology, public humanities, and so on) even if the substance of it remains oriented towards sociology. Under the platform ecosystem we all, as Healy (2017: 780) puts it, 'face the challenge of figuring out how to work successfully in a latently public, ambiently visible way'. This is true across disciplines and reflects the institutional changes we have considered in previous chapters and will return to in subsequent ones.

The past of public sociology

In the first instance of its use, in H. J. Gans' 1988 presidential address to the American Sociological Association, public sociology was ambivalently referred to initially as 'lay sociology', later as an attribute of sociologists who engage in popularizing the discipline for a broader public ('public sociologists'), and finally as 'public sociology' per se (Gans 1989: 5–7). What is remarkable and also quite puzzling about the birth of the term, however, is that it came into being almost accidentally, given that in Gans' speech and subsequent script as an article for the American Sociological Review, public sociology, unlike 'lay sociology' and 'public sociologists', is neither highlighted for emphasis, nor does it seem to feature as anything special, other than as a simple word used in passing; it is actually only mentioned once. Even if the term is used much more precisely in the specialized literature which has proliferated since Burawoy's (2005) intervention, we cite the example of Gans' presidential address to signify how the term can be used in relatively careless ways even by those who, as a matter of intellectual history, made a profound contribution to the evolution of what we term public sociology. Unlike Burawoy's (2005) project to inaugurate a new era of public sociology, mapping it out in relation to other forms of sociology in order to plot a route forward, Gans merely sought to signify a type of sociological endeavour as part of a larger argument. Seidman's (1998) use of the term is equally irregular although he does infuse it with a normative purpose. So does Agger (2007) who has grand aspirations for it as a successor script in sociology, pregnant with the possibility of re-orienting the discipline's emphasis from 'social facts' to 'literary acts', echoing Mills' (1959: 8) hope and promise for sociology to translate 'personal troubles' into 'public issues'. Michael Burawoy (2005) on the other hand, inherited both the term itself as well as its idealism from Agger, and partly from Seidman, presenting it as a neologism armed with a revolutionary aim to reconfigure the entire discipline, without acknowledging these past uses of the term.

There was a historical ambiguity built into Burawoy's project from the outset, seeing itself as naming what had not been named (*traditional public sociology*) and rendering visible what had largely gone unseen (*organic public sociology*) while remaining at a strange distance from past attempts to render this activity visible. This isn't an attack on Burawoy's achievement but rather an illustration of how the historiography of public sociology has been ambiguous from its inception. It sought to express the reality of public sociology as an existing professional practice without a name. This existence of public sociology despite its namelessness is best described by Patricia Hill Collins (2007: 101), where she admits to have been 'doing a sociology that had no name' prior to Burawoy's popularization of the term. This can be found throughout the discipline's history. Indeed, it is remarkable to read the minutes and correspondence in Keele University's Foundations of British Sociology archive where the public orientation of sociological work is seemingly axiomatic, as opposed to being something which must be popularized and pursued. In fact the vision of Victor Branford, Patrick Geddes and their collaborators that 'sociologists could join with playwrights, poets, and other artists to write and present sociological knowledge and understanding in a way that is both accessible to a general public and could motivate them to join in a strategy of social change' feels remarkably contemporary, as does their advocacy of participatory methods so that 'those most affected by contemporary conditions' could become involved in a way that 'would allow them to participate in the formulation of social policies' (Scott and Bromley 2013: loc 2063–2119). There remains much historical work to be done exploring the inspiration that can be found in sociology's archives for the contemporary practice of public sociology.

However, if we simply frame 'public sociology' as naming a subterranean tendency, we miss the performativity of the term. This popularization also sought to reconfigure sociology as a professional field, providing visibility and prestige to activities undertaken by sociologists in a manner liable to transform the opportunity structure they confronted. It was an attempt to change how the discipline of sociology operates, based on an analysis rooted in the character of American sociology even though Burawoy later sought to extend far beyond this. It is a term which now has widespread recognition, even if this goes hand-in-hand with a semantic slippage from a technical usage (for example, distinguishing between public and professional sociology) through to a vernacular one (as a general term for sociologists doing public facing work).

This creates a space in which problems can thrive. It encourages us to rehearse our intuitions about publics and our relationship with them while reassuring us that we are undertaking a recognized and delineated practice (public sociology) rather than a messy and precarious enterprise which requires our reflexivity in the fullest sense. In the last chapter we considered how social media is imagined within the academy (*platform imaginary*) and the assumptions about our work which have emerged around legacy platforms of scholarship (*scholastic disposition*). We argued that the scholarly orientation encourages an approach to social media that creates difficulties when it comes to building an audience, negotiating filtering mechanisms and thriving in the acoustics of social media. These problems are far from insurmountable and we argued that dislodging outputs, expertise and knowledge from their preeminent position goes a long way towards clearing the field of conceptual detritus that hinders the fullest exercise of our reflexivity in relation to these new contexts for our public action. But the tendency of public sociology to implicitly embody what Arribas Lozano (2018) describes as a 'dissemination model' further inclines us towards this platform imaginary by encouraging us to see social media in terms of its capacity to get our knowledge beyond the walls of the ivory tower so that it can help address social problems.

There is still much we can do in this mode and this chapter explores how social media can be taken up within the existing framework of public sociology in fruitful and exciting ways. However, in subsequent chapters we loosen our grip on the term somewhat in order to smooth over the problematic oscillation between the technical and vernacular uses of it. In this book we neither seek to dissolve the term nor secure it with a new meaning, particularly not one centred around the assumed brave new world of digital technology with all the ideological baggage that framing would carry (Carrigan 2019). Instead we want to use the term in a way which is consistent with this ambiguity, recognizing how the manner in which it is poised between technical specification and idiomatic shorthand is a product of its own meandering history. This legacy is what public sociology must address in the present and it has often failed to do so, leaving us with what at times feels like a chasm between the practice of public sociology and arcane debates taking place within a voluminous literature. As Healy (2017: 772) remarks acidly, much as German critical theorists 'succeeded in unifying theory and practice – in theory' the public sociology literature 'succeeded in unifying professional and public sociology, in professional journals'. In response to this trend our approach could be characterized as quietist in Rorty's (1989) sense: we want to gently sidestep the conceptual thickets of the public sociology debate in order to turn to practice but without collapsing conceptual discussion *into* practice. We want to recover the *doing* of public sociology in a way that ensures this remains an object of theoretical reflection, as opposed to a crude actionism which would claim the problem is too much theory and too little activism. The platform ecosystem brings new challenges for public sociology which require theoretical reflection. The challenge, as we see it, lies in recalibrating the relationship between theory and practice in a way which is adequate to these new conditions and allows us to reconstruct public sociology for them.

The present of public sociology

In 2004 the American Sociological Association's erstwhile president, Michael Burawoy, endorsed 'public sociology' as the theme of its prestigious annual meeting; a neologism that paved the way for a lively debate between sociologists over the discipline's raison d'être. Although present, by allusion rather than by name, in the work of sociologists like C. Wright Mills, Alvin Gouldner, W.E.B. Du Bois and Jane Addams, the term 'public sociology' was mobilized by Burawoy in his presidential address to describe and foster a sociological ethos of publicly relevant and engaging sociological practice. As Blau and Smith (2006: xvii) observe, this gave 'a sense that the floodgates had at long last been opened and that they were liberated to profess a sociology that was relevant, critical and publicly responsible, if not in partnership with publics'. The popular appeal of Burawoy's speech, 'For Public Sociology', transcended the confines of the 2004 ASA meetings, resulting in publication in the *American Sociological Review* soon after the event, while the *British Journal of Sociology* republished the original paper and dedicated its next volume to hosting replies to Michael Burawoy with contributions from a host of distinguished scholars, followed by Burawoy's own response to his critics. 'For Public Sociology' soon appeared in multiple languages, sparking open and broad discussions between professional sociologists and a web-based database of books, papers, symposia and videos compiled by Burawoy at his Berkeley webpage. It was characterized by a fundamentally ethnographic sensibility in which Burawoy turned the ethnographic eye inward on his own profession in order to see how knowledge can be turned outwards by doing public sociology.

It is not our intention to summarize Burawoy's 11 theses or the voluminous literature which these provoked but rather to convey its appraisal of public sociology and the work this sought to do in shaping its future. This entails understanding how the public sociology Burawoy sought to champion relates to the professional practice that characterizes the core of the discipline. In Burawoy's mind sociology should remain professional above all, with this supplying true and tested methods, accumulated bodies of knowledge, with specifically oriented questions and conceptual frameworks. Research in professional sociology is conducted within research programmes that define assumptions, theories, concepts, questions and puzzles and allows these to be openly contested by critical sociology. Critical sociology examines the foundations, explicit and implicit, normative and descriptive, of the research programmes of professional sociology and hosts critical debates within and between research programmes. Most importantly, critical sociology is credited by Burawoy for giving us the two fundamental ontological questions that place the four sociologies in relation to each other; 'sociology for whom?' and 'sociology for what?' Inspired by Alfred McClung Lee's 1976 ASA presidential address, Burawoy revisits the 'sociology for whom' question, wondering whether we are simply talking to ourselves (an academic audience) or we are also addressing others (an extra-academic audience). He goes on to ask 'sociology for what' where the question mark this time examines the very substantive matter of sociology, that is the direction of the knowledge(s) produced within the discipline. This is in contrast to policy sociology which is undertaken in service of a goal defined by a client and positions itself in defence of sociological research, human subjects, funding and congressional briefings. He suggested the differences between them can be usefully characterized in terms of the distinction between 'instrumental' and 'reflexive' knowledge; the former referring to puzzle-solving professional sociology or the problem-solving of policy sociology, while the latter interrogates the value premises of our profession and society stressing the need for a dialogue between academics and various publics about the direction of research programmes and society too.

These four types of sociological knowledge constitute a functional differentiation of sociology spelling out who does what, but also four distinct perspectives on and of sociology, each trying to advance its own research initiative while recognizing their cohabitation in the same grid. Each type on its own would have been useless, in Burawoy's thinking, without its leaning to and borrowings from the others. A useful metaphor to explain this productive tension within the discipline is to imagine each type as a soldier fighting a different battle for the same war, where professional sociology would provide the ammunition and would be the discipline's trooper, policy sociology would assume the role of the engineer while critical and public sociologies would function as the guardian and the moralist, respectively. The lived careers of sociologists unfold in the agonistic interdependence between these sociologies in a manner that can imbue their existence with an ambivalent character while also shaping the constitution of the discipline as a whole. Burawoy (2005: 13) emphasizes this with reference to a number of sociologists from W.E.B. Du Bois and C. Wright Mills in the 20th century to James Coleman and Chris Jencks in the 21st century, to illustrate this mobility within and between the quadrants, with their unusual combination of public, critical, professional and policy moments in their careers leading to a tension between institution and habitus. Each of these entails a different mode of justification which supplies these trajectories with a distinct texture, as movements between them involve differing conceptions of why we do what we do and what it means to do it effectively. Professional sociology justifies itself on the basis of scientific norms and is subjected to peer review; policy sociology justifies itself on the basis of its effectiveness and reports to clients; public sociology advertises its relevance and is accountable to a designated public, while critical sociology supplies moral visions and stands in front of a community of critical intellectuals.

In an earlier chapter, we encountered Burawoy's (2005) distinction between traditional public sociology and organic public sociology. The former is the familiar preserve of the public intellectual who uses mass media to talk and write about matters of public concern with the intention of reaching an audience beyond the academy. The publics involved in these debates are 'generally invisible in that they cannot be seen, thin in that they do not generate much internal interaction, passive in that they do not constitute a movement or organization, and they are usually mainstream' (Burawoy 2005: 7). In contrast the latter is a matter of sociologists working 'in close connection with a visible, thick, active, local and often counterpublic' with Burawoy (2004: 8) citing examples such as 'a labor movement, neighborhood associations, communities of faith, immigrant rights groups, human rights organizations'.

Even though Burawoy presents the two as complementary, he sees a tendency towards elitism within public sociology which has helped the spectacle of (usually) white men talking to dispersed audiences dominate the imagination of the public role sociology can play, in the process marginalizing the organic public sociology often undertaken by much more diverse sociologists and going unrecognized by the disciplinary mainstream (Burawoy 2002). For example in an imagined open letter to C. Wright Mills, Burawoy (2008) takes issue with what he claims was the propensity of Mills to 'talk down to publics'. While he frames this as typical of a traditional public sociology that has tended to involve 'books written for but not with publics', it is a distinction which ought to be revisited with a view to social media because the detachment which Burawoy sees as the basis of this elitism is precisely what is undergoing a subtle transformation driven (inter alia) by social media. Following Bacevic (2019a, 2019b, 2019c), we are interested in the institutional and imaginative (re)construction of this distance and see it as eroded by the tendency of social platforms to facilitate interaction across distinct sectors of social life. We need a conception of public sociology which is adequate to the platformized boundary work which this entails.

Traditional public sociology

Print media

If traditional public sociology tends to be exhausted in the imagination of sociologists by op-eds in papers of records, the proliferation of new modes of publication is exciting and important. Online publications which feature academy commentary have proliferated in recent years. Aeon, Open Democracy, Slate, Quartz, Current Affairs, Public Seminar, Jacobin, Real Life and the New Inquiry are just a few examples of the many outlets which recruit academics, often without the constraints of length and style which tend to be attached to the op-ed. These are joined by expanding online supplements to familiar magazines and newspapers. Furthermore, there is a vibrant ecology of academic blogs, ranging from the small and amateur through to the large and professionalized, which traverse sectoral boundaries and inevitably attract at least some interested non-academic audience even when their content is unapologetically academic. This crossover potential can be seen most strikingly in the hosting deal the Monkey Cage political science blog signed with the *Washington Post*, effectively incorporating itself into the global newspaper's online stable.

Even if the traditional op-ed retains its lure, there are many advantages to publishing with online magazines: freedom from the news cycle, more space to make an argument and the likelihood a well-received piece will be published elsewhere (Stein and Daniels 2017: 44–45).

The last point reflects an important feature of an online ecosystem in which formal and informal syndication agreements are common: blog posts are republished across a network of connected sites, with larger sites often relating to smaller ones as reliable sources of content. This is particularly pronounced with an initiative like The Conversation where syndication in the mass media is often an outcome and professional journalists work with academics to produce pieces in a style which renders this more likely. However, it often takes a more quotidian form where blog editors have informal reposting relationships between themselves or a number of online magazines cooperate where they have overlapping interests. Under these conditions articles travel, through social media and republishing, in a way which would have been difficult to conceive of in a past media environment. In the most straightforward sense, there are simply more outlets willing to publish social scientific analysis than was previously the case. Whereas Wolfgang Streeck (2011) could ask a decade ago whether sociology had a 'demand problem', quite the opposite is now true when there are more forums than ever for sociological research to be published for varying sizes of public audience.

There are reasons we ought to be cautious about this. For example, The Conversation has generated controversy in recent years for its policy of refusing access to those without a university affiliation, with their distinctive funding model of subscriptions by universities exercising a constraint over their operations. It's not our intention to intervene in this controversy, as two authors who have actively supported The Conversation and remain interested in the potential of this model. However, the case illustrates key issues which are at stake in traditional public sociology within the new media ecology. Who labours to produce content? How is this labour reimbursed? What value is added to this labour? Who benefits from it? In the case of The Conversation, its tight cleavage with the university system means the labour falls under the rubric of the impact agenda; universities are in practice buying access to editorial support and a distribution platform for their academics to undertake activity which is now expected as part of their occupational role. The added value comes from the editorial expertise provided, with a professional journalist working with each academic on a one-to-one basis, as well as the promotional expertise they have accumulated.

We shouldn't lose sight of how an underlying transformation in publishing, with less staff being expected to produce more copy, means there is more demand for authors than ever before (Abramson 2019). At risk of putting this too bluntly: are academics just overly verbose journalists who write for free? Even if it would be simplistic to answer 'yes' to this question and simply move on, it is a reminder that we must remain attentive to a political economy of digital publishing which is still unfolding, as struggling publishers adapt to an environment now transformed by social media (Caplan and boyd 2018, Fourier 2018). It is crucial that public sociology remains reflexive in this environment so that we can reflectively adapt and seek to intervene in shaping a landscape that is still far from settled. We need to sustain a professional awareness of these changes, including criticizing them when necessary. The risk is that we otherwise confront them as a series of individualized opportunities to get our research 'out there' without attending to the aggregate consequences of embracing these developments.

Social media can make academics more easily discoverable by the media. The role which learned societies and communications offices once played as gatekeepers to expertise is steadily eroding as a simple internet search will often prove quicker and easier for journalists or broadcast researchers seeking expertise relevant to their work. It's important to stress that this is a new relation with the media rather than the disintermediation promised by the cyberutopian prophets – the role of gatekeepers changes rather than being eliminated. Existing media players are more powerful than ever, as gatekeepers to online audiences and mediators of message, even if the manner in which they exercise this power has changed (Couldry 2012). Interactions of this sort are not dependent on social media but having a personal presence on these platforms can be a valuable way to mediate the relationship. What matters is the digital footprint: the traces which an academic leaves about their work online which might be found by someone in the media and encourage them to make contact. What might otherwise seem to be a narcissistic concern for online identity can actually be a crucial practice of curating one's identity, ensuing a digital footprint expresses a desirable narrative and making it less likely a reader will infer unhelpful conclusions on the basis of it (Carrigan 2019: 150–173). A platform like Twitter is well suited to building relationships across institutional boundaries, facilitating a thin relationship to be sustained that can be activated for collaboration at a later date.

However, the interface between the academy and the media can also be rather messy. Many social scientists with a large digital footprint have found themselves emailed by a journalist with a deadline and a request for a quote, in some cases specifying what they would like the academic to say to an uncomfortably specific degree. While this might not be problematic in itself, these requests can often betray a lack of research (having little to no relevance to one's topic of study) and be framed in a panicked tone which asks for a response within hours. This clash of temporal regimes can be jarring to those party to it, not least of all for journalists who often find the glacial pace of knowledge production in the academy frustrating when they are forced to engage with it. This can be a problem for ambitious projects which seek to bridge the gap between research and journalism, as was the case for the Reading the Riots project undertaken by the LSE and the *Guardian* after the English riots of 2011 (Carrigan and Brumley 2013). The increasingly porous interface between the media and the academy can also be a problem when it leads journalists to report on tweets, in some cases opening up the academics involved to online abuse when their tweets are taken out of context. But this is unlikely to change given the uptake of social media by journalists and academics, rendering it the new normal to which public sociology must adapt. This in turn calls into question the existing relationship between the two groups, in which academics relied on journalists to translate their research for a general audience (Stein and Daniels 2017).

Books

Thus far we have focused on magazines and newspapers, exploring how this traditional preserve of public sociology has been changed by the proliferation of new outlets and a transformed environment in which they operate. Books are no less significant, either as a route through which traditional public sociology can be undertaken or as a vector through which social media is making itself felt in the circulation of knowledge. While one of our central arguments is that public sociology is likely to be ineffective in the platform era if its imaginary remains dominated by the book, it won't have escaped your awareness that this is an argument you are reading in a book. It's not so much that we need to leave behind 'old' ways of doing public sociology in order to embrace 'new' ones but rather adapting to an environment in which the former and the latter are possible moments in a broader trajectory of publicness (Healy 2017). The characteristics of platforms which we encountered in Chapters 2 and 3, particularly their visibility and spreadability, render our everyday orientation towards publicness much more important in relation to the publicity of our outputs than was previously the case. In fact success at the traditional undertakings of public sociology increasingly depends on a willingness to engage prior to and following the publication, as publishers look to the 'platform' (in the sense of an existing audience and ability to command attention) an author brings with them when making commissioning decisions

(Thompson 2010: 86). Much as the visibility accumulated through social media can be transformed into academic capital under certain conditions (such as when the capacity to be an 'engaged academic' is valued by institutions), it can also be transformed into media capital when publishers are concerned about the crossover potential of academic books in a crowded marketplace (Couldry 2003).

Stein and Daniels (2017: 82–83) reflect what this means in practice when pitching books to publishers who are concerned about an author's capacity to attract and sustain a relationship with an audience. There is a profound opportunity to deepen engagement with an audience through these dialogues which surround the publication process but we should also recognize how they are driven by the competitive pressures of an attention economy, necessitating a form of brand management which is an emotionally and temporally costly undertaking that remains unpaid by the publishers who benefit from it (Marwick 2013). It's also an enforced sociality which is much easier for white European males such as ourselves who are rarely objects of online abuse, ranging from the draining accumulation of chronic mansplaining through to criminal levels of harassment which are a recurrent feature of platforms for women, people of colour, queer, trans and differently abled scholars (Carrigan 2019: 121–149). If we remain fixated on the outputs, talking merely about new online magazines we could write for and new outlets through which to promote our books, it would be difficult to understand the platform ecosystem and what it means for different groups within the academy who are seeking an audience. This is why we need a sociology of publics in Burawoy's (2004) sense, helping us understand the shifting ontology of public life and what it means for the aspiration towards public sociology. However, it also has a more instrumental purpose, facilitating the mental mapping necessary to negotiate what Beer (2013) describes as the politics of circulation encountered across digital platforms: who gets heard, why they get heard and how what they say travels. This is another way of talking about what we considered in the last section as the acoustics of social media (Margetts 2017a). Decentring our focus away from outputs is not a rejection of their importance but is inter alia a strategy for better ensuring their successful circulation of an expanded array of publications (books, chapters, papers, essays, blog posts, podcasts, videocasts, tweets) in an information environment as rife with opportunities as it is challenges.

In fact, books are a particularly interesting output through which to understand the shift in the politics of circulation underway and what it means for the familiar outputs of traditional public sociology. As

Stein and Daniels (2017: 74) reflect in a thoughtful appraisal of the possibilities and pitfalls involved in writing books of social science for popular audiences:

> While some scholars may see such books as outside the bounds of academic knowledge production, they are in fact sophisticated translations of social science for general audiences. These works of popular social science were widely reviewed, generating a host of new conversations about the nature of urban poverty, the changing roles of men and women, the politics of intelligence testing, and Americans' false fears and assumptions, among other topics.

There is a remarkable public hunger for books of this sort, even if it might fall short of the audience that greeted some of the canonical works of traditional public sociology (Carrigan 2019: 95). There has also been a rich vein of popular social scientific writing in recent years produced by journalists drawing on academic research. Perhaps the foremost figure has been Malcolm Gladwell, whose most popular books have sold millions of copies. He was the recipient of the inaugural American Sociological Association Award for Excellence in the Reporting of Social Issues in 2007. The *New York Times* columnist David Brooks, occupying a similar intellectual niche to Gladwell, came to be awarded the same honour in 2011. The ASA's (2011) award statement illustrates how sociological knowledge comes to be represented in the work of such public figures, observing that 'his columns have described or otherwise promoted the work of scholars including Manuel Castells, Christopher Jencks, Lisa Keister, Annette Lareau, and Robert Wuthnow'. Given the body making the award, it is understandable that it is concerned with the presence of sociological themes in the author's work. However, there are other influences at work, particularly social psychology, which point to the ambiguity involved in seizing on journalists and opinion formers as champions of the discipline, even if encouraging outreach of this sort is nevertheless a valuable activity.

We should be cautious in our engagements with Gans' (2016) 'presenters'. Even if we were to count such figures uncritically as public proponents of sociological thought, we would still confront a public sphere saturated with psychological and economic analysis exemplified by a title like *Freakonomics*, a collaboration between a 'rogue economist' and a journalist which had sold 4 million copies worldwide by late 2009. It subsequently spawned a sequel, a documentary, a podcast and a consulting group. Prominent behavioural economists figured in the latter project, particularly Daniel Kahneman who became a best-selling author himself with his *Thinking Fast and Slow*. This summary of his lifelong research, foundational to behavioural economics had sold over a million copies by 2012. Sociologists face an intellectual marketplace which is extremely crowded by other disciplines, as well as journalists popularizing social science. In the face of this challenge, skilful engagement with social media is as much the price of admission as it is an opportunity to get your research 'out there'. However, this isn't a matter of compulsively seeking followers but rather understanding the platform ecosystem so as to be able to use it to your strategic advantage. This is what we think of as **platform literacy** and it's necessary to negotiate the challenges and opportunities which are opening up for the practice of public sociology.

Reviews

For example, it is still far from clear what role social media is coming to play in the reviews, conversations and political discussions likely to flow from such books. There has been an exciting emergence of digitally native review sites, ranging from the public-literary (LA Review of Books) through to the scholarly-academic (LSE Review of Books). This has been supplemented by literary journals undergoing something of a renaissance, encompassing the existing (*London Review of Books*) and the new entrants (n+1), as well as a tendency for academic journals to move their book reviews onto free to access sites (*Theory, Culture, Society*). However, there are also dedicated platforms for 'lay' book reviewing, as well as countless conversations about books taking place on mass commercial social media platforms. For example, there are 85 million registered members of Good Reads and this is merely the most popular of a number of book platforms (Statista 2019). We also shouldn't forget the role reviews play on a platform like Amazon, even if there remain many questions about the significance we should attribute to them (Stone 2013). Even if the audience for popular social science books has in one sense fragmented, in another sense it has become much more open and connected.

Social media offers exciting opportunities to build multifaceted conversations with such a readership, making it possible to supplement books which tend to be devoid of jargon and distant from the literature with pathways into scholarship that interested readers might follow. It's undeniably the case that some topics simply have much greater capacity to incite public interest than others (Stein and Daniels 2017: 65).

This has been our own experience as sociologists whose work on asexuality (Carrigan 2011) and UK grime and drill music (Fatsis, 2019a, 2019b) has attracted much public interest but our other work on social ontology and history of public sociology has attracted much less. Furthermore, epistemic hierarchies make themselves felt in the attention economy such that it will often prove easier for economists and psychologists to attract an audience then it will be for sociologists and anthropologists. Nonetheless, we shouldn't treat these hierarchies as fixed, even as we take them seriously as practical constraints. The evaluative cultures which platforms are giving rise to, even if they are largely predicated on thin social relations, suggest that participation in them could play a role in rendering these hierarchies mutable. Skilful engagement with review sites, particularly smaller and more specialized ones, offer important opportunities. The same is true with a view to the podcasting boom and the sustained influence of YouTube, with podcasts and channels existing across an incredibly diverse range of topics that have an interest in academic work. These include podcasts produced by mainstream media organizations which provide avenues for academic engagement, if for no other reason than there's more channel space which needs to be filled (usually with less budget with which to fill it). Perhaps more excitingly, it includes a thriving ecology of grassroots podcasts which are increasingly media operations in their own right through their use of crowdfunding platforms, often pushing beyond the frontiers of the traditional media and offering exciting avenues for academic debate and discussion. These include popular podcasts established by academic with vast audiences. For example, the Talking Politics podcast based at the University of Cambridge's Department of Politics and International Studies has been downloaded over 5 million times while the Philosophy Bites podcast has been downloaded over 40 million times. As we will discuss in greater depth, when these are successful they have consolidated a bond with an audience. The theoretical significance of this will have to wait for another chapter but we wished to underscore the practical opportunity it offers.

It's important to reiterate the extent to which engagement can be read as a form of emotional labour which the attention economy renders necessary, increasingly expected by book publishers and suggested by magazines and newspapers (Marwick 2013). Sharing updates, responding to messages and filtering content can be a time consuming process, particularly if it is undertaken with a resigned sense of necessity. It can often feel like work and in an important sense it is work. These platforms come with their own sunk costs, leaving one more or less committed to a platform where one has invested time in building connections. This engagement can't be reduced to a transaction but much of the behaviour of academics on it becomes somewhat inexplicable if we deny the contours of strategic conduct. It's a necessary feature of accumulating visibility within the platform ecosystem and until we become comfortable talking about that necessity, it will remain difficult to provide support and guidance to each other on how to negotiate it.

Organic public sociology

Platforms collapse the distance between author and reader in the manner analysed by Stewart (2018) and Seymour (2019) while also rendering it necessary to shout in order to be heard, at the very least suggesting to publishers that you exhibit an independent potential to be heard. However, there remains an ambiguity about the point at which self-promotion in this sense bleeds into public engagement. If your engagement with an audience is centred around a matter of common concern, is talking to them about a piece you wrote on this topic *really* self-promotion? It is a notion with a transactional connotation that belies the affective richness of online interaction (Papacharissi 2015). If what you are doing is an expression of what matters to you, in Sayer's (2011) sense of motivating your activity as well as imbuing it with meaning, characterizing it in terms of a transaction is an alienated (and possibly alienating) way of understanding your own behaviour. This isn't to deny that self-promotion exists, it's rather to interrogate how we frame the concept and its implied relationship to promotion which lacks the implied strategic element. Too often there's an implicit moral psychology lurking within the notion, suggesting a clear division between instrumental rationality and value rationality, which obscures rather than clarifies the practical dimensions of using social platforms for public sociology.

Social media platforms exist in part to choreograph interactions around shared interests, simply because this is a reliable means to keep users engaged with the platform. This means that building an audience can be a matter of value rationality as much as instrumentality, helping us see a way to transcend the antinomy introduced in Chapter 3: for public sociologists acting out of a commitment to a cause, building an audience on social media is organic public sociology. It is a particularly *thin* form of it but its value shouldn't be underestimated. Under conditions of social distancing, it is also the only form of audience building which is likely to be accessible. This doesn't mean we should be uncritical of the activity, let alone the corporate platforms on which it depends. However, it does suggest we ought to recognize its potential uses while avoiding any a priori judgement that 'online' organization is inherently inferior to 'offline' organization.

It's not a replacement for the other forms which organic public sociology can take but it has the potential to function as a powerful precursor to them, including a fuzzing up of the boundary between inside/outside that is usually entailed by a scholarly orientation. Interactions with them could easily be perceived as transactional, often involving little more than ensuring the mutual flow of information across sectoral boundaries. These minimal units of social interaction, particularly pronounced on a platform like Twitter, often give rise to unfamiliar forms of ambient knowledge that shouldn't be underestimated. While each particular insight may be trivial, it nonetheless contributes to what Reichelt (2007) calls 'ambient intimacy': a background of awareness about other people and their lives, facilitating a degree of acquaintance with peripheral social connections which would otherwise be precluded by constraints of time, energy and geography. This is something which can feed back into 'offline' relations, as the bonding of occasional meetings is reinforced by an undercurrent of mediated connection. This can be supplemented by more direct forms of engagement that could lead to any number of developments depending on how the interaction proceeds.

It might help to offer an example of what this entails in practice. One of us spent a number of years undertaking research with the asexual community, fascinated by how their experience complicated orthodox understandings of sexuality and frustrated by the complete absence of this group from the existing literature on the sociology of sexuality (Carrigan 2011, 2013). There are plausible reasons to believe there have always been people who do not experience sexual attraction but until the internet it was difficult for members of such a dispersed group to find each other and share their experiences. The role that digital platforms have played in the formation of this community, through the Asexuality Visibility and Education Network bulletin board (founded in 2001) and the range of social media platforms which emerged in the ensuing years, ensure a degree of organization that would otherwise be unlikely. This includes outreach initiatives with researchers and the media, seeking to raise awareness and encourage engagement, ranging from the collectively planned through to the individually spontaneous.

This means that research is read, discussed and sometimes criticized in ways that are particularly visible in the relatively small field of asexuality studies (Carrigan et al 2013). This can be enormously beneficial in providing opportunities for familiarization, interaction and learning that can feed directly into the research process. Under these conditions a slide into advocacy occurs easily through the opportunities for work with the media, contributions to campaigns, speaking at events and participation in public conversations which ensue from the increasing density of connections with the group in question. But it can also be difficult for those researchers who expect to work at a distance from those they are writing about and are unprepared for the latently public character, to use Healy's (2017) term, which work in relation to such a proactive online group inevitably comes to possess. This isn't just a matter of social platforms eroding the boundary between the university and other sectors, it's the agency of those we write about responding to our representation of them across these increasingly porous institutional divides.

If we insist on thinking in terms of research/dissemination phases (outputs), experts studying non-experts (expertise) and the accumulation of knowledge as inherently efficacious (knowledge) then the coordinates of this process remain difficult to grasp. But once we decentre these elements from the pride of place they enjoyed with legacy platforms then a new mode of organic engagements becomes legible in which research and advocacy merge into one another, at least when it comes to already constituted publics like the asexual community. Social media offers new ways of identifying and beginning to engage with groups, of supporting groups and of making this activity visible within the academy in a way that might draw others into their remit (Pausé and Russell 2016). Social media is changing how such groups can come together, particularly in their initial stages, by offering new opportunities and challenges for assembling similarly-concerned people in time and space (Carrigan 2016). It's a complex and exciting process which we struggle to grasp, either theoretically or practically, if we remain wedded to the categories of legacy scholarship. But it's also a challenging undertaking which can't be assumed to be successful simply in virtue of the communicative powers of social platforms (Shephard et al 2018). It requires careful reflection and sustained work in order to develop reliable and adaptable strategies to guide what we are doing. Most of all it requires platform literacy so that we understand how social platforms facilitate and frustrate such undertakings, as well as how we can act in ways which encourage the former and avoid the latter.

A similar point can be made about students, a group who have been invoked within the literature as a significant public for sociology, with whom our relationship is changing as social media cuts through the ivory tower (Burawoy 2005, Gans 2016). In the British context, student engagement is prized throughout the academy, framed by management as the barometer of success under conditions of marketization. Yet forms of student engagement which fall outside of this managerial conception are readily derided as pathological, leading to sanctions which may in some cases go as far as police involvement and legal action. Such examples are comparatively rare, usually confined to truncated periods of upheaval within the campus life of an institution, while being all the more illustrative for being exceptions. They reveal the narrow confines within which 'engagement' is encouraged, suggesting what is in fact hoped for is predictable action from individual students, rather than the collective assertion of a student body in pursuit of self-derived objectives. What is sought is *involvement*, the weakest sense of engagement, without the participation crucial to the stronger sense of the term (Kelty 2020).

There are exciting opportunities for public sociology with students in this context. For example, cases of students seeking to exercise an influence over the curriculum have proliferated in recent years. These range from university wide campaigns, such as Liberate The Curriculum by the National Union of Students in the UK and the Decolonise The Curriculum movement, through to discipline specific campaigns, such as the Cambridge Society for Economic Pluralism and the Post-Crash Economics Society. While students calling for curriculum reform is a familiar occurrence, with much earlier roots in the expansion of higher education coupled with the radicalizing influence of new social movements, it is worth noting how these campaigns have drawn on social media in pursuit of their aims, as well as how the issues they address have been debated through these platforms by the wider academic community.

For instance Rethinking Economics, a global network of campaigns to diversify the teaching of economics with its origins in conversations taking place at the University of Sydney in the 1990s, enjoys a substantial following across social media: 16,800 Twitter followers, 18,930 Facebook followers and 852 YouTube subscribers at the time of writing. The latter seems particularly significant, as a diverse array of 22 full-length lectures facilitate the circulation of substantive academic perspectives far beyond the confines of the rooms where these events were held. The Decolonise The Curriculum movement, working to overcome the eurocentrism of the curriculum, grew in recent years across universities in the UK, with the Rhodes Must Fall in Oxford campaign being a crucial vector in its development. As Sabarantam (2017) notes, 'contestations over the politics of knowledge are as old as universities themselves and in this sense the present student campaign is itself a manifestation of the fusty old academic tradition – to challenge received wisdom, to ask questions about society and to generate the insight needed to change the world'.

What makes these campaigns noteworthy are the speed with which they've spread, the visibility they have accrued and how effective they have been in many cases. Participation can range from encouraging debate within seminars, adapting reading lists and participating in events through to organizing campaigns and engaging in public advocacy about these issues. However, this is complex and challenging terrain. The rise of 'free speech' as an organizing principle for the political right, with the university as its crucible as Davies (2018) observes, means that advocates must tread carefully when think tanks, pressure groups and attack journalists listen in to a once opaque ivory tower which is increasingly made of transparent glass (Carrigan 2017b). Furthermore, there is no reason to be confident these mobilizations will be in pursuit of progressive causes, as projects like Professor Watchlist encourage conservative students to report on the perceived bias of their professors. Given the likelihood that the COVID-19 crisis will only entrench political polarization, we can plausibly expect such undertakings will grow as they seek to take advantage of the rapidly declining logistical costs associated with intervening in campus politics.

There are opportunities for organic public sociology with students which digital platforms open up but they simultaneously contribute to an environment in which such involvement or its absence are increasingly likely to be contested. This further erodes the distinction considered in the previous chapter between 'in here' and 'out there' such that politics becomes either something we engage in once we leave the ivory tower or something we do through our scholarship which is elevated to politically efficacious status through our faith in speech acts (Bacevic 2019a, 2019b). It is a difficult context which is likely to become more so with time, even if the contours of these changes vary between national systems. Though we must recognize when considering the upsurge of student activism and the possibility of our contribution to it that, as Bhambra (2016) points out, 'the marketization of the public university entails an attack on precisely this diversity within the institutional forms of knowledge production'. Sociology is a discipline which grew, particularly in the UK, through the expansion of higher education (coupled with the influence of new social movements) and its intellectual character has always been bound up in the dynamics of that expansion (Williams et al 2017).

This is why the transformation of the sector poses such a challenge for public sociology: the encounter Burawoy (2004) describes between the discipline and 'diverse publics' risks becoming decreasingly likely, intensifying a broader set of pathologies afflicting the discipline (Holmwood 2010, Beer 2014). This is why the university figures prominently in the coming chapters because it remains the grounds from which sociologists employed within it undertake public sociology, even if these endeavours can't easily be captured by a sense of the university's boundaries. Students as publics embody this powerfully by reminding us that the politics taking place 'in here' (marketization, metricization and managerialism) influence the relationship we have with publics who we tend to think of as 'out there'. In this sense public sociology can provide a frame for political activity within the university, particularly the defence of the public university, without being confined to the university and those who work within it.

The role of social platforms in this is more obvious than ever given the **crisis platformization** which COVID-19 has necessitated, with universities rapidly pivoting towards online operations to cope with the requirements of social distancing. Digital platforms have enabled a rapid pivot towards online operations to cope with the requirements of social distancing, with this transition being a short sharp shock disrupting the personal and collective routines on which organizations depend. However, the same platforms provide us with the means to collectively make sense of this transformation, as well as exercise an influence over them. We are suggesting that public sociology be seen as part of such an undertaking, refusing a clear boundary between 'in here' and 'out there' in order to investigate the conditions of our labour in a rapidly changing academy and what this means for our potential undertakings.

The future of public sociology

In these terms social media seems like an obvious benefit for public sociology. However, there are many problems which we have only touched on here. In part this is because we don't intend the present volume as a manual: Carrigan (2019), Mollett et al (2017) and Stein and Daniels (2017) each perform this role in different ways. Our focus will be on conceptualizing the sources of these problems rather than on enumerating the practical difficulties which academics typically encounter in their use of them. In doing so we want to move beyond a focus on how individuals can use platforms for their own purposes, characteristic of so much of the scholarly and grey literature on social media for academics, in order to consider how we can collectively build projects which take advantage of the opportunities while mitigating the problems of platforms. This will be the first step in moving beyond a public sociology which is tied to the legacy platforms of scholarship in order to develop a framework which is oriented towards the problems and prospects of social media. These are platforms which it should be remembered emerged at around the same time as Burawoy's (2005) ASA address (Healy 2017: 771). Facebook was founded a few months before, YouTube the following year and Twitter the year after that. Now that the full significance of these platforms appears clear, it is necessary to rethink public sociology in light of them. Particularly when we remain dependent on them at the time of writing for intellectual conviviality, as social distancing means that face-to-face conferences, seminars and workshops remain untenable. Even if this situation will prove to be a fleeting occurrence, this radicalized dependence on social platforms should be an experience we learn from as we seek to imagine what scholarship looks like under changing circumstances.

We can take inspiration in this challenge from platform cooperativism, the diverse and growing movement which seeks to develop equitable and participatory alternatives to corporate intermediaries. As one of its initiators Scholz (2017: 191) has put it, 'platform capitalism is getting defined top-down by decisions made in Silicon Valley, executed by black box algorithms' but platform cooperativism can provide 'a new story about sharing, aggregation, openness, and cooperation; one that we can believe in'. There are examples which can be seen in a wide array of sectors, ranging from transportation through to photography and time-banking. In some cases these projects have been backed by trade unions resisting the encroachment of digital platforms into a sector, in others they are supported by city governments eager to find alternatives to municipal disruptions and others still have been driven by alliances of producers within particular fields. These initiatives share a concern to utilize the affordances of the platform structure, supporting interaction between parties for a specific purpose, while rejecting the notion that the data this generates should be extracted and utilized for private gain. This helps illustrate how problems are not inherent in technology but reflect their design and deployment in particular contexts.

We can already see examples of these within higher education. Humanities Commons was developed by the office of scholarly communication at the Modern Language Association, with funding from the Andrew W. Mellon Foundation. Its explicit focus is on 'providing a space to discuss, share, and store cutting-edge research and innovative pedagogy – not on generating profits from users' intellectual and personal data'[1]. A project like this is exciting and embodies the potential for platform cooperativism in higher education, suggesting the scale of what might become possible as ambition grows and resources become more easily available for work in this area. In doing so, we avoid the temptation to frame platforms as an intrusion from the outside, reproducing what Bacevic (2017b) identifies as a common trope: if we are constantly looking out towards the enemies who are perceived to be at the gate, we mystify our own role inside the university and our responsibility for it. This is why the sociology of the platform university figures so heavily in the subsequent chapters, as we need to understand the interpenetration between digital platforms and university operations if we wish to intervene in this landscape (Robertson 2019).

However, as well as building platforms which operate as alternatives to commercial offerings, we should not lose sight of how existing technologies can be deployed and repurposed to further collective ends. This involves the other sense of platform, as a position from which to speak, which it might be necessary to recover. For example, larger academic blogs tend to represent a platform in this sense, with the collective behind them having designed and built an infrastructure, using a WordPress installation on a private server and a Twitter feed for dissemination, which enables individual authors to reach an audience which the project as a whole assembles over time. There are many examples we can find of platforms in this broader sense, including many which are unlikely to be noticed beyond the field in which they operate. These initiatives range across online magazines, podcast series, YouTube channels, Twitter accounts and many other forms. Under conditions of social distancing they have become the main means through which intellectual exchange occurs within the academy, replacing the social infrastructure of conferences, workshops and seminars which are so familiar that we rarely reflect on them *as* infrastructure.

These initiatives are dazzling in their diversity but if we see them as instances of the same category, academics using the affordances of digital media to build platforms from which to speak and influence, a rich ecosystem of creative and collaborative activity soon becomes recognizable around us. It is a social infrastructure for scholarship which has emerged haphazardly but should now be an object of our care and concern, particularly given its necessity under the crisis conditions which exist at the time of writing. In this sense, cooperative platforms aren't intrinsically about building technical infrastructure, as much as the most exciting and high profile cases might involve this, but rather finding ways to work together to leverage what digital environments allow us to do for communal ends which express our commitment.

However, the most significant feature of these collective endeavours is how they mediate the problems of platforms, creating the possibility that digital engagement becomes a shared undertaking rather than an individual pursuit. It is this possibility and the preconditions necessary for it which we turn to next.

6

Making Sociology Public

The range of ways in which sociologists are using social media is constantly expanding, leaving it difficult to make definitive statements about emerging practice. If we look carefully enough we can find examples of any social media platform we can think of being used by sociologists, even if it might be little more than a fleeting experiment or an activity with little reach beyond a limited network. But pointing out that sociologists are among the users of most, if not all, platforms provides us with little help when trying to conceptualize the sociological uses of social media. An attempt at such a declaration also encounters the obvious question of what it means for their use to be 'sociological'. This is a problem which plagues the research literature on social media as it is far from self-evident where personal use ends and professional use begins (Carrigan 2019). In fact it is precisely this boundary which the uptake of social media within higher education is destabilizing, as the line between what happens 'inside' the university and what happens 'outside' it comes to look increasingly unrecognizable (Bacevic 2019a).

This has implications for how we conceptualize public sociology because if we persist with a common sense concept of getting beyond the ivory tower, any use of social media comes to appear as if it is public. If sociologists employed within universities have conversations between themselves, concerning professional matters and conducted in an obtuse idiom, does it become 'public' purely by virtue of taking place on platforms which originate and operate outside the university? But if we go to the opposite extreme and restrict our definition of public sociology to initiatives which seek to engage with publics as a deliberate undertaking then we miss out on a grey area which has great significance for what it means to do public sociology in an age of social media. Existing categories obscure a diffuse publicness which characterizes the use of social media by sociologists even when no explicit attempt is being made to pursue this (Healy 2017).

If the decentring of *outputs*, *expertise* and *knowledge* we advocate is to be viable, it requires a firmer grounding in the institutional conditions in which sociologists work. These assumptions constitute a scholastic disposition which is deeply embedded in professional culture within higher education. They reinforce an ideology of social media that has its origins beyond the academy, in the self-presentation of platform firms and the willingness of optimistic commentators to reproduce them and tendency of pessimistic analysts to reproduce the underlying assumptions in their critical screeds (McChesney 2013). However, overcoming them isn't simply a matter of wishing them away because a platform imaginary, emerging from the combination of the scholastic disposition and the ideology of social media, risks being reproduced by the institutional environments in which sociologists undertake their online activity. This is the context in which we need to understand the problems of platforms and how collective projects of public sociology might succeed in mitigating them. In keeping with Burawoy's (2005) original sensibility, it requires that we turn the sociological eye inwards in order to see how social media platforms are received within universities qua organizations, as well as what this means for the organization of work within them and the role that the metrics inherent to platforms perform in the ensuing shifts in organizational culture.

Social media in higher education

Sceptics of social media warn against the narcissism it can generate, particularly a concern for winning attention at the cost of intellectual merit. For example, in a much criticized *Times Higher Education* piece, Egan (2014) warned of 'our narcissistic craving for others' approval' and how 'we crave evidence of the esteem in which we are held'. Social media firms exploit this need through the continuous feedback they offer, ensuring users engage for longer and return regularly to provide the data which they need to sell adverts. It was widely attacked on Twitter, including by those who openly acknowledged they had only skim read the piece. It certainly featured overstatements which should be criticized, such as the claim that social media presents a 'threat to our mental health' matching that which fat and sugar-rich diets pose to physical health seems untenable given the evidence of a much more complex reality (Orben et al 2019). However, the broad contours of Egan's argument reflect what can be found within the most celebrated scholarship on digital platforms (Van Dijck 2013, Tufekci 2017, Vaidhyanathan 2018). The alacrity with which Egan's (2016) argument can be written off as the technophobic ramblings of someone unable to accept this brave new world speaks volumes about how polarized this debate has tended to be within the academy (Carrigan 2019). If we want to think seriously about how social media can be taken up in the cause of public sociology, it's crucial that we engage with the problems of platforms as well as celebrating the opportunities they offer. If we frame them as 'tools' this too easily becomes a matter of inventorying the strengths and weaknesses of different services. This is a mistake because it fails to grasp the interconnectedness of these features, suggesting the balance of upsides/downsides is a contingent matter rather than an inevitable feature of platforms being designed in specific ways.

To achieve a broader view requires that we situate their use in organizational terms, supplementing the analysis we offered in previous chapters of the institutions of legacy scholarship. This means we must reject what Van Dijck and Poell (2018) refer to a 'social media-as-tools approach'[1] in which these platforms are treated as instruments that can be picked up and put down at will, motivated by their capacity to enhance or disrupt the learning experience (Selwyn and Stirling 2016). While there are many questions concerning individual practice which must remain within our grasp, detaching these from structural issues about how practice is organized within organizations will ensure our answers remain superficial and truncated. The fact that academics are subject to regimes of performance management,[2] involving the evaluation and ranking of their activity, invites the obvious question of how social media will be incorporated into this (Woodcock 2018). As Healy (2017: 779) writes in a thoughtful reflection on social media and public sociology:

> While it can be great to have new modes of scholarly interaction and engagement recognized as such, there is also a clear administrative downside. Once your dean or department chair believes that your social media nonsense may actually be a good thing, they will want to measure it. Once they measure it, they want to rank it.

The rapidly developing field of **altmetrics** has sought to facilitate such measurement, developing a range of metrics that track the circulation and impact of research outputs online through indicators such as social media mentions, references in blog posts and policy documents (Erdt et al 2018). The fact that Taylor & Francis, Wiley Blackwell and Sage all feature Digital Science's Altmetrics product illustrates its creeping institutionalization.[3] It seems increasingly likely that Altmetrics will define the broad category of article level metrics in a manner akin to Google's domination of search. Bookmetrix is a parallel platform which tracks reach, usage and readership for individual chapters. They track influence much more rapidly than traditional citational measures, as well as identifying forms of influence which do not result in a citation. The issues that can be raised with these systems are significant: there's a risk of sampling bias in making inferences from social media, the criteria for identifying blogs to track is unclear,[4] there are risks inherent in depending on social media data[5] and the system can be gamed in real time by those with sufficient online influence. However, it needs to be taken seriously as a means through which online influence comes to enter into performance evaluation, even if this is a matter of journal performance and private assessment rather than formalized management procedures at present. It operates much more rapidly than citational analysis because it relies on the temporality of social media to register influence, in (near) real time from the moment of publication, as opposed to the glacial pace of scholarly publishing in which influence can easily take years to register as public citation.

This highlights how the temporality of online publishing differs for academics and how this might exercise an influence over its incorporation into performance management. As Stein and Daniels (2017: 33) observe, 'for academics, whether and how people read their work is disconnected from their professional success'. It is the fact of publication which counts, getting something 'out there' to satisfy the analogue criteria of being published, with any ensuing engagement simply being a bonus. There is a risk of overstatement here because citational measures, as well as the peer engagement they (fallibly) track, increasingly play a role in professional outcomes for academics. However, this has tended to be distant and retrospective, a matter of assessing how one's standing has developed over time, as opposed to being a live concern in the writing process. In part this reflects the aforementioned glacial pace at which citations accrue over a matter of years. Or fail to, as is the case with an unnervingly high percentage of publications within the social science and humanities (Remler 2014).

It's easy to remain (relatively) phlegmatic about this process when it operates so slowly. An uncited publication lingers as a growing disappointment over a matter of years. In contrast an unnoticed tweet or unread blog post has the power to inculcate disappointment with a much greater immediacy. It sits, unread and unloved, surrounded by activity which assures you that it will soon be forgotten because there is so much else it competes with for the fragmented attention of social media users. Engagement either comes, or fails to, immediately, as opposed to trickling in over months and years in a manner only likely to register with the author over time when they stumble across a citation or check their Google Scholar profile.

The influence of Altmetrics bridges this gap by incorporating publications through legacy platforms into the time horizons of digital platforms. This has the potential to subtly influence the experience of publishing, the expectations placed on it and the meanings found through it. It can insert online visibility as a concern into the traditional chain of actions associated with publishing, encompassing everything from a mild curiosity about how an article is performing in Altmetrics terms through to a deep strategic commitment to increasing its visibility. However, it also provides a means through which social media can be incorporated into the core responsibilities of academics. This is informally underway within many contexts, as competitive job markets mean that activities perceived as advantageous are liable to be seized on in an accelerating fashion (Müller 2016, Vostal 2016). This contributes to a situation in which academics increasingly feel they ought to be on social media, animated by parallel fears of missing out and being left behind,[6] without clarity about the appropriate contours of this engagement. This is particularly pronounced when it comes to engagement which generates political controversy, with universities benefitting from the visibility which their academics accrue while often disowning them if something goes wrong (Bacevic 2019a, McMillan Cottom 2015). In this sense institutionalization *can* seem like a desirable process, formalizing and regulating an informal and uncertain undertaking that has grown messily in only a few years. However, its incorporation into formalized assessment has implications for the freedom of academic speech which we need to take extremely seriously (Carrigan 2019: 138–140). If the value of an article comes to be tied by an institution to its online visibility, this leaves academics worryingly bound into social platforms.

There are two routes through which social media could be incorporated into performance management. Firstly, altmetrics scores could be tracked in order to assess influence by universities that conceive of their 'third mission' in increasingly technocratic terms (Cooper 2017). If knowledge exchange and research impact are institutional priorities then the capacity to follow the circulation of knowledge through social media, mass media and policy making will prove enticing. Particularly if this can be used as a basis to infer influence, even if the inference might be grounded in assumptions which are methodologically questionable. Secondly, social media metrics could be regarded as a proxy for impact *capacity* and social media engagement as a proxy for impact *willingness*. The metrics provided by social media platforms promise objectivity, even if the link between online popularity and social influence remains profoundly uncertain. This is liable to prove enticing for those tasked with institutionalizing engagement within their universities,[7] evidenced by existing examples of social media metrics being incorporated into the reporting of research in naive and uncritical ways (Jordan and Carrigan 2018a). There is a risk that a dissemination model is 'baked into' the institutionalization of social media if the accumulation of followers is valorized as exemplifying a capacity for impact, providing institutional ballast for the platform imaginary we discussed in the previous section. It can't be stressed enough that social platforms have been designed to incentivize the pursuit of popularity, framed reductively in terms of one's quantifiable prominence, as part of a hierarchically stratified attention economy.

While the methodological sophistication of altmetrics and the specialized literature on research impact give us reasons to hope this won't be the case, we must consider the potential disjuncture between sophisticated policy and naive practice. There is a risk that a naive metrics culture emerges, conflating online popularity with online influence,[8] despite the repeated warnings of specialists that 'dissemination and impact aren't the same thing' and 'metrics don't tell us how research has been used', and so on. This follows from the performativity of metrics. By representing what is popular they also shape what is popular and this is as true of highly cited papers as it is of viral YouTube videos (Burgess and Green 2018: 63). Their meaning and interpretation by those who fall within their remit is an expression of their influence but it is also one which often outstrips the expectations of those designing the system (Beer 2016a: loc 2403, Couldry et al 2016). The influence of metrics on behaviour will tend to outstrip initial intentions under competitive circumstances in which strategic actors struggle for advancement within hierarchies defined through these rankings. In other words, people compete over their position within a ranking once it becomes a means through employers evaluate their worth. This should leave us extremely concerned about the potential influence of social media being incorporated into performance evaluation, not least of all how it will leave academics approaching social media in a manner which intensifies the problems of platforms: pursuing the logic of competitive visibility rather than finding a way to use the platform in a sustainable and satisfying way.

The fact most of us have yet to reach the stage of the (possibly apocryphal) professor who adds an H-index to their email signature illustrates how the cultural hegemony of metricized assessment is much further from being the case than is often assumed. It helps us see how the introduction of a range of new metrics into academic life (follower counts, retweets, daily hits, video views, engagement rates) doesn't mean we have retreated yet further from the ephemeral ideal of scholarship that lurks spectrally over an accelerated academy, compounding the misery of those within it while providing little resources for meaningful resistance[9] (Vostal 2016). A fixation on how many times a tweet has been retweeted certainly *can* be evidence of social media's capacity to hijack the deliberation of users in order to leave them wallowing in ephemera against their better judgement (Williams 2018). However it can also express aesthetic pleasure in a thought that has been constructed so parsimoniously that it resonates with others in spite of its complexity. A fixation on how many times a blog post has been read can express a narcissistic concern for popularity as an end in itself, with the risk that meaningful evaluation of quality is replaced by reductive quantitative measurement (Van Dijck 2013). But it can also reflect excitement that one's intellectual labour is being seen and heard, offering an exhilarating escape from the invisibility which so many feel within the regimented star system of the academy.

It's important that we grasp how varied orientation to these metrics can be because it helps avoid the risk of falling back into generalizations which (unintentionally) shut down the space in which we can have meaningful dialogues about metricized assessment and how we can and should relate to it. If we declare that metrics are nothing more than a vector of neoliberalism, it becomes impossible to give voice to the ambiguity and ambivalence which defines many people's experiences of them. It assumes a uniform outcome to a messy process with heterogeneous results, ranging from those evaluating their self-worth in metricized terms to those whose self-evaluations are utterly detaching from these rankings. It seems likely most of us exist between these two extremes, recognizing the significance of metrics as currency for career building while remaining at least somewhat alienated from their implications. This is why it's crucial that we understand how platform architectures seek to shape user behaviour (**platform literacy**) while exercising our capacity to individually and collectively reflect on our relation to these architectures in a way that shapes our own action (**technological reflexivity**). These are capacities which academics need to develop in order to *use* social media rather than *be used* by it, negotiating the problems summarized in Table 6.1, in circumstances where a narrow framing of its possibilities is liable to constrain the exercise of their agency.

The problems of platforms

What we have analysed as the scholastic disposition in previous chapters goes hand-in-hand with what we term the **forgetfulness of technics** (see Table 6.1 for a summary of their intersection). It is a product of a sociotechnical apparatus, the legacy platforms of scholarship, fading into the background in a manner which leads us to forget their own origins. Hall (2016a) considers this tendency in relation to philosophers like Jacques Derrida and Bernard Stiegler whose radical ontological and epistemological stances sit uneasily with their privileging of writing and 'associated forms and techniques of presentation, debate, critical attention, observation, and intervention' (Hall 2016a: 63). They proceed as if there's little relationship between the content of their ideas and the means of their circulation. In fact they are far from alone in this.

We suggest, drawing on Hall's (2016a) argument, this reflects a distance from and lack of concern for the platforms through which knowledge circulates, as opposed to the simple fact of it being 'out there' beyond the imagined boundaries of the ivory tower. In part this reflects the normalization of the legacy platforms for scholarship, with successive cohorts having routinized a process of publishing which changes little from their perspective beyond the increasing sophistication of the devices they use. There is an established routine through which the activity is undertaken, anchored by the weight of expectation which surrounds the publishing process. The fact that 'backstage' elements have undergone radical change manifests in practical problems which are the familiar substance of academic shop

Table 6.1: The problems of platforms and our proposed solutions

Forgetfulness of technics	The scholarly orientation
Establishing rhythms for our use of social media which facilitate *skholē*	Technologically passive academics reproduce the parochialism of platforms
Developing cultural armour to escape the social media machine	The personalism of platforms and the objectivity of scholarship
Negotiating the politics of platforms and the toxicity it generates	Dual consciousness as a barrier to reflexive institutionalization
Technological reflexivity	**Platform literacy**

talk: declining standards in copy editing, increasing waiting times and expanding promotional expectations on the part of publishers. But this is more often cathartic grumbling than a sincere attempt to understand the reasons for these difficulties. This distance persists even as we grow jointly dissatisfied by the process, with those who seek to exercise a real influence over the system coalescing into academic subcultures which are insulated from the broader academic community by terminological specificity and technical knowledge.

In fact it is rather striking how widespread ignorance of academic publishing remains among (some) academics given its centrality to their occupation. This is symptomatic of a broader ignorance of the role of the technical systems in scholarly practice, punctuated by outbursts of irritation when routines are interrupted by their sporadic failure. As Judith Butler (2015: 20) has put it, 'The dependency of human creatures on sustaining and supporting infrastructural life shows that the organization of infrastructure is intimately tied with an enduring sense of individual life: how life is endured, and with what degree of suffering, livability, or hope.' It might seem like a category error to describe the technological infrastructure of the university in these terms but if we take the aspiration towards what Sennett (2008) calls 'craft' seriously, recognizing the aspirations towards vocation which can linger on in even the most mundane work – which in fact can only be constituted *through* such work – the subdued intimacy marking our dependency on this infrastructure becomes more obvious. There is a profound mundanity to matters like working email, reliable Wi-Fi, the capacity to print or access to journals. But this mundanity is the ground on which the achievements, realized or otherwise, anchoring our life as a whole begin to take shape. This has opened up new forms of inequality during the pandemic, as a shift towards remote working has left university staff with wildly different working conditions, ranging from luxurious home offices with superfast broadband through to shared rooms with unreliable internet access unable to cope with multiple video meetings at the same time. This makes it more urgent than ever for us to recover infrastructure as a crucial factor in the nature of academic labour.

If we hope to address the problems of platforms then it is necessary to transcend the scholastic disposition by developing platform literacy and overcome the forgetfulness of technics by developing technological reflexivity. These are the loci of the issues which platforms pose for scholarship, including its specific manifestation for public sociology which we turn to in the following chapters. There is a **social particularism** to our use of these platforms which shapes the exercise of our agency in relation to them, in the sense that there are precise characteristics about *us* which condition our engagement and experience: there is no general user, even among those who share the same occupation (Macintyre 2013: 256). As Marres (2017: 152) puts it[10] 'one doesn't just participate in "digital culture" or "life online"; one also participates in a specific conversation, an event or a community, and one adopts the role of "user" of platform X or "subscriber" of service Y'. Their use is tangled up in the thickets of our own existence, with participation able to serve ends deriving from organizational and institutional imperatives beyond participation itself (Marres 2017: 153). The institutions of legacy scholarship, with the pride of place they give to outputs, expertise and knowledge draw a veil[11] over this entanglement.

In the previous chapter we explored how platforms pose challenges to scholarship which force us to draw back this veil. If we can do this it provides us with the grounds through which to develop these new capacities, platform literacy and technological reflexivity,[12] which will help us negotiate the problems of platforms and provide the foundation for digital public sociology.

The scholastic disposition

Platforms are parochial places in spite of their international scale. Their interactions easily traverse national boundaries but communication across linguistic barriers is a more complex issue, particularly as platforms have territorialized with expansion. We now confront two webs at the macro level: one in the Latin alphabet (with English dominant) and another in Mandarin (Vaidhyanathan 2012: loc 2519). However, the meso and micro dynamics of this are much more complex. For example, YouTube features an enormous range of country and language options, with filter by location the default option for mobile users. While these options can be changed, geolocation of content cannot because of its centrality to copyright protection. This means that it is 'increasingly unnecessary for Western, English-speaking users to encounter mundane cultural difference in their experience of online video' (Burgess and Green 2018: 131–133).

This parochialism can be compounded by the research process through which knowledge about platforms is produced. For example, Papacharissi (2015: 40) reports being forced to leave 400,000 Arabic tweets out of a corpus compiled to study the role Twitter played in the Egyptian revolution because the analytics software being used could only support Latin characters. Even if this was methodologically defensible in this instance, it points to a much broader problem in which contingent barriers to *cultural* internationalism mean that *structural* internationalism remains an unrealized opportunity.

This creates problems when we consider the status of English as a lingua franca within international higher education and what this means for the circulation of ideas (Jenkins 2013). This anglophone bias reflects the dominance of North American universities in finance, publications and infrastructure, even if this is not the sole cause of it (Keucheyan 2012: loc 469). It creates a bias for ideas to be expressed in English in order to ensure they receive a substantial audience, requiring intensified labour (posting in multiple languages or through multiple accounts) if one is to avoid being restricted to a linguistic sphere.[13] There are projects like Global Dialogues and Global Social Theory which suggest how we might begin to overcome this parochialism (Carrigan 2019: 137–138). But what's important to stress is that they are projects. If we see social media through the lens of speech acts then we risk naturalizing the constraints of this environment as a demographic fact of language, as opposed to it being a design decision by platform firms being compounded by the faux internationalism of the academy. If we remain individualized in how we imagine our use of platforms then technologically passive academics will inevitably reproduce the parochialism of platforms, seeing them as an external horizon for our individual action rather than something we can collectively change. If we come to see these as objects of intervention then we can begin to plan collective projects which leverage an understanding of platforms in order to mitigate these constraints.

There is a tension between the personalism of platforms and the objectivity of scholarship. As Davies (2018: loc 3680) observes, the 'delicate interplay of anonymity and public identification' found in peer review 'is the legacy of the seventeenth-century etiquette in which experts took great pains never to impute bad character or intentions on the part of their peers'. In contrast social media not only encourages self disclosure but sustains a record of these disclosures due to what boyd (2014) describes as the 'persistence' which characterizes updates on the platform. As Davies (2018: loc 3680) notes these can easily be 'weaponized' but they also nudge us towards a situation 'where it becomes virtually impossible to judge them on the basis of their public words alone'. A similar dynamic is underway within the journalistic field. Social media fits easily with the disposition of columnists expected to offer their own perspective on the affairs of the day. However, it is more disruptive when it comes to the practice of reporters whose inevitable insertion of personal reflection into real time updates sits uneasily with the orthodox conception of objectivity. This conveys a contextual richness which can be framed as an epistemic gain but it confronts difficult questions concerning the role of the reporter and the status of their reporting (Papacharissi 2015: 49). It is not that social media undermines the established way of doing things by replacing 'old' with 'new', but rather that the 'old' must be recalibrated under 'new' conditions: there's no value judgement inherent in the terminology we've adopted of legacy scholarship.[14] This will be a difficult undertaking if we insist on a stark dichotomy between the two but a dialogue becomes feasible as soon as we can fuzz up this distinction somewhat, informed by an appreciation of how platforms encourage personal disclosure and facilitate personalized forms of exchange which have significant implications for orthodox conceptions of scholarship.

A useful concept here is what Stewart (2018) calls the 'dual consciousness' surrounding social media use by academics. Social media is experienced as an enjoyable environment outside the constraints of the academy which nonetheless impinges on one's academic life and work. There is a tendency to simultaneously see social media as a strategic object from the perspective of a professionalized academic ('I can build my visibility within my discipline through Twitter') and as an immersive experience from the perspective of a user ('It's fun to keep in touch with people from conferences'), without being able to bring them together in a sense of social media as a novel vector through which familiar aspects of academic life now unfold. We oscillate between these two perspectives rather than experiencing them as dual aspects of how we relate to social media as academics.

This is a barrier to reflexive institutionalization because it stops us acknowledging that we have vested interests in our activity through social media platforms, such as the value which an employer might place on our perceived online influence or lack thereof. If we can recognize the incentives which platforms create for us and the events through which these operate (platform literacy) then it becomes possible to develop norms and expectations surrounding social media in a deliberate manner, as opposed to letting them emerge chaotically in the aforementioned institutional context. These could be scholarly norms which support collective and creative uses of platforms, encouraging collaboration rather than competitive individualism. However, doing this requires that we learn to discuss social media in ways which draw together the ludic and the strategic, as opposed to the current orthodoxy of compulsively oscillating between them.

Forgetfulness of technics

The concept of 'social media addiction' is liable to provoke the ire of sociologists. However, if we distinguish between a clinical sense and a colloquial sense of not feeling in control of one's use then the term becomes much less problematic (Williams 2018: 113). We need to take these experiences seriously, even if engagement with them has tended to be expressed in unpersuasive terms of 'dopamine hacking' and 'lizard brains' that reproduces exactly the behaviourism critiqued in the platform itself (Tarnoff and Weigel 2018). Seymour's (2019) invocation of the *chronophage*, the creature that eats time,[15] helps us frame the issue in a more sociological way: these platforms have been designed around the imperative to increase the time users spend on the platform. They are often accessed through devices that embody the same principles of persuasive design, encouraging us to keep them close and return to them throughout the day. If we are not watchful their inducements can lure us in against our better judgement, leading us to return more often and for longer than we would otherwise choose to (Pang 2013). There is a whole category of software which has emerged around the problems many people experience in this respect, with Apple even incorporating comparable functionality into recent versions of its mobile operating system. What does this mean for sociologists? It is a question of what Bourdieu (2000: 1) called *skholè*: 'the free time, freed from the urgencies of the world, that allows a free and liberated relation to those urgencies and to the world'. It is the condition which enables thinking in the (slightly inflated) manner we tend to associate with scholarship. The tension between skholè and social media exists in the tendency of platforms to encourage return, the cognitive stickiness which promises to fill idle or frustrated moments with a potential reward (Gilroy-Ware 2017). It is not a difficult problem to resolve but it does require a solution: establishing our own rhythms for platform use rather than subordinating our existing rhythms to the platform. It requires understanding the constraints of our craft, the techniques and processes through which we undertake our work in a quotidian sense, as well as the ways in which platforms can undercut these.[16]

This is a matter of reflexivity in Archer's (2007) sense because it sits at the interface between the platform (its promises and problems) and our working life (its commitments and rhythms), challenging us to calibrate the relationship between them. If we can do this then it becomes easier to escape what Seymour (2019) calls the *Twittering Machine*. This is more than establishing satisfying and sustainable rhythms to our use (Carrigan 2019). As we have seen in previous chapters, social platforms incorporate a tremendously powerful affective machinery that can be difficult to escape. In an environment saturated with what BuzzFeed founder Jonah Peretti described as 'contagious media', it can be challenging for non-contagious media to win an audience. When content can be modulated in terms of its viral potency by those with sufficient data and expertise, the capacity to be heard comes to seem obviously unequally distributed. When user responses can be inferred in an affective ontology available to some actors but not others,[17] the ability to make predictions about the behaviour of audiences is increasingly one sided (Abramson 2019). A competitive situation defined by platform incentives and the capacity of some to exploit them risks pulling ever more actors into the vortex, in the hope of being heard above the din (Beer 2014).

It is possible to keep a reflective distance from these pressures by being aware of the platform's capacity to modify behaviour, operating through the metrics of the 'popularity principle' and the susceptibility of users to recalibrating their strategic projects in these terms (Van Dijck 2013). To do this involves 'no longer praying at the altar of virality', as Caulfield (2016) memorably puts it, necessitating an acceptance that a loss of influence may ensue from no longer pursuing it at all costs.[18] This opens up the possibility of richer, thicker, deeper engagement which can't be tracked by a quantitative measure of 'influence'; being *listened* to rather than simply heard. It will often mean less reach and alternative conceptions of what success looks like can play a part in this. Adorno's description of Benjamin's ideas as 'radioactive', such that '[e]verything which fell under the scrutiny of his words was transformed', provides a sense of what this can look like (Benjamin 2014: loc 395–410). Rather than focus on the virality of our writing, the breadth of its circulation, we can seek to maximize its transformative potential. This entails a form of reflexivity which the instrumental pursuit of quantified reach will inevitably squeeze out. In a sense this can be seen as the cultural armour necessary to fight our way out of the social media machine without abandoning it entirely (Seymour 2019). It involves learning, as the late Mark Fisher put it, to develop an instrumental relationship: to *use* it rather than *live* inside it (Fisher 2018). To see it as a means to *accomplish* our ends while denying it the capacity to *define* those ends.

If we can develop this reflexivity then the politics of platforms, increasingly characterized by abuse and harassment, becomes more tractable. The social media machine isn't inherently productive of them: BuzzFeed's 'no haters' ethos and Upworthy's saccharine positivity emerged out of the same concern for viral transmission that is increasingly seen to encourage the worst of the internet (Abramson 2019: 108). However, the ubiquity of harassment is increasingly well established, with Duggan (2014) finding that 73 per cent of adult internet users in the United States have seen someone be harassed in some way online,[19] while 40 per cent have personally experienced it.[20] Twenty-five per cent of Black Americans and 10 per cent of Hispanic Americans report being harassed online because of their race/ethnicity (Duggan 2017). Young adults (18–29) are more likely to experience harassment and young women (18–24) are overwhelmingly the targets of the more extreme behaviours. To a certain extent this reflects a racist and misogynistic society in which harassment is already rife, with platforms offering an outlet for this. However, the form this outlet takes is a consequence of design decisions undertaken as part of a corporate strategy rather than inexorable features of the underlying technology. Twitter and YouTube in particular have produced online ecologies which have incentivized viral celebrities who feed on controversy (Carrigan 2019: 127–129). Public pressure has provoked technical changes which address these problems: minimizing the visibility of hateful content through algorithmic intervention, increasing the role of human moderation, expanding the means available for users to filter their own experience. These have been supplemented by collective projects which address the problem through advice for individuals, guidelines for institutions and technical interventions. For example, BlockBot was produced by a group of feminist developers frustrated by Twitter's continued refusal to address its harassment problem. It enables users to mass block a continually updated and collective sourced lists of serial harassers (Watters 2015: loc 1339–1420). Technical projects operate within the fluctuating constraints of platform APIs with all this entails in terms of their room for action and their sustainability over time (Vis 2016). Even if they can't substitute for meaningful action by the firms themselves, predicated on taking responsibility to avoid providing a platform for these behaviours,[21] it nonetheless contributes to mitigating the problems in the absence of concerted action by those who are ultimately profiting from the dangerous environment they have helped to create.

These interventions could nonetheless be dismissed as tinkering around the edges and they're often informed by a deterministic understanding which fails to grasp the agency of users in relation to what is often described as the toxicity[22] of online environments (Isin and Ruppert 2015: 112). Even the most sophisticated empirical treatments inevitably evacuate the issue of political complexity by reducing a diverse range of phenomena into a uniform category such as 'online hate' (Johnson et al 2019). Even though platforms fall short of the sociality which social media ideology would suggest, they still facilitate more interactions between a more diverse range of people than was previously the case. What's more significant are the conditions under which this takes place: accelerated and anormative[23] communication driven by structures which rewards controversy with visibility. Furthermore, what boyd (2014) describes as the 'persistence' and 'searchability' of social media content means that past interaction can be dredged up with ease, as part of a chronic weaponization in communicative exchanges which often descend into something approaching (cultural) warfare (Mayer-Schönberger 2011, Davies 2018).

In the following chapter we look in more depth at the epistemological character of platformized social life in order to better understand why the politics of this are so complex. We suggest this can be understood through the lens of platform governance with public sociologists having a (minor) role to play as digital citizens in steering debates about these issues away from simply technologizing the problem (structuralism) or reducing it to the figure of trolls[24] (voluntarism). But it's also a field which requires a much more prosaic reflexivity because of the risks it creates for public engagement and how unevenly those risks are distributed in classed, racialized and gendered terms (Phipps 2014). As McMillan Cottom (2015) puts it those whose 'social locations conform to the hegemonic ("natural") embodiment of intellectual critique' (a white male at an elite university) enjoy a perceived authority which often isn't accessible to their female and minority colleagues. This is why reflexivity about platforms can't simply be how we can best use them to our advantage. It necessitates a much broader reflection on what we are using them for and how this can serve collective purposes that overcome the inequalities they generate.

Building platforms for public sociology

The research literature on social media in higher education has tended to be preoccupied by how individuals take advantage of the affordances of these platforms or struggle with their constraints. We can see the same tendency in research on social media in education, described as Selwyn and Stirling (2016: 4) as preoccupied by 'good news, "best practice" and examples of "what works"' reflecting an underlying hope that social media will prove 'capable of initiating significant shifts in how people learn and engage with education'. Even the growing evidence base produced by empirical research which is being undertaken with greater frequency[25] largely ignores the question of collective use, reducing it to networked scholarship or the power of connection. The reasons for this absence are easy to grasp if we consider them from a methodological perspective, reflecting a reliance on sample surveys to grasp the extent to which a new technology is diffusing within a specific population that is compounded by how established the method is within educational technology and information science. However, from a theoretical standpoint it is more puzzling, as to use social media as a collective[26] represents a distinct form of engagement, with its own creative potentials and relationship to the organizational context in which it is being taken up. What's particularly interesting for our purposes are those projects which come to be well established, taking on an existence over and above their initiators and coming to enjoy an identity which is more or less independent of them.[27] There is a rich ecology of collaboration emerging across networks of academics using social media regularly, one we are unlikely to see anything but a fraction of unless we are deliberately searching beyond the boundaries of the niches we have come to occupy by virtue of our field, discipline and interests more broadly.

We suggest these initiatives can be usefully thought of in terms of building platforms: collegial projects which utilize the affordances of social media to pursue a collective agenda. The forms these take are familiar: Facebook groups organized around a particular topic, multi author blogs devoted to a field of inquiry, online magazines committed to making academic research more accessible, podcast series which explore a topic in a specific way or YouTube channels which collect academic talks in a given area. In some cases, these are funded but in many they are not. There are many examples of universities or research funders providing the financial support needed to keep the project going, something which seems likely to increase with time albeit in an uneven way. For example, it remains to be seen whether funders will prove to be content with what they might perceive as the relatively low return on investment, in terms of viewing figures which often fail to exceed the low hundreds,[28] though this underscores the need for scholarly platforms of the sort we advocate which can help make these public. With so much content being produced, there's an increasing need for bodies with a wide purview (funding councils, learned societies or scholarly publishers) to provide resources for platforms which aggregate, organize and promote this material. In some cases, these are run directly by the university, something which we have no desire to dismiss but that in an important sense becomes a different undertaking, with unique objectives and constraints, to those we are examining here. The projects we are most interested in for present concerns are initiated by collectives, operated by collectives and pursuing an agenda defined by collectives. They represent a crucial part of the digital landscape which has yet to be fully appreciated. They serve a number of purposes which we can sketch in the abstract:

- **They provide access to an audience:** Building an online audience is an activity which takes *time*, no matter the purpose of the undertaking or which social media platform is being used for it. It is an uncertain and messy process which requires ongoing reflexivity (Carrigan 2019). This sits uneasily with the restricted time frame inherent to what Ylijoki (2016) calls 'project time'. Projects proceed towards a goal in a linear and cumulative fashion, often with outcomes delineated at the start of the undertaking. This imposes a limited time span and strategic restrictions which make it hard to build a significant audience in the context of a project funded for a handful of years. Even if the lifespan of the project does not prove to be a barrier,[29] the framing of these engagement activities in relation to core research creates a bias towards a dissemination model, reducing it to sharing the project's research to the greatest possible audience. If your primary goal is pursuit of numbers then this tends to squeeze out the more subtle and relational aspects of developing an audience online. It is even more difficult to undertake this *without* funding in the context of an accelerating academy where intensifying workloads are ubiquitous (Carrigan 2016, Vostal 2016). To the extent platforms have an existence outside project time[30] they can relieve the temporal pressure which social scientists face when using social media: making it possible to ensure an audience for online activity without the necessity of maximizing online engagement with a rhythm that is unsustainable and precludes skholé.
- **They provide access to a *specific* audience:** In many cases the sheer fact of an audience might be insufficient and what matters is the specific audience who have gathered around a particular publication. The impact imperative can play a role here, leaving certain groups strategically important for those who are seeking to exercise a particular influence on the basis of their research. This can intensify the temporal demands of engagement by making it a more specialized process. Platforms can relieve this temporal demand by ensuring access to an audience in the manner described in the previous bullet point. However there is an element of uncertainty inherent to building platforms in this sense, with the groups which coalesce around a platform not always being the one that

was originally intended. This might be a problematic undertaking for a funded project with a particular goal in mind but it can be a benefit if this audience coalesces around an external platform which makes itself accessible to others through guest posting, curating and publishing their materials.

- **They mediate interaction with these audiences**: When scholars engage through a platform it tends to create a distance between themselves and the audience, even if this might pale in comparison to that associated with legacy media. A strategic concern to use online publication to increase one's own visibility can mitigate this somewhat by linking a piece to the author's social media presence when it is promoted etc. But the meditation still changes the character of the interaction particularly when the platform has a clear sense of mission animated by the commitments of an underlying collective. This can help ensure a sense of purpose that counteracts the siren song of the social media machine and its capacity to leave people returning more often, for longer and doing more in a way corrosive of their original intentions. It also mediates the politics of platforms though a number of means: moderating comments without an author seeing them, accumulating expertise on intellectual positioning, taking stands in support of authors in the event they are attacked etc. It also means audiences confront collective scholarship rather than the personalism of platforms, short circuiting the antinomy between subjectivity and objectivity which runs through the epistemic culture of digital platforms (Davies 2018).

- **They filter abundance for these audiences**: By selecting material to publish platforms sieve through the overwhelming choice available and reduce the cognitive demands placed on social scientists. Instead of information overload, keeping track of an issue becomes keeping track of a handful of platforms. This makes it easier to establish a rhythm of social media use which is sustainable and facilitates skholé. They also have an important role to play in mitigating inequalities of status and visibility within the academy, being capable of reproducing these online or combating them in powerful ways through their decisions about which voices to amplify. This can erode the power of the social media machine by reducing the perceived necessity of embracing the logic of the platform in order to accumulate visibility for oneself. It can also transcend the parochialism of platforms by providing new forms for global exchange, even if the realization of these possibilities is still in its infancy.

- **They ensure the quality of what is published:** The role of editorial intervention might be contested as the quantitative explosion in online publishing creates a pressure for publications to maximize their outputs and minimize the time spent producing them.[31] There remains a lack of certainty about the intellectual standards relevant to producing digital artefacts and how they relate to the expectations attached to the familiar forms of legacy publishing. But this is a matter of the qualities of what is published as much as it is meeting a threshold of quality. What makes this material specific? What project does it serve? How does it express this mission? Those who are maintaining a platform inevitably encounter scholarly questions posed by social media, inviting responses through their actions which are often discussed in public forums.[32] In this sense they are contributing to the reflexive institutionalization of digital platforms, ensuring a conversation emerges about what these platforms are *for* and how we ought to use them.

- **They ensure the capacity to be counted**: Intermediaries can ensure that a piece of work is recognized either formally or informally in a manner which is significant for the producer. For instance this might be a matter of being recognized as an 'academic' blog, either by an institution which restricts what can count as an academic publication or informally by a real or imagined peer group who restrict their assent to publications which are recognized as properly academic. A review process can play a crucial role here, with established academic blogs rejecting pitches and finished pieces, ensuring a level of quality which is recognized by readers and contributes to the perceived prestige of what is published. This role in incorporating digital scholarship into existing evaluative infrastructure, both organizationally and collegially, contributes to the reflexive institutionalization of digital platforms, exercising an influence over how the uses of these platforms are related to the exercising norms and expectations of scholarship.

There are a number of reasons for the significance we accord to them. Firstly, they represent a collegial bulwark against the bureaucratization of social media, ensuring the existence of projects which are at least to some extent driven by motivations that evade and exceed the prevailing incentives of the accelerated academy (Vostal 2016). Secondly, they are a barrier against some of the more destructive tendencies to be found in the contemporary digital landscape, ensuring to some extent that challenges are not borne by isolated individuals but rather can be negotiated by a group. Thirdly, they jointly constitute a source of novelty which inspires other projects, ensuring that platforms are populated by organized groups who through their sheer presence unsettle the assumption that social media is used by influenceable individuals whose behaviour leaves them ever more open to analysis and intervention (Marres 2018). Fourthly, insofar as they are sustained and recognized, they come to constitute the archetypes through which the utilization of digital media in higher education is understood by others.

We are still a long way from something like a group blog having the institutional recognition of a scholarly journal but increasingly the former does enjoy recognition which exists on a spectrum with the latter, even if the intensity of that regard and the extent of its sources may still vary considerably. In this sense they contribute to a collegial institutionalization of social media, establishing what these platforms mean for scholars and how they can be used in scholarly ways. This won't necessarily interrupt the bureaucratic institutionalization described earlier in this chapter but it can be an important counterweight to it which provides the foundations in which digital public sociology can flourish.

It is not impossible to construct these platforms individually but there are obvious downsides: it will be difficult to build an audience, it will be a much more onerous undertaking and we will be left more open to abuse. However, this is a conceptual sketch of the purposes they serve rather than an empirical analysis of their characteristics or a guidebook about how to build and maintain them. It is intended to stress the significance of their collective existence. Even if any one such project might be tiny in its scope, their collective emergence represents an important and timely development in the meditation of social science. The long tail distribution which characterizes social media can be a source of collective hope because of the aggregate significance of what we do, hence our repeated insistence on talking about this as a general phenomenon rather than focusing on isolated examples, as well as a source of individual despair because of the limited reach of the vast majority of undertakings. In this sense we are trying to open a discussion about the significance of these collective projects; one which highlights practical questions without getting reduced to practicality.

To take this discussion forward will involve technical skills, even if their designation *as* technical will decline in salience with their creeping ubiquity. The forcible transformation of many university teachers into online content creators during the COVID-19 crisis, producing short form video content and engaging asynchronously with students, has pushed some aspects of digital scholarship which might have been seen previously as 'technical' into mainstream practice. The intensive collaboration it has mandated with other forms of expertise within the university (educational technologists, learning designers, audiovisual producers) simultaneously changes the character of technologically-oriented activity, even if too much of this load still falls on individual academics as part of a spiralling burden of digital labour. It remains an open question whether this problem will persist beyond the crisis that holds at the time of writing, though the collaborative character which *can* characterize these activities suggests that political organization around them needs to extend beyond academic staff and encompass other digital labourers within the university.

There are also questions of funding and sustainability which remain, encompassing how to hook into legacy institutions while also finding ways to take advantage of emerging systems of micropayment and crowdfunding. But there is much more to it than this and a preoccupation with the perceived technical factors impedes the wider array of questions which are confronted in such an undertaking. Consider a comparison with a journal. There are all manner of tasks involved in operating a journal which would be deemed technical by many: acquiring DOIs, operating workflow management software, ensuring the journal is indexed and typeset effectively, and so on. But these only become actionable tasks against a backdrop of a collective commitment, in which a group of people have oriented themselves to the operation of an established organizational form, with familiar roles such as editor and editorial board member, in order to periodically produce an output oriented towards an anticipated audience. The technical aspects are (recurrent) moments of a project. The project cannot be reduced to them, even as it couldn't proceed without them. There's a tendency for the technical aspects of these undertakings to crowd out consideration of the socio-relational context which explains why those challenges are confronted in the first place. It's this broader discussion of what these undertakings are for and the expectations we should have of them which has been our concern in this chapter. This is the terrain on which we believe conversations about the practice of public sociology will increasingly need to take place.

Making Platforms Public

At the heart of our argument is a simple observation: there is an inherent asymmetry built into platforms. What makes them exciting at the level of social research, the real time data they unobtrusively generate as a by-product of user behaviour, can look rather sinister at the level of political economy[1] (Mantello 2016, Wood and Monahan 2019). They are, as Marres (2018: 437) says, 'an environment in two halves'. The front stage is a remarkably engaging place full of inducements, provocations and distraction while 'a veritable army of social data scientists who monitor, measure, and seek to intervene in this behavioural theatre' lurk behind the curtain (Marres 2018: 437). The users are *known* but the platform affords them little capacity to become *knowing* in turn (Kennedy and Moss 2015). This is what we have called, following Seymour (2019), 'the social media machine' and any account of digital public sociology needs to grapple with its implications in a systematic way. These are not tools we can pick up and put down at will but rather systems we can operate *with* and *through* that will simultaneously be exercising an influence over us, encouraging us to return more frequently and stay for longer when we do (Van Dijck and Poell 2018).

What Srnicek (2017) calls platform capitalism provides us with an exciting machinery for making public but it is one we are liable to be used by if we are not careful in our use of it. We offered the concepts of technological reflexivity and platform literacy to identify those characteristics necessary to thrive as public scholars under these conditions. Each of these involves leaving behind the assumptions of legacy scholarship concerning outputs, expertise and knowledge in order to embrace platforms in a way which leaves us prepared for their problems. What we describe in the next chapter as digital public sociology is an approach with its foundations in the space this opens up, taking advantage of the room we have to build on once legacy assumptions have been dispensed with.[2] In entering this space, we begin to see how sociology transforms in changing conditions, with our modest conception being one contribution to what we hope is a broader debate about the socioeconomic shift that has been variably defined as data capitalism, digital capitalism, surveillance capitalism and platform capitalism. To use Burawoy's (2011) terms: what 'companion sociology' should we expect for the digitalized capitalism we see unfolding at such a critical socioeconomic juncture (Robinson 2018)? Is there a risk that a data-driven sociology, adapted to the methodological and infrastructural realities of platform capitalism, could become a source of legitimation rather than critique (Skeggs 2019)? In this sense the argument we are making addresses one aspect of a wider set of questions which a changing environment poses for sociology as a discipline (Savage and Burrows 2007, Halford and Savage 2017).

However, there is a danger when using a concept like platform capitalism in relation to higher education that we position it as 'out there', impinging on the university from outside. In doing so, we take the boundaries of the university for granted when it is precisely these which are being reconstituted by the uptake of digital technology (Bacevic 2019a). It should be stressed that the digitalization of the university is not a new phenomenon, as many once disruptive technologies (online journals, word processing, electronic communication) have faded into the background as an unremarkable feature of organizational life. Each of these had enormous implications for the existing sociotechnical apparatus within the university: online journals eroded the centrality of physical space in how libraries facilitate access to scholarship, word processing minimized the role for clerical assistance in everyday scholarly operations, and electronic communication sped up the internal life of the university. The fact these are now so unremarkable as to escape notice illustrates the ease with which a technology can disrupt existing arrangements before being consolidated then taken for granted by successive cohorts of academics. As we argued, this reflects a broader forgetfulness of technics among academics (Hall 2016a). The result is a misconception about one's own work, particularly the reliance on technical systems which have to be maintained[3] and which can be *changed*. It is in the operation of this imagination that the exercise of our agency is encouraged or relinquished, as the sociotechnical horizon of our action either fades from view or becomes an object of our collective interest.

The platform university

What *is* new about the contemporary wave of digitalization within higher education is the platform model which digital services are increasingly taking. Williamson (2019) suggests a number of causes for this: striving for ever more granular measurement for performance management, the expansion of alternative providers,[4] the unbundling of universities into discrete functions, intensifying marketization and continual internationalization with the competitive pressures this brings. The demand for platforms reflects a number of practical challenges faced by university management rather than an overarching sense of platformization as a desirable outcome for the system as a whole. It also reflects a broader enthusiasm for digital technology among university leaders (Hall 2016b). This is particularly pronounced within the UK where intensifying marketization, the consequence of the policy agenda following the Browne report in 2010, increased the (structural) competition between universities for student numbers and the (cultural) competition between university leaders keen to demonstrate the potential of their institution to rise up the league tables (Holmwood 2010, McGettigan 2013). The obvious implication which their perceived success or failure has for their own remuneration and career prospects should not be overlooked. The fact their spiralling salaries come at a time of stagnant remuneration elsewhere in the sector goes some way to establishing the class dynamics of the contemporary university.[5]

In a parallel analysis of the American system Burawoy (2016) describes what he terms the 'ascent of the spiralists': a class of university managers who spiral into their positions, often from outside higher education and with a distrust of the sector's norms, with the intention of rapidly moving upwards and onwards to more senior positions elsewhere. The insightful analysis of Davies (2018) suggests this might typify a broader pattern of elite mobility but it's important to consider the particular forms it takes within an increasingly polarized university. Parker (2014) provides us with a vivid auto-ethnographic account of working under a regime of 'change management' at a prominent business school led by an incoming dean from an investment management firm. His experience led him to wonder about the propensity of academics to exit under intolerable working conditions. However, this assumes the capacity to spiral onwards and upwards into a satisfactory job elsewhere, suggesting a privilege which is likely confined to professors.

There is a risk of overstating the role of digital technology in these matters. If we frame it as what Vostal (2014) calls a 'mega-force', intruding from outside the university in a way that inevitably brings about change, we inadvertently reproduce the ideology of Silicon Valley in which technology acts and the world adapts (Watters 2014, 2015, 2016). The reality is much more ambiguous. For example, university led digital technology projects can be a source of prestige, including for spiralists in university management who lead on their development and implementation. But they can also be a source of profound risk, in common with IT projects across sectors which tend to overrun and can be enormously dangerous when a spiralling project compounds the existing problems an organization faces (Flyvbjerg and Budzier 2013).

It is easy to see why platform models might prove attractive in light of these risks. There are turnkey solutions for a whole range of university functions: student recruitment, student engagement, alumni management, room allocation and staff recruitment among many others. In many cases these have been designed specifically for the sector, enabling the (near) immediate implementation of what might once have been the outcome of a costly development process. Enterprise systems emerged in this environment as a replacement for what had usually been a mix of distinct pieces of software which were difficult to integrate. They made it possible to replace this jumble with a single layer of software which could execute functions across the organization, once a process of customization and configuration had been completed (McAfee and Brynjolfsson 2017: 32–33).

It's interesting to contrast these older enterprise systems which required capital investment, as well as implementation and maintenance as a major staffing cost, with contemporary Software as a Service (SaaS) models in which a service is centrally hosted and licensed by subscription.[6] Even though it would be overstating matters to suggest this means services can be switched without cost, SaaS models lack the sunk costs involved in designing bespoke solutions and/or implementing enterprise systems on a local infrastructure. It reduces the staffing costs involved in provision, outsourcing maintenance and support functions while often providing a superior user experience. SaaS services are easier to iterate, meaning improvements can be introduced with little to no imposition on users, as well as relying on user feedback and user data generated across a diverse range of contexts.[7] While a platform which has been designed for the whole sector inevitably entails at least some degree of 'one size fits all',[8] there is still room for customization even if this entails shifting demands in the expertise which universities must have available to them in the maintenance of their infrastructure. They also entail familiar concerns about data ownership and data safety which place demands on the capacity to negotiate service contracts which are adequate to these concerns. The transition towards platforms in this sense represents a radical outsourcing of digital operations in which the internal focus shifts from providing services through the maintenance of local infrastructure to administering the provision of services by external providers. There is a risk of overstatement here and we are not attempting an empirical appraisal of the shifting cultures of IT service within universities but rather to capture the contours of a change underway in an ideal typical fashion.

This is not the only platformization process underway within the university. By this we mean the insertion of platform-based intermediaries into a routinized social activity within the university. There are many other forms which this can take and they result in dynamics which can vary immensely while still being subsumed under the category of 'digital technology', leaving us with an analytical challenge about how to schematize platformization. For example, Robertson (2018) provides a schematization with a focus on knowledge production and Komljenovic (2018) explores new social relations created by academic social networks like Academia. Edu and ResearchGate. We need comparable schemes for other core features in order to understand the politics of platforms unfolding within universities.

This is particularly significant when we consider the crisis platformization that took place during the COVID-19 crisis, as universities were forced to vastly extend their online operations in an extremely short space of time. If we are correct that platformization has significant implications for the university, beyond the consequences of any individual platform that is adopted, it's essential we find ways to talk about and exercise an influence over these decisions. The speed with which Microsoft Teams and Zoom have become ubiquitous features of academic life is startling, not least of all when we consider the security concerns with the latter which have been well documented. The capacity of the two firms to scale these products at speed during the outbreak of the COVID-19 crisis highlights characteristics of platform capitalism which are now interconnected with core university functions. Without Microsoft's existing cloud computing infrastructure or Zoom's capacity to quickly expand its external cloud computing provision, it simply wouldn't have been possible for these firms to expand their user base so rapidly while maintaining the reliability of their services. Without these services, it's unclear whether the pivot to online learning could have taken place or the core operations of the university could have been sustained to the extent they were during lockdown. There's an inherent risk in writing about the consequences of a crisis of this scale while remaining, at the time of writing in November 2020, deeply lodged within it. Nonetheless, it's difficult to avoid the sense that we've passed a threshold during the COVID-19 pandemic in which the platform university has gone from being a speculative object to an institutional reality.

Daniels and Thistlethwaite (2016) observe a tendency to confuse the transition from *legacy* to *digital* scholarship with the tension between *democratization* and *commercialization* within the university. This astute observation makes the cultural politics surrounding technology within the university much more legible, helping us see what is at stake for both sides in an ever more polarized debate. On the one side we have those who 'dismiss the rise of digital scholarship as just another victory for the forces of neoliberalism' and on the other we have those who 'get swept away by the rhetoric of the disruptive potential for digital technologies to transform all of higher education "with just one click"' (Daniels and Thistlethwaite 2016: 17). These are obviously sketches of outlooks which tend to be more complex in practice but they capture something important about the debates we tend to have about the digital university. This is the reason for our focus in the last chapter on the concepts of technological reflexivity and platform literacy: the capacity to reason practically about *our*[9] relationship to technology, informed by an understanding of how platforms shape the action which takes place through them, sometimes in observable and explicit ways but usually in unobservable and implicit ones. Unless we can develop these capacities it will be difficult to ensure the success of public sociology undertaken through social media because of the problems of platforms discussed in the previous chapter.

However, to develop them requires that (1) we cast off the cultural assumptions of legacy scholarship, without rejecting legacy publications, and (2) we develop these capacities in relation to the organizational circumstances we work within. This isn't a matter of scaling the walls of the ivory tower, as much as recognizing the university as the grounds from which our work has public implications: in the ambient sense described by Healy (2017) as increasingly characterizing all our work within a digitalized university and in the thicker and sustained sense which has tended to dominated our conception of what engaged scholarship entails (Cooper 2017). Unless we do so it will remain difficult to grapple with the pronounced challenges we face 'out there' because we've failed to grasp that platform capitalism is 'in here' too. In fact if the remote working mandated by COVID-19 becomes the norm then this distinction between 'in here' and 'out there' breaks down because the physical space of the campus becomes less significant in the operations of the university.

The epistemic chaos of platform capitalism

The unbridled enthusiasm with which social media was once greeted can now seem jarring and anachronistic, as breathless excitement about 'Twitter revolutions' has fallen away to be replaced by dark visions of ubiquitous surveillance, computational propaganda and planetary scale harassment (boyd 2017, McNamee 2019 loc 3298–3313). As the director of the Oxford Internet Institute put it, 'social media has had a bad press recently' (Margetts 2017c). The Edelmen Trust Barometer (2018) found trust in platforms had decreased in 21 of the 28 countries surveyed, with the steepest decline in the United States. Nonetheless, it is instructive to revisit the claims that were once made, as they still linger on in the social imaginary while academic opinion continues to turn towards the threats social media might pose (Couldry 2015). If the early treatments of social platforms were naively optimistic, there's a risk that has been called the 'techlash' goes too far in the other direction. Instead of investing these sociotechnical forms with the power to save or doom us, we need to treat them as objects of analysis rather than focal points for cultural politics.

The ubiquity of social media sometimes makes it difficult to stop and take stock of the fact that even the most well-established of these platforms are a little over a decade old. Early advocates of social media like Shirky (2007, 2009) saw it as an inexorable force which would circumvent traditional organizational structures, facilitating a mass outpouring of creativity and collaboration from previously isolated people who had been yearning for something which could bring them together (Couldry 2014). Many of these gains were understood to be political, with the election of Barack Obama in 2008, the Iranian protests in 2009 and the Arab Spring in 2010 being attributed to the influence of social media, as well as its perceived empowerment of so-called 'millennials'. It meant the end of information monopolies and the hierarchical control of communication, as the removal of gatekeepers liberated the people to come together (McChessney 2013: 7). But we are now in the grip of what Pasquale (2016) describes as a 'darker narrative of platform capitalism [which] balances the sunny optimism of neoliberals'. This is the context in which what Gorwa (2019) designates 'platform governance' becomes an ever more prominent concern, as scandals accumulate around the corporations variously described as the 'FAANGs' (Facebook, Apple, Amazon, Netflix, Google), 'the Big

Four' (Amazon, Apple, Facebook and Google) and the 'Frightful Five' (Amazon, Apple, Facebook, Microsoft and Alphabet). Concern about their dominance is often supplemented by the backlash that firms like Uber and Airbnb, once called 'the sharing economy', increasingly engender in municipalities around the world (Stone 2017). The optimism which platform firms once inspired is in increasingly short supply, with the force of their (cultural) promises seemingly in steep decline even while their (structural) influence grows (Srnicek 2017).

In this chapter we focus on the claims made about social platforms. This is only strand of what has been called the wider 'techlash' but it is a prominent one. Social media is blamed for the populism sweeping through the world, upending old certainties and undermining old institutions. McIntyre (2018) presents it as a crucial tool which has been used to bring about 'post truth', exploiting cognitive biases for partisan purposes. d'Ancona's (2017: 97) account of the 'awesome force of social media' issuing in 'the ultimate post-modern moment' is emblematic of what is at risk of becoming orthodoxy among liberal commentators. The 'torrential outpourings' and 'viral power of social media' are assumed to be of immense political significance but it is rarely specified exactly how the quantitative facts of social media lead to such urgent political consequences (d'Ancona's 2017: 59–64). In fact one could argue this is an ironically *populist* form of argument, in its implicit conception of a golden age interrupted by an intrusive element that undermines the smooth unfolding of our collective life: a powerful new tool to be exercised by 'the singular agent behind all the threats to the people' who is seeking to undermine the liberal order (Žižek 2009: 280, 2018).

What we describe as the **epistemic chaos of platform capitalism** is an attempt to get beyond this impasse by elucidating four tendencies concerning social media before turning to what these mean for the role of the social sciences in public life. It should be stressed though that this chaos is not a failure of social media (Vaidhyanathan 2018). It is an *expression* of the model which underlies the success of the major commercial platforms: accumulate as many users as possible, as quickly as possible, optimizing the platform to have them return ever more often to spend ever longer there (Lanier 2018). It is something which the firms themselves are grappling with in their increasing turn towards fact checking and initiatives intended to counter 'fake news'[10] (Marres 2018). What has been called the COVID-19 infodemic of misinformation has made this issue more urgent than ever, with the real possibility that a vaccine will be undermined by widespread reluctance to take it as a consequence of ideas circulating online (Cinelli et al

2020). It is something which users face as their daily routines interface with increasingly unstable environments. Crucially for our purposes, it is something which *sociologists* confront as the meaning of objectivity and expertise undergo a profound change under these conditions.

- The immediacy of communication means that established norms lose their force, even if they don't vanish entirely. For example, Papacharissi (2015: 43) observes 'the temporal incompatibility of Twitter with our conventional definitions of what is news, what separates fact from opinion, and subjectivity from objectivity'. Events on the ground can be reported in real time, without a temporal bulwark which permits reflection, evaluation and filtering. The inevitable clarifications, criticisms or contestation only contribute to the cacophony of the stream, enjoying no attentional privilege at the point at which the audience might simply have moved onto something else. If we understand objectivity in terms of methodological procedures rather than ontological relations, there is reason to conclude that social media *tends* to move too fast for objectivity, at least in the traditional sense. It also poses challenges for practitioners of objectivity such as journalists and academics, encouraging the insertion of personal reflection into what would be expected to be disinterested accounts (Papacharissi 2015: 45). This can be factually enriching and convey more of a context but it erodes the ability which norms of objectivity would otherwise have to adjudicate between competing parties. It increasingly feels as if there are *no* disinterested parties and this means attempts to invoke objectivity will often be perceived as providing cover for sectional interests. The fact that expression of solidarity and assertions of fact tend to blur together under these circumstances[11] only compounds the problem (Papacharissi 2015: 50). Objectivity doesn't vanish as a norm but its capacity to ensure agreement on underlying facts rapidly declines (Davies 2018, 2020).
- The fact that established actors do not enjoy more legitimacy by virtue of *being established* suggests a degree of democratization at work. However, these actors tend to have the resources necessary to dominate the news stream which flows through digital platforms, by posting more and being able to ensure what is posted has the qualities necessary to thrive online. In this sense the means through which their influence is reproduced has changed but the fact of that influence hasn't. What Burgess and Green (2018: 30) describes as the 'myth of mass democratization as a direct effect of technological change' foregrounds the declining authority of established voice but

obscures the new inequalities of visibility which are emerging. The ease of entry for new voices co-exists with emerging hierarchies which govern *who is heard* and *who is listened to*. The pertinent issue in this sense is not the fact of making public but the *cacophony* which ensues when the costs involve drop so precipitously. Existing name recognition,[12] resources for communication,[13] willingness to follow platform incentives and a skill in doing so are the crucial factors. The apparent democratization of social media involves the simultaneous creation of new hierarchies concerning who is heard and who is listened to.

- There is a lack of normative consensus about the purpose of platforms. As Marres (2017: 156) puts it, platforms 'bring diverse audiences and constituencies into relation by way of the digital – users, journalists, advertisers, software developers, campaigners' necessitating their capacity to adapt to this diversity. The routines of platformized interaction, such as 'likes' and 'retweets', exhibit a strange duality: they are determinate so as to facilitate *counting* yet polysemous so as to preclude fixed meanings (Gerlitz 2016). What Marres (2017: 156) calls the 'multi-interpretability of action' is crucial to 'their ability to engage heterogenous actors'. In this sense there is a degree of openness built into platforms in order to ensure a fixed sense of their use doesn't prevent the sustained growth of their user base. This openness invites commentary about what the platform is for,[14] which always has the potential to amplify disagreement because there's no ultimate arbiter establishing what it means to use a platform properly. This is particularly interesting when it comes to use by professional groups, as well as interactions *between* professional groups that invoke norms about the platform e.g. between academics and journalists on Twitter (Carrigan 2019: 104). There are converging, if not necessarily shared, professional circumstances which mean there being a 'correct' way to use a platform (as a journalist, as a politician, as an academic) is not a prima facie absurd notion but the aforementioned underdetermination of platform categories means that it's difficult to establish this in practice. It is necessary for professional groups to establish norms about the professional use of social media[15] but the design of platforms makes it nearly impossible to do this in a comprehensive and final way.[16]

- How do users cope with an environment in which binding objectivity is largely absent, new voices emerge alongside opaque hierarchies and there is little possibility for agreement on what constitutes appropriate comportment? The forms of strategic conduct which emerge under these conditions can play a crucial role in intensifying the underlying problems, contributing to an acceleration of the social media machine: it can be rational for an individual to shout louder in order to be heard above the cacophony but this only makes the collective environment more cacophonous (Bucher 2017: 36–37). As Marwick (2013) documents, there are assumptions about self-promotion and visibility built into platforms which have their origins in the extremely specific conditions of Silicon Valley within which these firms were incubated. Not only are these inscribed into the platform itself but the epistemic difficulties users confront over time further incentivizes their embrace in order to survive the epistemic chaos: strategic engagement as a means to ensure *any* visibility rather than the single minded pursuit of visibility as an end in itself. This has been compounded by political economic trends which are exogenous to the user culture of platforms, while having their origins in platformization. Far from liberating the creativity of cultural producers, platformization has made it increasingly difficult for them to support their activity (Lanier 2014). The means through which platforms sought to 'protect' copyright holders against privacy in fields like musical production have depressed their incomes to a profound degree (Taplin 2017). What Abramson (2019) describes as the 'wrenching transition' underway in news media has led to a massive expansion in freelancing under increasingly untenable conditions. The epistemic chaos of the platform is an inflection point through which other tendencies inevitably pass, in the process compounding the underlying chaos.

These tendencies create an epistemic environment which is immensely challenging for the social sciences. Apparent threats to the integrity of social scientific knowledge proliferate amid a broader crisis of expertise (Davies 2018, 2020, Drezner 2018). This has only become more significant during the COVID-19 crisis, to the extent that misinformation has the potential to extend the most significant public health crisis in over a century (Cinelli et al 2020). There are many other examples we could point to here: the flat earth movement, the proliferation of conspiracy theories and climate change denial are simply three of the most jarring. Each can seem like an egregious attack on factualness that is pre-modern in its implications. However, we encounter a more nuanced reality if we look slightly further into them. Within the flat earth movement there is a passionate commitment to empirical inquiry, built around the practice of DIY field experiments (Paolillo 2018). It's a pre-modern empiricism which distrusts anything which can't be seen with one's own eyes but it's an empiricism nonetheless. Within the alt-right media there is a passionate commitment to investigative journalism, built around an enthusiasm for the information sources which the internet has generated (Abramson 2019: 337–338). It is a jarring facsimile of what this looks like elsewhere, oscillating between cynicism and childishness in its willingness to draw connections between discrete elements absent any justification for this inference. But it is a commitment to investigation, nonetheless. Within climate change denial there is a proto-sociological fixation[17] on the vested interests of climate scientists lurking beneath their purported objectivity (Andrejevic 2013). This doesn't mean we are refusing to take these seriously as problems. In fact we would suggest that taking them seriously *necessitates* closer scrutiny, including reflexivity about our instinctive reactions to them and the wider purposes these might unintentionally serve. If we simply dismiss them as pre-modern throwbacks we fail to grapple with the peculiarly modern conditions which have generated them. As Seymour (2019: loc 2320) points out, 'the "fake news" trope is like a conspiracy theory in that it asserts a huge epistemological gap between the knowledgeable elect, and a mass of deluded "sheeple"'. But the idea that somewhere there was a *knowing lie* which others have been deceived by evades the more unsettling question: why is there such an enthusiastic embrace of these ideas in the first place?

Seymour (2019: loc 2320) suggest they function as a 'shorthand political sociology, explaining how their lives got so bad, and how official politics became so remote and oppressive'. It would be naive to imagine we could simply meet this need with longhand political sociology, reproducing the deficit model which was embraced by the public engagement agenda in its early years. But it does help explain why we cannot merely hurl facts at our adversaries, as Davies (2018) so memorably put it, in the expectation they will *eventually* acquiesce to the authority of what we are saying. A ready to hand diagnosis for this can be found in the 'backfire effect' in which being presented with falsifying evidence can actually strengthen belief (MacIntyre 2018: 778–812). However, attributing this to a psychological mechanism fails to do justice to either the empirical variability of its operation or the role of the context in which evidence is presented and accepted or rejected. It also underestimates the difference between laboratory studies with their inevitably contrivances[18] and everyday settings in which debate and discussion occur. Treating these issues through a psychological lens lends credence to approaches which see these problems as expressions of cognitive propensities that can be ameliorated through action leading to better informed individuals. However, in spite of the hopes of the nascent fact checking industry, it seems unlikely that contemporary polarization over matters of fact can be resolved through the provision of *more* facts. Nor through *better* facts or a corresponding change in the seriousness with which people *treat* facts. The problem, as Davies (2018, 2020), convincingly argues, is the erosion of factfulness itself as an institutional form grounded in trusting disinterested experts.

If there's any meaning to be found in the cliche of post truth, it is surely the increasing awareness among the powerful of the apparent erosion of the capacity to consecrate facts, even if the belief they once could relied at least in part on being imagined by themselves and others as being at the heart of public affairs (Couldry 2014). As Boczkowski and Papacharissi (2018: 4) put it, 'Journalism no longer has a monopoly on deciding what's news' as a consequence of the direct connections which social media opens up between groups that previously relied on journalists as mediators, though 'perhaps, it never really did'. The faith in facts as a solution to the problems of factfulness carries the dream of a return to this role, how it was perceived by others and how it felt to be occupying it. If only we can improve the quality of our facts, ensuring we have the *best* facts, it is hoped that things can return to normal. As Marres (2018) provocatively reminds us, 'we cannot have our facts back' and the incessant call for their return leaves us swamped with centrist nostalgia[19] and failing to address the pressing normative questions which now confront us: 'what ideal of public knowledge should we invoke? What role for facts in the public sphere should we strive towards?' (Marres 2018: 424).

These are the pressing questions which the epistemological chaos of platform capitalism pose for the social sciences. While media literacy projects undoubtedly have a role to play in addressing these challenges, it's far too easy for them to take on a technocratic orientation that evades philosophical inquiry by seeking to elevate deficient individuals in order to render them adequate for factfulness. If we see the problem as resolvable through technical intervention, we inevitably miss the deeper underlying shift which is underway. Not only is a renewed commitment to factfulness unlikely to be successful, ignoring as it does the underlying social epistemological changes described previously, it also 're-instates a highly problematic normative hierarchy of knowing and un-knowing subjects, which ultimately stalls the quest for a thriving knowledge democracy' (Marres 2018: 424). Even if social scientists are a minor part of this knowledge apparatus, the ease with which social media encourages the public making of knowledge claims by those with traditional bases of (academic) authority means that we cannot help but become embroiled in the ensuing politics.

The fetishization of factfulness creates incentives and opportunities which it's important to understand if we have a vision of social science as exercising an influence over public affairs. Halford and Savage (2017) suggest we have seen a transition in public intellectualism in recent years in which predominantly theoretical thinkers have tended to be supplanted by those with a more empirical orientation: Thomas Piketty, Robert Putnam, Kate Pickett and Richard Wilkinson. But they use their respective 'data assemblages' to construct big picture arguments which recast pressing issues in new ways. These are narrative deployments of factfulness rather than facts which merely speak for themselves (Gitelman 2013). The mastery of data is the methodological condition for their theoretical arguments but it also confers an epistemic legitimacy on its reception and a pedagogical efficacy through the visualizations used to convey it (Halford and Savage 2017). The success of the aforementioned authors in winning attention and influencing public debate offer a sign of what traditional public intellectualism needs in order to thrive under these conditions. But it does nothing to ensure a genial reception and the cottage industry which Pickett and Wilkinson's *The Spirit Level* provoked among right-wing think tank researchers is a startling example of this, with attacks proliferating of wildly varying levels of sophistication. These tend to revolve around tendential methodological disputes which are of little interest to the casual reader but cumulatively obfuscate the issue so as to cast doubt on the evidence base on which these arguments were made. In doing so, the over-abundance of putative facts generates a pervasive 'data smog' that can lead to epistemic withdrawal on the one hand ('who can really say what's true?') or performative certainty on the other to hide from the growing sense that no one can really be sure (Shenk 1997, Andrejevic 2013).

Social platforms accelerate this process, creating a culture in which facts are sought while ensuring their offering near inevitably meets with contention. It offers an environment in which those offering facts are rewarded with visibility, as users making a provocative claim on the attention of others, while the likelihood of those facts adjudicating disputes in the expected manner continues to decline. This has varying implications for disciplines and the different intellectual currents within them. A particular vision of political science has come to the fore under these conditions, heavy on polling and voting data while light on qualitative evidence and theory. It might seem a boon for the discipline that an influential cohort of political scientists find themselves regularly invited onto television and quoted in the media, coupled with having social media audiences in their own right which allow them to talk directly to large numbers of followers. However, as Allen (2020) argues, this is much more ambiguous than celebrations of political science's visibility would allow. The political scientists with a media platform inevitably become figureheads for the discipline through their presence in the media and participating in the unfolding of events in real time as participants in an enormously visible back channel within the 'political class'. Reflecting on the treatment of Jeremy Corbyn, left-wing leader of the British Labour Party, by the media, Allen diagnoses an 'epistemic snobbery' animated by an idea of serious people with serious thought. They are cast as purveyors of facts, giving answers rather than asking questions. As Allen (2020) observes, 'given increasing pressures on media outlets to generate content at relatively low cost, academics are likely to look like a budget-friendly option whenever a talking head is required in the newsroom'. What might seem like an exciting opportunity can equally be cast as an intensification of the underlying over-production of facts, with epistemic constraints and consequences which are subtle yet significant.

These platforms seem exciting to critical social scientists because many see it as more urgent than ever to speak out, in order to counter organized interventions by think tanks and campaign groups serving commercial interests. These interventions have been part of corporate lobbying for much of the last century, originating out of a sense that the case for business was not being heard before gradually coalescing into an international think tank system that exercises tremendous power (Phillips-Feinn 2009, Medvetz 2012). One tactic routinely adopted has been the cultivation of doubt concerning issues which have been scientifically settled, restraining or reversing action by claiming the issue in question is insufficiently understood. While the tobacco industry led the way in 'merchandising doubt', it has been taken up across a range of sectors with varying degrees of success (Oreskes and Conway 2011). One particularly striking example is the nascent attempt to cast doubt on the relationship between junk food and obesity (Dolgon 2017).

These interventions often have an online presence, relying on the affordances of digital media to sow the seeds of doubt, whether with particular stakeholders and gatekeepers or directed at a slightly fuzzy idea of the general public. It can be tempting therefore for critical social scientists to respond in kind, using these same affordances to repudiate the misleading material that is being generated. However, the risk involved in such a response is that it makes a perverse contribution to the underlying goal of the doubt merchants, furthering the deterioration of the public sphere into adversarial claim and counterclaim in a manner which erodes the capacity for consensus formation. Even if the evidence base is firmly on the side of the counterclaim, it produces an environment in which a cacophony of voices dispute what might in reality be as settled an issue as one can feasibly be. To approach social media in terms of the exchange of speech acts in defence of knowledge only intensifies what Boland (2018) calls the 'cacophony of critique'. This doesn't entail passivity in the face of epistemic pathologies but it does mean we should resist immediate and individualized responses in order to pursue strategic and collectivized undertakings. Research will always be contested under these conditions and we need to grapple with what this means rather than simply hurling facts at our perceived adversaries in the hope it will eventually reinstate the integrity of factfulness.

The contestation of research

This contestation of research isn't going to go away. As Stein and Daniels (2017: 154) put it, 'The only sure way for scholars to escape any and all controversy is by doing unremarkable work that contributes little of broad interest, or work that is so inconsequential – or impenetrable – that it's incapable of ruffling anyone's feathers because so few people care about it, or understand'. In fact this could easily be regarded as overly optimistic given the existence of social media accounts such as Reel Peer Review which aggressively seek out work that they deem absurd and impenetrable in order to subject it to public ridicule. Even if their modus operandi leaves them as an outlier, in that they actually *read* the papers[20] before mocking them, it nonetheless reflects a broader tendency in which a range of disciplines have become embroiled in a culture war which they did not expect. The critics of these disciplines would say that they sought a culture war and what we see now is merely the other side fighting back. But the salient fact is the increasing unavoidability of conflict for those working in disciplines which are deemed to be avatars of 'woke' culture and affiliated to social justice warriors. In fact, as Evans (2019) observes, 'The war on gender studies is a pillar in the authoritarian critique of liberalism' that the ascendency of right-wing populism around the world is pushing into the public sphere. It's difficult to know whether we should be more unnerved by a fake bomb being left outside the National Secretariat for Gender Research in Gothenburg, Sweden or effigies of Judith Butler being burnt in Brazil before she was attacked at São Paulo airport when returning from a conference. These are undoubtedly outliers but they illustrate the potential for the polarization we see at present to lead to some dark places, with at least parts of the social sciences coming to be tied up in them in ways we cannot avoid.

There is a growing infrastructure in place to challenge the perceived politicization of the university that could render the contestation of research a much more prosaic and ubiquitous matter. CampusReform is an online magazine, operated by the Leadership Institute, intended to 'report on the conduct and misconduct of university administrators, faculty, and students'. It styles itself as a 'watchdog' committed to fighting back against 'the outrageous discrimination and abuse conservative students face'. It seeks donations because it 'doesn't have the corporate funding of mainstream media organizations – who repeatedly refuse to cover these stories'. However, the Leadership Institute receives funding from a wide spectrum of conservative organizations in the United States, including the Charles Koch Foundation (Vogel 2017). It was founded to teach 'political technology', increasing the effectiveness of conservative participation in public policy and its campus activism can be understood against this background. It encourages the submission of confidential tips, from those who 'know of some kind of abuse on campus', feeding into the content featured on the website. It is a partner of Turning Point USA which maintains a Professor Watchlist intended 'to expose and document college professors who discriminate against conservative students and advance leftist propaganda in the classroom'. This features short profiles, supported by links ranging from mainstream news sites to CampusReform itself, detailing the alleged infractions of the professors concerned. This includes salaries for professors working at public institutions. The profiles themselves are strikingly thin and they invite the suspicion that the purpose of the watchlist is as much to be seen to be engaged in this scrutiny as it is to build a comprehensive database. However, their modus operandi is less important for present purposes than is their use of digital media and the impact their existence might have on how academics interact using social media platforms.

CampusReform accepts pictures, documents, video and audio as attachments for their tips. In contrast, TurningPoint USA only includes an option to upload video or photographic evidence to support a submission. It also solicits news sources but there's little evidence of how its standard of 'credible source' is operationalized, suggesting being published on an established website is considered sufficient evidence to support a tip. In this sense they reflect the broader epistemological characteristics we encountered earlier in the chapter. Their claim to objectivity is sustained by having the resources to select from the epistemic chaos of platform capitalism. There is so much material in circulation which pertains to higher education that pursuing an agenda is a matter of sifting through the mess in order to craft a narrative, as opposed to establishing the facts of the matter in order to adjudicate on disputes. If these are an insurgency into what is perceived a strong hold of the liberal left, what the theoretical wing of the 'alt-right' describe as the 'cathedral',[21] they are matched by a macro-politics which has sought to attack the social sciences through legislative means. This can range from a strategic concern to prioritize 'hard skills' and employability through to attacks on 'useless research' up to the cultural warfare we see embodied in a figure like Jair Bolsonaro.

It is not our intention to map this issue in a systematic way but simply to point to a broader tendency for social science as a whole to be contested, as well as particular social scientists and/or their work being directly targeted through the new means of political engagement which social media has opened up. It raises the question of how the legitimacy of sociology, as a discipline so prominent in these attacks, can be ensured and what this means for the corporate organization of the discipline and the individual orientation of sociologists. A particularly clear expression of this challenge can be seen in the Assistant Dean of Social Sciences at Endicott College, Joshua McCabe, calling on Twitter for a 'professional organisation focused on scholarship' in the face of a statement calling for the American Sociological Association to 'continue to emphasize social justice in sociological inquiry'. McCabe's point was misread by some as indicating an attack on public sociology as such, despite himself being active in such activity, as opposed to a call for neutrality in the professional association. In a later reflection, Fabian Rojas, a prominent blogger at the popular OrgTheory blog, astutely discerned the practical issue at the heart of the dispute. He described this as the McCabe Query:

> What if you were on Fox News or the Rush Limbaugh Show and a hostile host said, 'why should I believe anything you say?' All of sociology is contaminated by politics. It's leading voices claim that it's the discipline of activism, not science. They claim 'objectivity' is misleading and they reject the idea that sociology can be scientific. Why shouldn't I believe that sociology is just choosing the evidence that suits your moral views? (Rojas 2017)

Holmwood (2007) helpfully stresses the distinction between 'individual commitment' and 'corporate neutrality'. It is inevitable that sociological research will be contested because of its engagement with matters of public relevance (Holmwood 2007: 62). In this sense the worrying tendencies we have seen are a radicalization of an existing dynamic in which sociological attempts to demarcate social life as its expert domain provokes the ire of lay actors whose competency to account for their everyday experience is affronted by these attempts. In this sense doubling down on claims to expertise misses the point in the same way as hurling facts at post-factual critics does (Davies 2018). It fails to recognize what Holmwood (2007: 63) describes as the *dialogic* character of sociological knowledge production in which 'we should expect a public contestation of our claims, just as we confront the claims of each other' with the implications that we should be 'rigorous in our practices, modest in our claims, and open to the surprise and pleasure of learning from others, including those we might construct as adversaries'. He argues that corporate neutrality is crucial to this undertaking because it creates the space in which that dialogue can flourish. This is the challenge we have sought to elucidate with social media. It creates the conditions for sociology to embrace this reactivity[22] but it carries with it novel challenges which our existing scholarly dispositions leave us ill equipped to address. Much of what we term 'digital public sociology' is a matter of tending to the conditions for this reactivity to take productive rather than deleterious forms. But this needs to be understood against the background of the increasingly technologized problem of publicness we confront when platforms are ubiquitous.

Public sociology and platform governance

There is one further actor we have yet to consider: the platform itself. Not in the sense of the background architecture of what we have termed, following Seymour (2019), the social media machine but rather the active and evaluative platform which *intervenes* against that background (Gillespie 2015). As Gillespie (2018: 4–5) points out,

> Platforms must, in some form or another, moderate: both to protect one user from another, or one group from its antagonists, and to remove the offensive, vile or illegal – as well as to present their best face to new users, to their advertisers and partners, and to the public at large.

This might be a straightforward undertaking in the abstract but when the scale of their operations meets the epistemological chaos (which is in part generated *by* that scale) it becomes an endeavour rife with dilemmas in which the strategic conduct of firms, modulating the user experience, the expectations of those users and the regulatory pressures emanating from beyond the platform require constant decision making.

Platforms exhibit a profound ambivalence about making these decisions. As Gillespie (2018) points out moderation is essential to their operation in order to ensure user experiences exceed a threshold which encourages them to return, itself only discernible through intervention and analysis. However, doing so acknowledges their agency, with the risk of casting doubt on their claim to be a neutral intermediary. Instead they 'prefer to emphasise their wide-open field of content and their impartial handling of it' (Gillespie 2015: 1). The cases that receive the most attention reliably illustrate the normative minefield in which they operate, with attempts to evade political responsibility only intensifying reaction to the (clearly political) decisions they make. For example, footage of the Syrian conflict was removed from YouTube after being flagged as violent before being reinstated after consultation with human rights groups (Burgess and Green 2018: 138–139). Each case of contested intervention, with the visibility that ensues from contestation, establishes a precedent which shapes expectations and contributes to the normative complexity of future decisions.[23] The fact these are often contested after automated processes only adds to the challenge, encountering ad hoc responses to manage the controversy that store up difficulties further down the line. Pasquale (2018) suggests platforms are exercising a 'functional sovereignty', comparable to the more familiar territorial sovereignty of states. In spite of the particularities which inevitably surround particular cases of contested intervention, these issues embody a broader challenge of the democratization (or lack thereof) surrounding the exercise of this sovereignty by platforms. As we saw in Chapter 3, consumer preferences are recorded by platforms through the analytical apparatus tracking user behaviour in real time.

This fails to treat people as reflexive agents capable of deliberative judgement (Carrigan 2019). It falls even further short of treating people as citizens or at least something akin to it. This might seem like a category error initially but its relevance becomes more clear if we consider the role that users play in the co-creation of platforms, as well as how it exceeds its empirical manifestation through the aforementioned analytics. As Burgess and Green (2018: 95) put it, 'the purposes and meanings of YouTube as a cultural system have also been co-created by its users – albeit not in conditions of their making, and with very uneven levels of agency and control.' Users feel a sense of ownership over the platform and the tendency of platforms to act as unaccountable sovereigns will often be experienced as an affront to this. This epistemic privilege the firms enjoy on the platform is part of the problem: they know what users do at scale in spite of what vocal users might be telling them. For instance, Facebook's transformation of the newsfeed in 2009 and introduction of Timeline in 2011 provoked furious reactions, with over 1 million users joining the group 'Change Facebook back to normal!' in order to protest the former (Van Dijck 2013: 52–55). Unlike the earlier Beacon controversy, in which user backlash to the automated sharing of their activity on external websites led Facebook to withdraw the feature within a year,[24] Facebook simply persisted until the resistance died down. The MoveOn campaign and class action lawsuits which Beacon provoked must play some role in explaining this difference (McNamee 2019: loc 940). But the more significant factor has been Facebook's increasing confidence in exercising its power. As Vaidhyanathan (2018: 73) puts it, 'Facebook's playbook has seemed to be to slowly and steadily acclimate users to a system of surveillance and distribution that if introduced all at once might seem appalling'. In this they have led the way in reducing platform governance to the imposition of a unilateral agenda and the strategic management of the ensuing dissent.

This can easily be cast in terms of structure and agency. The increasing prominence of this theme in data studies suggests a trend which is likely to grow, as sociological theory is brought into dialogue with the empirical challenges of platform capitalism (Kennedy et al 2015). However, it remains crucial to recognize that the user base is itself structured, in order to avoid romanticizing it as the life world in contrast to the system of the platform. For example, Burgess and Green (2018: 122) draw attention to the boundary 'between the YouTubers as a core group of "lead users" and an imagined "mass" of ordinary users, and the ways these have changed over time'. The core group is in turn divided between the small number who have proved very successful as YouTube partners and the wider community of lead users (Burgess and Green 2018: 120–121). A perceived distinction between media partners and users complicates the imaginary of YouTube yet further (Burgess and Green 2018: 116). While the YouTube partners programme marks out celebrities, the star system itself is not unique to YouTube. In fact it is inherent in mass commercial social media platforms for whom celebrities, made on the platform or emerging outside of it, provide an important vector for generating engagement. In this users have a vested interest in platforms but they won't all have the same interests. In fact the interests of an aspirant celebrity and a casual user are likely to be in tension in many instances; for example, if a tweak to the algorithm to improve user engagement lowers engagement rates for high volume posters.

For users to exercise agency over the platform isn't inherently a positive thing. Reddit's reform minded CEO Ellen Pao being forced out by a concerted campaign of sexist abuse and personal threats illustrates why we should be wary of seeing user agency as axiomatically positive, even if a case can be made that this propensity of this user base reflects what was wrong with the past governance of the platform.[25] But such a case nonetheless needs to be taken seriously as an example of collective action by users in relation to a platform which sought to transform the environment they had contributed to co-creating. To use the term 'community' in relation to online interaction carries a great deal of ideological baggage with it (Turner 2006). However, there *are* sustained relationships over time between people who share a converging, if not necessarily common, orientation towards the platform. This is far from true of the entire user base, hence the importance of recognizing how it is itself structured. It's also a judgement complicated by the reliance of a platform like Facebook on existing relationships. Nonetheless, if we recognize there is something which *feels* like community then we are confronted with questions which are immensely familiar yet obviously alien. Consider Brunton's (2013: 9) reflection on the conditions for online community:

> Yes, you may have a 'community,' with all the emotional baggage that term entails in its dense interlace of shared interest and solidarity, but your community is also a particular arrangement of hardware and software. Your community needs electricity. It is rack-mounted servers, Apache, and forum software, perhaps funded by advertising revenue, volunteers, or corporate largess. (In the case of The WELL, for instance, it was that temperamental DEC computer and six modems in a leaking, poorly insulated office by the sea, a 'community' that was always crashing or threatening to overheat.) Your community may be someone else's property and subject to someone else's laws. Perhaps, like GeoCities – or Imeem, Lively, AOL Hometown, OiNK, and so on, in the necrology of dead user generated community platforms – your community will one day disappear with little or no warning, user generated content and all. Until it evaporates like a mirage due to a change

in business plan, how is your community to police and maintain itself, and how are the rules to be decided?

What he identifies as the 'uneasy balance between the group and the means of their existence at a group' pervades social media (Brunton 2013: 10). This is a site of great promise for a (public) *sociological* approach to platform governance. Platform governance tends to be individualizing when we consider governance *by* platforms because their interventions tend to be undertaken at the level of the individual user (Gorwa 2019: 857). They tend to be framed as narrow and corrective because of the aforementioned reticence of platforms to accept the responsibilities incumbent on them (Gillespie 2010). For all their technological novelty, this confronts us with a classic nemesis of sociological reasoning: individualizing and technocratic treatments of communal issues. How can sociologists contribute to making platform troubles into public issues? What we've offered in this book is only an initial sketch but it suggests an important, if minor, role to be played as digital citizens in steering the meta-debates we've seen platforms give rise so as to move them away from simply technologizing the problem (structuralism) or reducing it to the figure of trolls (voluntarism). In doing so it becomes possible to push towards a recognition of the multilayered character of platform governance beyond the respective spheres of state and firms (Gorwa 2019). Can we do justice to the community and help negotiate this uneasy balance between the groups which emerge through social media and their reliance for this existence on infrastructure which precedes them and remains outside of their direct control? Only time will tell but this is the challenge to which digital public sociology must address itself in the longer term.

8

Assembling Public Sociology

In the previous chapters we have engaged with the voluminous literature which has emerged around public sociology, suggesting it is an example of a scholastic predisposition towards *thinking* rather than doing. It should be stressed at the outset that we don't believe that thinking about public sociology serves no purpose. Even if we did it would be impossible, if not embarrassing, for us to admit that now that we have written an entire book on the topic. Despite this book's theoretical tone, however, its intention is actually practical. We therefore concur with David Mellor (2011) who argued that '[w]e don't need to debate public sociology anymore; we need to get good at it'. Stating this book's objective in such a bold and forthright manner might seem imprudent or careless even, yet much of the sentiment behind Mellor's arresting phrase captures our own argument for a sociology that can be(come) public only if it reinvents itself as such. Yet, what do sociologists need to do to make their discipline 'public'? What does it mean to be good at public sociology? What does it mean to do it well? How would we know that we have done this? Once we start asking such questions, it becomes clear that the answers depend on how we define our terms, how we envision the practice of public sociology and what the key attributes for such a role may be.

In our view, becoming good at public sociology involves a process of weaning ourselves off our professional(ized) or institutional(ized) identity to acquire a taste for a more public or civic purpose to our scholarship. Such a shift from a professional to a scholarly identity or role for sociology and sociologists may sound vague, idealistic or unrealistic. But it is seen here as the first step towards resisting the trappings of professionalization and giving ourselves permission to (re)define what sociology is, who it is for, who we are, as well as what we do and how we do it, according to our intellectual and civic preoccupations rather than our professional occupation. To put it bluntly what we oppose is the way that 'professionalization leads to privatization or depoliticization, a withdrawal of intellectual energy from a larger domain to a narrower discipline' (Jacoby, 1987: 147). Furthermore, we object to a process of 'institutionalization' which 'encourage[s] the professionalization of sociology' through the 'standardisation of study areas (e.g. organizations, crime, demography, urban, political), the consolidation of a technical language, specialization, the canonizing of a theory tradition, the mathematization of research, and the belief that only science yields social knowledge' (Seidman, 1998: 299). What we aspire to instead is a radical attitude towards the institutional environments we inhabit, and a different relationship with public life. This entails adopting what Harney and Moten (2013: 26) provocatively describe as a 'criminal' stance towards institutions that have transformed knowledge into a commodity, a job and a certificate; tailoring it to the specifications of university rankings, degree qualifications, research grants, professional associations, conferences and career prospects. Against such a brazen hijacking of scholarship by metrics, citations, workload models, transparent costing data, research assessments, teaching quality assessments and commercial university league tables (Burrows, 2012), we side with Harney and Moten (2013: 26) who urge us to 'abuse the hospitality' of such institutions, 'spite' their 'mission' and 'be in but not of' them. While most of us cannot afford to opt out of the academic market altogether, we can nevertheless explore possibilities for transgressing its boundaries and subverting its rationale through the work that we do both within as well as outside and beyond it. In this sense we have sought to blur the line between public action as sociologists and as citizens, itself being transformed by the role of digital platforms in re-territorializing the university as an institution with fluctuating boundaries (Bacevic 2019a).

This final chapter will outline our thoughts on how public sociology can realize its aspirations by becoming a reality in practice through a consideration of how we can use sociology for the invigoration of civic, associational life with the aid of our disciplinary knowledge and the affordances of digital platforms. The urgency of this undertaking has only increased with the COVID-19 crisis, as we confront a scarred and suffering social world. This raises the question of the contribution that sociology can make towards a project of post-pandemic reconstruction akin to the reconstructive ambitions which animated the founders of the discipline (Scott and Bromley 2013).

To realize such an ambition we shall endeavour to distil the book's overarching argument into three main propositions that aim to sum up the contributions of the previous chapters in the light of our vision for a public sociology that produces civic-oriented knowledge and strengthens public life. The first of these three propositions discourages us from engaging with public sociology as specialists in a disciplinary subgenre of the same name, urging us instead to think of it as **sociology in public**; by creating opportunities for offering sociological knowledge as a good to be shared in public with anyone who is interested through community education initiatives. By becoming sociologists in public we can jettison the patronizing assumption that public sociology is a branded good that we export in order to increase its visibility, raise its public profile, augment its professional prestige and advance the career of sociologists who are thrust into the limelight as visiting dignitaries rather than as coexisting members of the public. Our second proposition invites us to approach digital platforms as a **digital undercommons** not so much for publishing sociological knowledge, by making material accessible to wider audiences, but for platforming or making knowledge available to encourage communities of people to coalesce around and build on the ideas that are exchanged. In so doing we aspire to a use of digital platforms as what we call **assembly devices**[1] that use online spaces to encourage participation within and beyond them. Our third and final proposition calls for our re-education as **public inter-lectuals** who converse with their fellow citizens instead of expecting them to be converted to our intellectual habits. The difference is one of emphasis in the mode of engagement with public life. 'Public intellectuals' are judged a priori to be distinguished thinkers whose interventions are often seen as authoritative, whereas the role of what poet Ebony Ajibade (1984: 51) calls 'inter-lectuals' reminds us of the importance of thinking and argumentation as something that is done with rather than to 'publics'. All three propositions serve to move sociology and sociologists beyond the limits of professional institutions, encouraging us instead to plug ourselves into digital platforms only to create social life with(in) as well as without them, not as sociologists who speak to publics who passively listen but as citizens with a sociological education. As we have seen, digital platforms unsettle the boundary between public/private and inside/outside the university (Bacevic 2019a). This makes the need for reflexivity more urgent than ever in order to be clear about the position from which we are speaking, who we are speaking to, and the role of platforms in mediating that exchange. It is a *technological reflexivity* informed by *platform literacy* but one which complements rather than replaces the existing routines and repertoires of public sociology.

Sociology in public

Public sociology has established itself firmly as a buzzword that frequently slips from sociologists' lips, especially since Michael Burawoy popularized, but did not coin, the term in his 2004 presidential address to the American Sociological Association's annual meeting in San Francisco. Our thinking about the relationship between the two words that are twinned to bring the term 'public sociology' into existence, however, has unfortunately yielded little by way of understanding what the term really refers to, or what the nature and prospect of that relationship between sociology and 'publics' actually is, has been, or could be. In fact, as Herbert J. Gans (2016: 3) put it, 'almost all' discussion on public sociology has hitherto 'dealt with sociology, virtually ignoring the public and the role it plays in the realization of public sociology'. Disappointingly, Gans (1989: 7) himself – who first used the term in his own 1988 presidential address to the American Sociological Association – is also quite vague about the term's meaning. We are therefore left to wonder who or what 'the public' is, what its connection to sociology might be, or how such a bond can be forged other than in a one-directional manner where sociologists address publics that are spoken to rather than engaged in dialogue or collaboration of any kind. While this observation is not intended as a scornfully derisive critique of an entire debate and everyone who has contributed to it, it nevertheless serves as a good starting point in identifying blind spots that recur in our thinking about the discipline we work within and the publics we want to reach out to. Despite heartfelt endorsements of an 'organic' public sociology 'in which the sociologist works in close connection with a visible, thick, active, local and often counter-public' (Burawoy, 2005: 7), most contributions to the public sociology debate avoid discussing sociology's relationship to 'publics' in any direct manner. What has dominated the existing literature instead is a plethora of suggestions on how sociologists can and should engage with media and social media, how to increase involvement in activism or community work, and how to inspire a radical pedagogy that is aimed at civic education. Laudable though such aspirations for public sociology may be, they are way off the mark. Such visions for public sociology inadvertently assume that there is something special about sociology that inspires 'the public's' imagination, or that there is something uniquely 'sociological' about the content or nature of such encounters with 'the public'. Such practices, however, are already known to us by their proper names (media/social media commentary, activism and pedagogy) and need no validation by, or a takeover from, sociology. To think otherwise would amount to an ontological and epistemological nationalism of sorts, which fails to recognize that there is nothing sociological per se in engaging or working closely with 'publics', and that there are other ways of contributing towards public life beyond and without sociology. Any failure to remind ourselves of that simply assumes that sociology somehow has a monopoly on ways of thinking and acting in order to bring about social change, which 'publics' and the communities they reside and participate in ostensibly lack.

This well-meaning but flippant and insulting ambition for public sociology actually runs the risk of alienating us even more from the 'publics' we wish to approach, and vice versa, but also overestimates sociology's contribution as a superior or singular one compared to other academic disciplines or other forms of knowledge and varieties of public participation. The remainder of this section will therefore attempt to resist sociology's self-indulgent exceptionalism, focusing instead on how to improve sociology's relationship to (its) 'publics'. This inevitably involves admitting sociology's limits and directing its energies to establishing a more humble, equitable and less one-directional or hierarchical relationship with a social world it takes so much from but perhaps gives so little in return. What is suggested here is a change of perspective that puts less emphasis on what public sociology does to publics but rather on how sociology can be in public. The entire public sociology debate has hitherto exhausted itself on how sociology can publicize itself and sociologize 'the public'; either by peddling its insights in the media and social media, involving itself in activism, community-based research and action, or through converting journalists, activists, and independent researchers to sociology. Sensing a faintly imperialistic undertone in such a conception of public sociology, what we propose instead is a much more humble, yet no less powerful, role and presence for sociology.

Rather than emphatically declaring that 'the world needs public sociology' (Burawoy 2004), we contend that it is sociology that needs a world that it can be a part of, not as a swashbuckling buccaneer but as a kindred spirit. The sociology in public that we envisage offers its services as itself, not as journalism, activism or any other form of action that already has another name or function, and as a subject matter that can be taught for free as a way of thinking about 'the social' in community education projects. The aim of such a sociology in public is to feature in public settings as a body of knowledge, in the spirit of skill-sharing and mutuality as a contributor to a process of exchange that fosters public life. This involves settling among or setting up community education initiatives, where sociology is taught without charge in public spaces not as a process of instruction or luminaries who address humble audiences, but as part of an exchange of knowledge and skills among fellow citizens. An example that illustrates how sociology in public can, and has, been part of concrete experiments in social change comes from the Free University Brighton (FUB). FUB was established in 2012 as a direct response to and a protest against the 2010 Browne Review, which announced the introduction of £9,000 fees per annum from 2012, thereby trebling the cost of UK higher education. The idea of setting up a community education project that would offer university-level education in the humanities and social sciences for free was also inspired by the Tent University which offered free lectures on a wide range of topics at the Occupy camp outside Saint Paul's Cathedral. Building on a long-standing tradition of alternative social movements that have fashioned egalitarian and solidaristic versions of the university, such as the London Free School or the Anti-University of the 1960s, FUB emerged out of the ferment that established similar initiatives in the 2000s. These include the Campaign for the Public University, The Silent University, the Social Science Centre in Lincoln, the Ragged University project in Edinburgh and Glasgow, as well as Cardiff and Liverpool's Free Universities. As an experiment in 'deschooling' (Illich, 1971) Free University of Brighton does not simply offer education for free, but also frees education from its institutional confines, in the spirit of the anarchist 'free skools' and the Black Supplementary Schools.

What singles out FUB for our attention is the fact that a team of sociologists, including one of this book's authors, have been instrumental in setting it up, teaching within it and volunteering for it as a practice of sociology in public. Sociology's role in this example and in such a context is not to install itself as a 'professional practice' or a 'public discourse', to use Holmwood's (2007) useful distinction, but to feature as a *public* practice. Sociology's presence in this and similar community education projects is not an intrusive but an inclusive one. Unlike public sociology, which is conceived as and behaves like a marketable sociological brand, sociology's function within FUB has been to promote free and publicly available education in sociology in order to empower community organizing and rejuvenate public life, not to promote itself or its practitioners as public figures to be revered. The difference between public sociology and our competing vision for a sociology in public, therefore, lies in the power differentials of sociology's relationship to and with its 'publics'. Where public sociology wishes to extend its influence, sociology in public aims at making a contribution. Where public sociology wishes to establish control over the spheres of activity it wishes to shape, sociology in public aspires to co-exist and collaborate with(in) the domains it seeks to be a part of without overshadowing them. Where public sociology seems reluctant to shed its professional identity by defining itself according to its institutional confines, sociology in public self-identifies as a civic practice. Where public sociology seeks to establish colonies, sociology in public wants to make a home in the public sphere. Where public sociology appears aggressively ambitious, arrogant and self-absorbed, sociology in public emerges as a modest, humble, cooperative, collaborative and equitable endeavour.

By pitting 'public sociology' against our own vision for a sociology *in public* we are not aiming at 'abolishing' public sociology, but simply expose what we perceive as flaws in the ways it is currently thought and talked about. We therefore revisit some key arguments we have already made about the public sociology we cherish in the form of five questions that serve both as a brief summary of our thinking about public sociology, and as concluding afterthoughts that reframe our thinking and open the public sociology debate up to more critical scrutiny. The intention of these five questions is both summative and restorative and is aimed at encouraging more dialogue between multiple ways of thinking (a) what public sociology is, (b) what is *public* about it, (c) who and what its 'public' is, (d) what public sociology's relationship to its 'public' is, and (e) whether professional sociology can ever be public.

What is public sociology?

Despite the term's popularity and ability to fire up our sociological imaginations, its precise meaning would elude anyone who tries to grasp it. It remains unclear whether public sociology is a kind of sociological scholarship that engages non-academic public audiences, whether it aspires to becoming a specific disciplinary subgenre, whether it can become a form of activism, or whether it refers to a certain attitude towards our subject matter which nudges us towards raising questions of immediate public relevance. While public sociology could mean any or all of the above, it is nevertheless important to clarify what it actually *is*. The reason for that is not merely conceptual but practical too. Without knowing *exactly* what public sociology is, it is difficult to think about how to practise it or demonstrate whether we are willing to do so beyond simply investing in an idea and a discursive trope, which has no specific empirical referent or any real grounding in sociological practice in and out of the academy. To make matters worse, public sociology, on closer inspection, can and often does seem like a metaphor, a pleonasm or a euphemistic misnomer. It is therefore not clear whether public sociology is used as a figure of speech (a metaphor) to express the mode(s) in which sociologists communicate (with) their publics, or whether 'public sociology' designates something which sociologists already do: thinking about, studying, teaching, creating and promoting publicly relevant work (a pleonasm). Unless, of course, public sociology is intended as a public relations exercise which aims at boosting the discipline's profile, without however changing the way it is practised (a euphemistic misnomer).

What is public *about public sociology?*

What remains equally perplexing about public sociology is the question of what exactly is so 'public' about it? Is it its name? Its reachability? Its way of doing scholarship? Its audience? Its funding? Its institutional environment? Its orientation, ethos and spirit? Much like defining the term, pinpointing what is public about public sociology could indeed be any or all the above or it could merely be used as a cipher for a wide array of activities that *are* public and are being *done in public* but have nothing to do with sociology per se. If the overarching aim of public sociological practice is to involve sociologists in community work or activism, what is distinctly 'sociological' about such engagement, and why is the term 'public sociology' needed to refer to what could otherwise be described simply as civic engagement? Until we can somehow demonstrate that we bring something uniquely sociological into our encounter with (our) publics, then public sociology loses much of its analytical potential and participatory currency. Unless, of course, public sociology is thought of as a fig leaf which conceals the fact that our professional practice may no longer be infused with public concerns; to the point that when we do something (in) public, we feel the need to call it public sociology. If this is the case then the very term itself runs the risk of being perceived as little more than a badge of self-flattery, a mere rhetorical gesture, a self-righteous posture and a self-referential endeavour.

Who and what is its 'public'?

If sociology is, or aspires, to be 'public', who and what is or can its audience(s) be? Who does public sociology speak to and who does it aim at speaking for? Who makes up public sociology's public? Is it our students? Our academic colleagues? Our funders? Or is it policy makers, politicians, NGOs, community groups and the general public? Indeed, it could be that any and all of the above could serve as public sociology's public, yet how do we know if they have any interest in listening to us? What's in it for them? How different is our message from that of other academics or non-academic knowledge producers? Also, who decides who and what public sociology's public is? Is it sociologists who decide or is it their publics? Who reaches out to whom? As what? For what? What demands do we pose on them and what demands do they place on us? (How) do we know whether what we want out of such encounters agrees with what our audiences may want from us? In the example of students as 'our first and captive public' (Burawoy, 2005: 263) in the context of mass, marketized higher education our students may, and often do, make sense of themselves and their learning experience as active consumers in search of job and career opportunities, rather than as enlightened scholars and politicized citizens. Similarly, other organizations we come into contact with as producers of specialist knowledge and research expertise may be motivated by their own selfish organizational interests rather than be interested in the scholarly or civic value of our work. It would therefore be naïve to expect or assume that they are receptive to or attracted by the work we do. This, therefore, complicates somewhat the choice of our audience and places limits on the impact we can actually have on our chosen audience(s), especially if they have not chosen to act as our public.

What is public sociology's relationship to its 'public'?

Public sociology could be likened to a 'sociable' or 'shared' sociology (Back, 2007: 163, 2016), yet its relationship to the publics it associates itself with remains unclear. Despite all good intentions to address 'different types of publics and [find] multiple ways of accessing them' or our willingness to 'create other publics' and 'constitute ourselves as a public that acts in the political arena' (Burawoy, 2005: 263, 265), most of our proposed ways of doing so reveal an exclusive and exclusionary relationship with our publics. This relationship often takes the form of something that we foist on rather than forge with the publics we seem so keen to reach. The problem with such a way of reaching out to publics is indeed in the assumption that this is a good way to establish a relationship with them. What kind of relationship is assumed here? Does it include and engage publics in dialogue or does it simply talk to, if not down at, them? Indeed, what is the meaning, nature, value and purpose of such a relationship when sociologists do the talking and their publics simply receive it? For any such relationship to flourish, its very nature has to be reciprocal and engage both parties in a situation where both are equally drawn to and responsible for lest we (mis)understand any association between two parties as a solo performance rather than as a mutual exchange.

Can professional sociology (ever) be 'public'?

According to Burawoy (2005: 10):

> [t]here can be neither policy nor public sociology without a professional sociology that supplies true and tested methods, accumulated bodies of knowledge, orienting questions, and conceptual frameworks. Professional sociology is not the enemy of policy and public sociology but the sine qua non of their existence – providing both legitimacy and expertise for policy and public sociology.

This way of conceiving the relationship of public and professional sociology makes sense, but it does not clarify whether the aim is to institutionalize public sociology within professional sociology or whether it is at all possible to publicize professional sociology. Making public sociology a part of professional sociology would make sense if public sociology is to function as a disciplinary subgenre. But such an ambition contradicts public sociology's aspirations to be carried forward as a 'social movement' (Burawoy, 2005: 25) if public sociology reproduces the institutional structure and function of its professional counterpart. Given that professional sociology's 'professional' status depends on institutional, techno-bureaucratic and managerial imperatives that package scholarship into something that is costed, audited, measured, appraised and sold as a commodity, it is hard to see how it could possibly dovetail with its public counterpart. Just as public sociology cannot be professionalized or institutionalized without losing its critical sting, professional sociology cannot be publicized without transforming the organizational infrastructure(s) within which it operates. For sociology to be 'public' it would have to give up its professional status if it militates against public engagement by narrowing sociology's scope, losing its critical bite or limiting its reach. Professional sociology cannot be publicized by rhetoric alone. It would either need to loosen the stranglehold that its institutional home has on it or to transcend it altogether. Professions draw their strength, legitimacy, prestige and power from their hierarchical relationships that sprout from their institutional soil, rather than from the public sphere, while public engagement depends on a horizontal relationship of mutuality and exchange. To put it bluntly, professional and public sociology can hardly hope to be anything other than mutually exclusive unless they are both reconceptualized in theory and reconfigured in practice. This would involve declaring public sociology as a branch of the professional sociology tree or as an outgrowth of sociology that happens *in public* as a civic rather than a professional practice, in the manner suggested by us in this book.

The digital undercommons

In contrast to a prevailing orthodoxy which sees digital platforms as powerful tools to 'escape the ivory tower' and 'get your research out there', we have argued for a more modest understanding which sees social media as a means of engagement but one which cannot be understood as a tool we can pick up and put down. Nor is it a neutral space in which we can come together for free exchange with equal others: an agora with the potential to heal the schisms of late modernity. In fact, it should be better understood in terms of what it seeks to do with us (the social media machine) and what we can do with it.

In this spirit, we propose a different engagement with and use of such platforms as assembly devices that gather scholars together to share ideas, voice views, and engage in 'study' (Harney and Moten 2013), while also initiating and rehearsing offline action, with all the dangers of surveillance that online life inevitably entails. By borrowing the concepts of the 'undercommons' and 'study' from Harney and Moten (2013), we aspire to a different ecosystem for the production and communication of knowledge, while also carving out a space for subversive study or (de)schooling, as a leisurely, unhurried endeavour which does justice to the etymology of the word 'school' (*skholé*). What is suggested here, therefore, is the use of digital platforms as a step beyond the limits imposed by our professional milieu. In thinking about digital platforms as alternative outlets for studying and thinking about the social world together, uninterrupted by the demands of our profession, we also see them as places where we can redefine what scholarship, research and public action mean to us and share ways to bring these about. As Astra Taylor (2014) puts it in the irresistibly quotable last sentence of her book's preface, '[i]f we want the Internet to truly be a people's platform, we will have to make it so'. The same goes for re-appropriating social media for the purposes of research, scholarship and 'study' not (only) as a set of procedures that allow a systematic investigation into an area of interest, but as a search for meaning and a desire to share ideas with colleagues and 'publics'. Appropriating their use in this manner involves overcoming platforms and finding ways to use them for own purposes rather than being used by them. This entails guiding their institutionalization within an increasingly platformized academy, finding ways to develop a user culture which can help realize their collaborative potential and suppress their competitive individualism (Carrigan 2019). Such a spectrum of activity requires building our own platforms, developing collaborative projects grounded in the affordances of existing projects through to simply initiating reflective dialogues about what we are using platforms for and the risks we face in being used *by* them in circumstances not of our making.

To realize such an ambition, we envisage the use of and function for digital platforms as an 'undercommons' which can host 'fugitive' (Harney and Moten 2013) activities that are suited to our priorities as civic-oriented scholars. These activities can range from creating a space for study as a community of scholars to disseminating research and making public interventions online and offline too. Instead of celebrating social media as places for merely publishing or transmitting 'public sociology', we are arguing for platforming our scholarship as a way of connecting with each other and with our 'publics' too. The difference between these two uses of and functions for social media lies in that we are not arguing for simply publishing material within a specified remit but call for providing a platform around which those who share an interest or concern can assemble. Platforming, in the way we understand and use the term here, is much more community-oriented and mission-focused at the outset; aiming at creating common spaces that draw together people with similar interests and concerns. Unlike publishing, which treats audiences as passive recipients of content in the hope that they might engage with and share the material that is being posted, platforming suggests the existence of a public which actively builds an online space for exchange or the consolidation of a public through the construction of such a space. Where publishing material in digital platforms uses them as advertising tools to broadcast information, platforming involves using digital platforms as assembly devices, which allow kindred spirits to come together and take part in an online community whose aim is to build connections online and offline too. Publishing relies on a digital platform to find, select or source a public through algorithmic connections that match a post with an audience. Platforming on the other hand, involves a conscious effort to reach out to target audiences for participation, acting against the fragmentation and individualization inherent in mass commercial social media platforms. Instead of treating audiences or publics as algorithmic artefacts, platforming creates a space for relevant content to be submitted, edited and made available.

To platform means having, or regaining, some control over what we do, how we do and where we do the things we want to do with digital platforms. While we certainly exercise much influence over the governance or the technical infrastructure of such platforms, though we should be *trying* to do this as *digital citizens* working as part of a broader collective, we can nevertheless shape the culture that develops within them through how we use them for our own purposes. Some examples of sociological platforming include The Society Pages, Discover Society, and The Sociological Review; all of which were designed as open spaces for the sharing of sociological research and commentary, and inviting a variety of contributions from blog posts to podcasts and videocasts, as well as fiction and sociological event reviews. Another sociological example is the Notes from Below online journal published by the Notes from Below Collective in the UK. It is inspired by the tradition of workers' inquiry, and their approach is described in terms of 'the class composition tradition, which seeks to understand and change the world from the worker's point of view' which is reflected by the journal's contributing authors[2]. The collective's political approach and theoretical orientation obviously predates digital platforms, but Notes from Below offers an instructive example of how platforms can support such an endeavour. The project is promoted through Twitter and Facebook, and is hosted by WordPress. It seeks crowdfunding through the Patreon platform, with 18 contributors giving $125 per month at the time of writing.

Building or using platforms as a digital undercommons for study can, therefore, take many forms. The aim being to subvert and respond to the restrictive and competitive environment of academic labour with a more expansive and cooperative virtual space for scholarship and thinking. Platforming offers a welcome respite from and an alternative to publishing and communicating research. Not only does the practice of platforming oppose forms of 'quantified control' (Burrows, 2012) through citation scores and other metrics that monitor academic performance but devalue scholarship. It also seeks to revive scholarship or study as 'an attentive and sensuous craft' as well as 'a moral and political project' (Gane and Back, 2012: 404). Or at least platforming can fulfil such ambitions if we develop the platform literacy and technological reflexivity necessary to thrive within a platform ecosystem. This, however, demands that we socialize social media and use their technical infrastructure for our own scholarly or political purposes. Most, if not all, digital platforms are built to inculcate habits in their users so that we stay addictively tuned in and seductively drawn to content that is algorithmically curated for us; we can, nevertheless, focus our attention and awareness on actively choosing what to do online in ways that serve our own interests, be they sociological, cultural, or political.

As Carrigan (2019) describes we can use social media as sites for research and scholarship by compiling and sharing reading lists on our area of expertise, sharing course handbooks and lecture material, or distribute bootlegged or non-paywalled versions of our work with colleagues across institutional and national borders. We can also test rough ideas and invite feedback from others outside the competitive, if not gladiatorial, arena of peer review or keep a community we are conducting research with informed about what we're doing. Such uses are consistent with the idea of study and scholarship as a craft and a public good rather than a guarder treasure that remains buried in inaccessible archives, or hidden away in sequestered university campuses. They also promote a more cooperative and collaborative spirit with which to *do* scholarship than our professional roles and institutional settings allow, thereby making it possible for us to retreat into the digital undercommons but only to connect with fellow scholars. Equally, the attitude and ethos we bring into digital platforms with a view to transforming them into a digital undercommons through our use of it can also be exploited as a training ground for civic and political interventions. One way of doing so is to use digital platforms as nonsense filters, conduits for nuance, and assembly devices or launch pads for sociologically informed citizens' journalism.

Although social media can be, and indeed are, used as tools for fragmentation and distraction, we can turn them into networks for engagement by actively intervening to filter out nonsense, outflank platitudes, point at facts, and salvage truths from irresponsible, misguided, ill-judged, and doctrinaire messages that fill our Twittersphere. Similarly, we can also use digital platforms as conduits for nuance in order to draw attention to important, yet often overlooked, details in matters of public, cultural, or political interest that may otherwise be drowned out in the noise of loud commentaries and media hyperbole. Combining the nonsense-filter and the conduit-for-nuance functions of our social media use also allows us to intervene directly in conversations about current issues by using our own research as a body of evidence with which to query and challenge widely held untruths. Using social media for such knowledge-based political intervention does not just clear the air by creating the conditions for an 'atmospher[e] of democracy' to flourish (Latour and Weibel 2005), it also allows us to use them as assembly devices which transform ideas into political initiatives online and offline too. This can involve campaigns, monitoring groups, the creation and spread of powerful hashtags that can mobilize action, and indeed promote a culture of sousveillance or counter-surveillance through sharing evidence of misconduct, corruption and social harm inflicted by elected politicians, the state and its law enforcement agencies. This resembles the function of citizens' journalism, as the production and dissemination of 'news' and media outside traditional media outlets, but adds a sociological slant on it by virtue of the research that can back up and bolster such initiatives further (Tufekci 2017: 42).

Public 'inter-lectuals'

Our focus up to this point has been on recentring sociology in the public realm, by creating opportunities for it to feature within it, while also exploring ways of repurposing digital platforms for sociological scholarship and political action. This last section will turn our attention to the practitioners of such public-oriented scholarship by refashioning their identity as what poet Ebony Ajibade (1984: 51) calls 'inter-lectuals'. Having already introduced sociologists as publicly engaged scholars and digitally literate curators of social media content, we now re-introduce them as civically minded custodians of the public sphere. In so doing, however, sociologists are not cast as public or organic intellectuals who divine what the world looks or should be like, but as public inter-lectuals who occupy public spaces as fellow citizens, interlocutors and listeners rather than privileged speakers of wise words (Townsley 2006, Fatsis 2018) The aim here is not to dismiss the intellectual stature of sociologists, but challenge the ways they channel it into more equitable ways than the conventional portrayals of public intellectuals allow. We are therefore keen to place more emphasis on what sociologists as public inter-lectuals can do, and who with, rather than who they are. Our presence as sociological thinkers in public is approached here as a desire to be(come) sociable members of and participants in the social world(s) we study, rather than simply contemplating them from afar with an aura of assumed authority or unwarranted superiority.

The difference between how public intellectuals are portrayed in the relevant literature and the public imagination (Fatsis 2018), and the way we understand them here lies in our demystified, if not irreverent, conception of their identity, function and role in public affairs. Instead of putting public intellectuals on a pedestal, we strip them of the exceptional status and privilege(s) they enjoy to bill them as just one of many equally worthy characters on the public stage. This is not to deny or trivialize the role of 'the intellectual' in public life, but to transform it into a reciprocal and equitable relationship where they act as thinkers in dialogue with people who also think, rather than intellectuals as sages who storm the public stage in a grand display of pomp. This is an important qualification given that despite most, if not all, attempts to publicize the intellectuals as 'embedded' figures (Baert 2015), such positions merely revisit and tired visions that are repeated in an endless loop and portray intellectuals as exceptionally gifted courageous truth-tellers who fight for social justice and against power.

Platforms provide an enticing opportunity to restage these prejudices by those who have, as Bourdieu (2000: 2) put it, 'excessive confidence in the powers of language' (see also Bacevic 2019b, 2019c). But we can transcend these temptations if we can dislodge outputs, expertise and knowledge from their pride of place in our professional orientation. This enables us to approach the interaction that social media enable in a dialogic way; informed by a platform literacy which ensures we understand how the underlying architecture of the platform shapes the form these events take, and a technological reflexivity which means we are able to understand how to negotiate our engagement in a satisfying and sustainable way (Carrigan 2019). To embrace social media in such a dialogical way ironically involves being suspicious of their capacity for dialogue, recognizing the ubiquity of what Winlow and Hall (2013: 73) describe as the 'cathartic opportunity to vent one's spleen accompanied by the sad recognition that in all likelihood no one is listening, and no one really cares'. It means approaching them as technologies of interlocution rather than platforms from which to speak, rejecting a view of social media as a window to the world through which we can channel our many discontents into an imagined public sphere. Platforms designed around what Van Dijck (2013) calls the 'popularity principle' reward speaking but not listening, encouraging a scrabble for visibility through the successful accumulation of engaging speech acts. In this sense, finding opportunities for dialogue involves cultivating the conditions for listening, as much as speaking. It involves overcoming the strange connotations carried by the notion of the 'lurker' and instead recognizing that lurking is a profoundly sociological thing to do.

Even if such technological affordances are new, the ambition itself is not and we can find inspiration from past figures to help us guide our way through the problems of platforms. Ironically, and somewhat paradoxically too, much of what follows establishes a dialogue with an essay written by a scholar who certainly fits stereotypical depictions of 'the public intellectual'. This mysterious, and hitherto unnamed, figure is Walter Benjamin, and the essay in question is 'The Story Teller', in which Benjamin frets about the role of print media and our 'dependence on the book', as a sign that we have become 'poorer in communicable experience' (Benjamin 2007: 84–87). The reason why Benjamin is chosen as an interlocutor in a book section on intellectuals as interlocutors, or inter-lectuals, is not because we plan to further ruminate on the issue of media or social media. Rather, he is chosen for the arresting insights that his essay offers as a commentary on communicable experience, which is the keynote of what follows. It should also be noted that Benjamin's cameo role here is also meant as a nod to Burawoy's (2005) 'For Public Sociology', which also begins and ends with a reference to Benjamin.

Unlike this book, Benjamin's essay sees technological change as a sociocultural shift that is experienced as an impoverishment rather than as an advance, fearing the replacement of immediate participation by mediated communication. Like us, however, Benjamin (2007: 91) is equally concerned by what happens when the 'gift for listening is lost and the community of listeners disappears'. Although Benjamin's essay is not a critique of public intellectuals, much of the sentiment regarding the enfeeblement of our ability to listen to each other as a mode of, as well as for, public participation resonates strongly with our argument about rethinking intellectuals as competent listeners and conversationalists in the public sphere. The importance we attach to this idea comes from our dissatisfaction with the dominant role that we assign ourselves as public intellectuals, this being primarily characterized as something we do to rather than with 'publics', thereby resembling a monologic recitation instead of a dialogic encounter. Such a narrow (mis)conception of what intellectual life amounts to and how it can be carried out in public does not merely betray a patronizing, condescending and patrician aversion to and attitude towards 'the public'. It also disempowers the 'public intellectual' by robbing them of the ability to function as a public person or a 'public character' (Jacobs 1961: 68; Fatsis 2018, 2019a) who engages in dialogue, rubs shoulders, co-exists with their fellow citizens in a relationship that involves speaking and listening.

This is why Ajibade's (1984: 51) creative wordplay is more suitable to our conception of public intellectual life as a process and a relationship that is made among (*inter-*) people who establish an understanding (*intellectus*) of and with each other by talking and listening to one another. Straightforward though this may seem, it is curious to note that our intellectual habits in defining 'public intellectuals' depart radically from such a dialogic and companionate relationship. The merits of rethinking 'the intellectual' and replacing them with inter-lectuals as both a mental and a social category allows us to rewrite the brief on how sociologists can and should behave publicly without courting the dangers of being seen, or indeed seeing themselves, as omniscient sages who deliver sermons to lesser mortals. It is therefore hugely important, or so we think, to reimagine what an intellectual in public is and does as immersing herself into the public realm and engaging in conversation with other members of the public who are (un)like ourselves. Failing to do so imposes barriers to our 'communicable experience', as Benjamin (2007: 84) would have it, while also assigning boundaries, establishing unnecessary distinctions and creating a distance between ourselves and the people who we otherwise seem to be so keen to communicate with, yet mostly treat as an audience to be reached and a public to address.

Much like public sociology, the way we define and conduct ourselves or act towards others, based on received ideas of who and what we are, determines what we can do and how to do it which is why a mental gearshift and change of perspective are required. Refashioning or rebranding ourselves as public inter-lectuals rather than public intellectuals is a good starting point, but it is not the only obstacle to being (more) public. To be public requires us to learn how to *become* public. For public life to be made, it has to be made possible. It cannot form itself around us without us doing nothing to bring it about. That is straightforward enough but important to remember lest we forget how barren life in public has become and how alienated from it we actually are. As we have already seen in the introductory chapter of this book, this is an age-old complaint about the disappearance of public life and the retreat into the private sphere. Alexis de Tocqueville's (1969: 506) description of 19th century individualism in America captures this pretty well by revealing it as a disposition which 'isolate[s]' people 'from the mass of [their] fellows and withdraw into the circle of family and friends; with this little society formed to [our] taste, [we] gladly leav[e] the greater society to look after itself'. To (re)launch ourselves as public characters or public inter-lectuals in the public realm, therefore, involves doing our bit; to recreate, revive, restage, reclaim and occupy that realm.

Regaining our ability to be public depends on our capacity to rethink and relive our identity as a public, as well as reclaiming the space we need in order to become public. The ubiquity of platforms means there is likely to be a technical aspect to such an undertaking, as creating space will often be as much a matter of finding breathing room amidst the hyperactivity of social media as the re(dis)covery of public space we discussed in Chapter 1. To reduce such an observation to its technical aspects, however, reproduces exactly the scholastic baggage we have spent so much of this book trying to clear away, with its tendency to frame thought as 'in here' and practice as 'out there' (Bourdieu 2000, Sloterdijk 2012, Bacevic 2019a). It is equally unhelpful to see this as a matter of 'old media' and 'new media' such that we are assumed to have entered a brave new world. In contrast, we have argued that while our techniques might have to be adapted to contemporary platforms, our ambitions often remain the same; recognizing this helps demystify 'the digital' and open it up as an object of the reflexivity we exhibit in other areas of our life (Carrigan 2018, 2019).

Sociologists need to become comfortable with being (in) public in our capacity as citizens by rediscovering public culture not just as our object of study but our civic base too. What this means inevitably changes as the sociotechnical constitution of civic bases changes too, but this is a matter of being mindful of the terrain we now operate on rather than throwing out everything we have done before. While such a public ambition applies to all citizens rather than being the sole responsibility of sociologists, we can claim to have something special we can bring to public life, beyond our specialist knowledge or our research expertise. Impossibly broad or hopelessly romantic though this may sound, the most important contribution to public life is our sociological imagination. Understood here as a quality of mind we bring not just to sociology but to our experience of the social world, our public presence and our interaction with others, our sociological imagination is likened to a tool with which to navigate associational life.

Enlisting our sociological imagination as a foot soldier in our attempt to re-engage with public life as 'something inalienable to' yet 'taken from us' (Benjamin 2007: 83) means immersing ourselves into social life as an exercise in attentiveness and sensation seeking. This inevitably opens up possibilities and creates opportunities for participation, sociability and interaction by virtue of the qualities we bring into our experience of public life through our bearing, our comportment, the people we meet or greet, and the places we pass by, walk around and reclaim as ours. This sociable way of being public through our presence in, our attitude towards, and our relationship with public life is captured rather well by two inspiring passages that we quote as a coda to this chapter and this book as a whole. The first comes from Randall Collins (1998), who celebrated the importance of acquiring a 'sociological eye' with which to find our position in relation to our surroundings. And the second is lifted from a short story by Sam Selvon (1998) who takes our sociological imagination for a stroll around the city and re-energizes everything that his narrator sees in a literary, yet so sociological, way of 'mak[ing] the familiar strange, and interesting again' (Erickson 1986: 121).

Starting with Collins' (1998: 2–3) appeal to the 'sociological eye' as an instrument for the re-enchantment of the social world:

> There is a sociology of everything. You can turn on your sociological eye no matter where you are or what you are doing. Stuck in a boring committee meeting (for that matter, a sociology department meeting), you can check the pattern of who is sitting next to whom, who gets the floor, who makes eye contact, and what is the rhythm of laughter (forced or spontaneous) or of pompous speechmaking. Walking down the street, or out for a run, you can scan the class and ethnic pattern of the neighborhood, look for lines of age segregation, or for little pockets of solidarity. Waiting for a medical appointment, you can read the professions and the bureaucracy instead of old copies of National Geographic. Caught in a traffic jam, you can study the correlation of car models with bumper stickers or with the types of music blaring from radios. There is literally nothing you can't see in a fresh way if you turn your sociological eye to it. Being a sociologist means never having to be bored.

In a similar vein, Selvon (1998: 164) digs just as deep into the minutiae of everyday life and transforms the protagonist of his story into a chronicler of 1950s London life that has much to teach us on how to be curious about the social world around us. He asks:

> What is all this, what is the meaning of all these things that happen to people, the movement from one place to another, lighting a cigarette, slipping a coin into a slot and pulling a drawer for chocolate, buying a return ticket, waiting for a bus, working the crossword puzzle in the Evening Standard?

This diversion from discussing the role of sociologists as public intellectuals might seem irrelevant or inconsequential, yet the alertness to our environment and our fellow citizens that these two passages describe fits our argument like a glove. Not only do Collins and Selvon gently persuade us to value the attentiveness of listening as much as the assertiveness of speaking, they also help us challenge the role of public intellectuals as privileged speakers of, or perhaps to, the human condition and replacing this idea with the practice of intellectual activity as an exercise in listening. This shift in modes of engagement with the public conveniently allows us to redraw and sum up the three main propositions that shape this chapter and our book as a whole, albeit in reverse order.

By retraining ourselves as inter-lectuals whose antennae are sharply attuned to the social world around us, rather than focused on imposing our voice to it, we can relate to and forge more meaningful relationships with the 'publics' we wish to come into contact with. In so doing, we can gain our fellow citizens' confidence and perhaps capture turn their attention to the work we do in and out of academia by pointing them in the direction of the sociology we do in public as teachers and community organizers in education initiatives or the digital undercommons we curate as spaces for making public interventions. Not only does this shift in our thinking bring about a welcome shift in our relationship with the work we do by bringing 'a bit of craftiness into the craft' of public sociology (Back, 2012: 34), it also helps us improve our relationship with our colleagues and our publics as a cooperative enterprise rather than a clientelistic mission in which we either become professional 'philosopher kings' who instil 'reason in human affairs' or policy 'advisors to the king' by succumbing to 'a functional rational machine' (Mills, 1959: 179–80), when we could be honing our sociological craft.

To conclude, this book has tried to explore and redefine sociologists' relationship with their 'public', their platforms (digital or analogue) and their own discipline by proposing an alternative to what has hitherto been offered in discussions of public sociology. As a counterpoint to this debate, now well into its teenage years, we have argued against a public sociology which travels from the academy to 'the public', writes itself into policy, or strengthens its professional portfolio often by alternating between those functions. What we call and stand for is a sociology which roams in public, creates its own spaces 'online' and 'offline', and socializes with its 'public' in a non-hierarchical, collaborative manner, which not only gives our discipline a boost as a publicly relevant professional endeavour but also creates the possibility for democratic citizenship and social change.

Our public sociology, therefore, sees itself as a technology for thinking about and interacting in public; drawing its strength from our 'sensitive perception', 'creative imagination', and 'adroit conceptualisation'

(Blumer 1972), and driven by the desire to lead scholarly and civic lives full of 'vigour of thought and thoughtful deed' (Du Bois, 2003: 189). This requires that we become adept with digital platforms, but not dominated by them. *They* are a means of *our* endeavours, an object of our critique but never an end in themselves. To focus only on 'the public' is mistaken but to restrict our concern to platforms and what we can do with them is even more dangerous. The public *and* their platforms are the terrain on which public sociology will operate in the coming decades. This text has been a modest attempt to map that terrain, clear away some of the conceptual detritus which hinders our understanding of it and develop orientation devices which can be picked up and used by public sociologists. We hope you have found it useful.

Notes

Chapter 1

[1] See Carey (1992: 25).

[2] For example, the extensive literature on filter bubbles, sparked by Pariser's (2011) original text, as well as the communicative capitalism literature, such as Dean (2010) and Hill (2015), express both themes in slightly different ways.

[3] For a good discussion of the tensions between interpretations of the public sphere and public society as both 'good' and 'bad', see Chambers and Kopstein (2001), Alexander (2006) and Putzel (1997).

[4] See d'Ancona (2017) and McIntyre (2018) for archetypal examples of this, from a political commentator and academic philosopher respectively. Green (2017) and Wendling (2018) delve more deeply into the reality of this connection which Nagle (2017) attempts to theorize in a still rather controversial text.

[5] Debates about civility in politics, online and offline, figure heavily in the media at the time of writing. Even if these are often unobjectionable in their own terms, it is important we consider what is assumed about the political and the platforms through which it is enacted by those making such calls (Mouffe 2000, 2005).

[6] See Carrigan (2014) and Uprichard (2008) for conceptual discussions of this.

[7] Veblen (1994), Fromm (2013) and Arendt (1998) come immediately to mind as thinkers who have notoriously warned against the dangers of conspicuous consumption, the obsession(s) of possession, and the emergence of the consumer society.

[8] For some good critical discussions of 'quality of life' offences and the 'broken windows' or 'order maintenance' policing used against them, see Roberts (1999), McArdle and Erzen (2001), Camp and Heatherton (2016), Vitale (2017), and Klinenberg (2018: Chapter 2).

[9] Earlier historical examples include the policing of the poor, 'dangerous classes' in Victorian England graphically explored by Henry Mayhew's (2005) journalistic sketches, and Davis (1989) and Storch's (2008) brilliant historical work on the policing of 19th century London's outcasts.

[10] For a good discussion of how 'the people' are often conflated with 'the mob', see Arendt (1967: 106–117).

[11] Details on where and when second line parades take place in New Orleans, can be found at the website of the community-run radio station WWOZ: www.wwoz. org/programs/inthestreet. A short snippet of a second line attended by one of the authors of this book is available at: www.youtube.com/watch?v=xJ_fXelisi8

[12] To find out details of the next Grenfell Silent Walk visit the campaign's Facebook page: www.facebook.com/GrenfellSilentWalk/. A recording of one such walks can be found on Monique Charles' YouTube page: www.youtube.com/watch?v=GAX4wT-LUO8.

Chapter 2

[1] The observation by Plantin et al (2018) that platforms unsettle the existing ontology of media studies is particularly relevant for our purposes, as we are making a parallel claim about platforms and the (implicit) ontology of public sociology.

[2] We use this term in an analogous sense to Holmwood and O'Toole's (2018: 83) use in their discussion of educational centralization. Their use concerns how proximate relations with intermediary bodies provide a 'scaffolding' that influences action in formal and informal ways.

[3] The fact that Uber makes it deliberately difficult to build a sustained relationship with a driver is telling here, as information about past drivers is presented sequentially within the interface. It is literally impossible to represent one's past relationship with a particular driver within the interface, even when both parties are aware of such continuity existing. It isn't possible to do this on the Deliveroo service which removes details of drivers immediately after the order has been received.

[4] For example, the possibility that Uber might *increase* the net amount of car journeys taking within an area. Should this be understood as the creation of something *new* or the mediation of activity which would have otherwise taken the form of walking or public transport? Furthermore, how should we conceptualize the potential impacts of the platform on public transport systems?

[5] For example, Chen (2018) concisely identifies why the model doesn't fit easily into other spheres of activity, drawing on his experience as a venture capitalist and past director of growth at Uber.

[6] The fact Uber operates an internal service called 'god view' which it uses to track customers in real time suggests an awareness of this dynamic, even if their reported willingness to use it as a party entertainment at internal events perhaps suggests something inherent to Uber rather than the platform model as such.

[7] See Savage and Burrows (2007) and Kitchin (2014) for appraisals of the social scientific significance of these developments. Pasquale (2016) and Carrigan (2018) explore the politics which follows from their widespread implementation and what this means for knowledge production. There is a powerful mythology associated with it which Andrejevic et al (2015) describe as the end of 'conventional forms of narrative and representation, promising to discern patterns that are so complex that they are beyond the reach of human perception, and in some cases of any meaningful explanation or interpretation'. See also Couldry (2014).

[8] For avoidance of doubt, we are not suggesting there is anything inherently commercial about machine learning. We merely wish to stress the significance of *contextualized implementation* for the character of a machine learning system.

[9] Though many commentators would suggest this merely compounds a tendency already found within Big Tech (Vogelstein 2013, Mason 2019).

[10] Orkut's lifespan was expanded for a long time by its success in India and Brazil.

[11] We expand on the significance of these services in the following chapter.

[12] Consider for example trade union activists using WhatsApp to coordinate during an industrial action, parents of children in the same year group at school or an extended

network of friends within a professional group. These are far from unusual uses of the platform which point towards its ubiquity, as well as the potential implications its affordances and constraints have for social organization within specific contexts.

[13] In fact, they can be used to *do* research, as Evans (2017) illustrates in the case of Tinder.

[14] Thanks to Katy Jordan for this comparison.

[15] For example, it would be difficult to make this claim of Borrow My Doggy, even if its design clearly reflects the data accumulated about how users approach the site and their communications seek to leverage this understanding in order to facilitate more successful 'matches'. It's important to recognize the exploitation of what Zuboff (2019) calls 'behavioural surplus' as a contingent rather than necessary feature of social platforms.

[16] Though we should remain cautious that this still remains a slightly nebulous term which, as Apperley and Parikka (2018), point out is playing a role in constituting a 'platform' as an epistemic object. As an intellectual trend its origin lies in game studies, particularly the Platform Studies MIT Press book series edited by Ian Bogost and Nick Montfort, supplemented by a more recent turn towards this terminology among analysts of social media who are predominantly (loosely) clustered around the Digital Methods Initiative's network.

[17] For all its computational sophistication there is still an epistemic bias inherent in data science in so far as that it seeks to understand future behaviour on the basis of *past* behaviour as evidenced through data generated within the platform. There is a temporal limitation here which has important connotations for how we interpret human action, with these interpretations being real in their consequences even if they fail to grasp the lived relationship between past and future (Pasquale 2016). But it also obscures the many extra-platform factors which cannot register within confines of the platform as a data infrastructure (Carrigan 2018). While platforms are seeking to overcome these limitations by purchasing data and linking these datasets together on a massive scale, it still reflects what Little (2016) calls the utopia of total social legibility: a belief the world can be read as if it were a book, if only enough data can be accumulated (Barnes and Wilson 2014).

[18] He draws an intriguing parallel between platforms and derivatives in this respect, hinting at a sociology of financialization in the platform economy.

[19] With the promise being this will keep users engaged by offering them a speed and ease of access which would be unfeasible. As Google's (2019) AMP page observes, 'Most mobile site visitors leave a page that takes more than 3 seconds to load. Yet most mobile sites miss that mark by an average of 19 seconds'.

[20] The fact Facebook users the terminology of platforms to refer to the environment in which third party developers can create their own applications and services complicates matters somewhat.

[21] At risk of stating the obvious, he is not writing this material himself. However, it *is* being written by people tasked with untangling his often far from clear thought processes. Losse (2012) provides a fascinating insider account of what it is like to be perform the role in relation to the man foremost among those she describes as the 'boy kings' of Silicon Valley. Even though his performances will clearly be informed, managed and supported by staff, we can legitimately infer more of Zuckerberg's authentic voice into public performances in which he responds to questions and engages in dialogue. The same is true of other tech founders who regularly participate in public events in the thickly networked milieu of Silicon Valley.

22   For example, as a consequence of the expansion of home working, coupled with the widely recognized unsustainability of the property market in the valley region.

Chapter 3

1   See Gerbaudo (2019) for an incisive account of the nascent mediating institutions (*platform parties*) which are emerging within this environment and unsettling what many commentators had taken to be established facts about contemporary politics.

2   The best expression of this can be seen in Facebook's warning of the potential for lost friendships when a user attempts to delete their account.

3   An impressionistic sense of this distinction can be discerned by comparing the relative sterility which many users find in LinkedIn with the thick sense of connectivity often associated with the early years of Twitter and Facebook.

4   Relevance can be inferred from descriptions of past behaviour but it cannot be explained without recognizing the evaluative capacities of the subject (Carrigan 2018). How else to explain why person X is engaged by a piece of content which person Y is left unmoved by? There are fascinating patterns which can be found at scale concerning the characteristics associated with different trajectories of engagement but these are still not explanations of these differences – why something is so rather than otherwise (Sayer 2011).

5   It could be objected that liking is often a matter of social signalling, conveying one has read and appreciated the sentiment, rather than evaluating the content itself. However, this itself points to the fact the social relationships maintained through platforms matter to users (Sayer 2011). What else would it mean to say that people care about what those they are connected to through the platform think of them? We cannot read back uniform motivations from the routinized interactions which platforms facilitate any more than we can assume the same practice has a uniform meaning across different instances of it (Archer 1985, Das and Hodkinson 2018). But if we lose sight of the fact that it does have a meaning then we contribute to reducing social action to social behaviour and render much of social media inexplicable, even if this move opens up sophisticated 'big data' tools for describing the empirical remainder (Carrigan 2018).

6   Even within platform studies a case can be made about the relative neglect shown towards users of the platform (Apperley and Parikka 2018: 354–356).

7   This invokes the crucial conceptual distinction made by Kennedy and Moss (2015) in an extremely important paper.

8   The fact that Klout was purchased for $200 million only to be shut down exemplifies the commercial landscape within which these firms operate. Lithium Technologies CEO Pete Hess (2018) wrote that the 'Klout acquisition provided Lithium with valuable artificial intelligence (AI) and machine learning capabilities but Klout as a standalone service is not aligned with our long-term strategy'. The firm's value lay in the data and the capacities which it developed to work with that data, as opposed to the services for end users.

9   Gerlitz and Lury make the important observation that influence as measured by Klout is not a linear phenomenon, as the reliance on an ordinal ranking between 1 and 100 leaves it a matter of *more* influence rather than the *most* influence. The meaning of the ranking constantly shifts as its objects of measurement do, compounded by the tweaks to the metrics being made by the firm for commercial reasons. They call this a 'participative metrics', designed to encourage and orientate

forthcoming activity, as opposed to providing a reliable measurement of activity which has already taken place (Gerlitz and Lury 2014).

[10] It used a virtual private network (VPN) to prevent access to listed websites for a specified amount of time. The result of the iOS change is that Freedom's operations can be switched on and off at will, removing the self-imposed period of disconnection which is the product's raison d'être.

[11] We are using the terms 'old media' and 'new media' here because they capture the epochal logic of the distinction. It follows from the argument we are making that the old/new contrast is analytically unhelpful.

[12] There is a thick layer of secrecy surrounding the shifting incentives of the algorithm which provokes a correspondingly thick layer of bullshit by those with a vested interest in exaggerating their own capacity to elevate a firm's ranking. The inevitable gaming which the material interest in getting on the first page of results carries means that constant change is necessary to ensure the user experience, namely finding what you want quickly and easily, which Google has sought to offer since its inception (Vaidhyanathan 2012).

[13] There is a risk of overstating this contrast. For example, after previously being granted a lofty position, about.com's traffic collapsed when Google began to prioritize more in-depth treatments of topics users were searching for (Abramson 2019: 73).

[14] We discuss this at greater length in Chapter 7.

[15] If the latter category seems insignificant, consider the unprecedented wave of militancy sweeping the technology sector. The narratives which platforms tell about themselves serve a crucial purpose within the company, offering a vision of a moral project to which employees can commit themselves. It would be a mistake to reduce the upsurge of labour militancy within big tech to a single cultural factor but there are grounds to suspect the diminishing hold of these narratives have played a part in encouraging the activism which we can now see.

[16] We mean platform in a broader technical sense here to refer to any infrastructure which generates digital data as a by-product of user activity. Social media is a particularly significant and interesting source of 'big data' but the history of knowledge production in this style precedes social media platforms and extends far beyond them (Beer 2016b).

[17] This includes a dependence on firms for access to platforms through APIs which are themselves far from stable, raising urgent questions about longer-term implications for the research ecosystem (Vis 2016). Much of the explanatory promise of 'big data' depends on liberating social data from corporate fortification (Margetts 2017b).

Chapter 4

[1] The role of a material infrastructure ensures that 'platform' means more than a social position (in the Bourdieusian sense), a social role (in the Critical Realist sense) or any analogous concept. Without this caveat, it would simply amount to the (trivial) insistence that communication always be treated sociologically, as conditioned by inequalities of capital between the communicating parties. Insisting on the role of material infrastructure doesn't substitute for this sociological framing but invites consideration of the interplay between social and material elements in establishing the position from which one communicates.

[2] These are far from the only properties and powers inherent in such a position, let alone the material infrastructure underlying it (Thompson 1995: 1–43).

However, they are the most significant for our purposes, as embodying the promise and pitfalls which platforms hold for public sociology.

3   To consider scholarship in terms of institutions encourages us to historicize the form which scholarship takes, rather than conflating existing forms with the *essence* of scholarship as such.

4   It depends on what we count as 'social media' and what we count as using it in a 'professional' capacity.

5   Even if the advice might be to avoid it, as has often be the case in the United States where concerns of tenure remain dominant in spite of only being reached by a minority of the academic workforce.

6   Even though our focus in the book is on public sociology, much of our argument is directly relevant to how publicness is conceived of within the social sciences more broadly.

7   This reflects a broader tendency of digital platforms driving metricization such that numbers figure heavily in how we think and talk about participation in social life (Marres 2017: 155–157).

8   This is compounded by the legacy of public intellectualism in which a small number of towering figures would broadcast to what was imagined to be an undifferentiated public (Carrigan 2019: 94–97). Baert (2015) documents the decline of the social and cultural conditions which facilitated this model of expertise, highlighting the necessity of the more concrete conception of publics which has accompanied the move away from the deficit model of public engagement (Maile and Griffiths 2014: 9).

9   The perceived plausibility of their claim does not mean they can *actually* ensure visibility in the manner they promise.

10 Thanks to Pat Lockley for initially pointing this out.

11 See Caplan and boyd (2018) for a more detailed analysis of how platform incentives bring about change within the media.

12 In the sense this is a strategic achievement involving the realization of one potential within social media, as opposed to simply being the successful use of this tool. In other words, what matters is not social media but rather *how we use it*. This is an obvious point but one which is easily forgotten in an environment saturated by the hype we encountered in the previous chapters.

13 Though the use of arcane language is too often framed as a problem that *other* people are prone to, pointing to an adjacent discipline using language of a form which is merely seen as 'technical' within one's own arena.

14 For a theoretical treatment of the idea we are invoking here, see Archer (1988). Logical relations don't determine thinking but they do condition it to move in particular directions by rendering certain outcomes tractable and others intractable.

15 These are often found in reflective pieces in journals which advocate rather than analyse social media as matter of academic practice. They are also found in the guidebooks mentioned earlier, even if claims about the nature of platforms as such tend to be diluted by their practical focus.

16 There is a tendency for the perspectives of enthusiastic early adopters to be heard disproportionately in these discussions, with partial observations repeated as orthodoxy simply through the apparent experience of the speakers and the confidence with which they speak in relation to a still uncertain field.

17 In this sense we use the concept in parallel to Taylor's (2004) account of social imaginaries. See also Couldry (2014).

18 A close reading suggests an aspiration towards sociable scholarship in this work which the available platforms couldn't facilitate (Pausé and Russell 2016).

19 The dictionary.com definition of scholar is 'a learned or erudite person, especially one who has profound knowledge of a particular subject'.

20 By this we mean respect for 'facts' as an institutional form (Davies 2018). While emphasizing the socially constructed nature of 'facts' is often taken as an anti-realist position, it is perfectly consistent with the idea there are *truths* in relation to which those facts carry a truth value. See Bhaskar (2010) for a detailed realist account of the social production of facts which demonstrates this understanding.

21 For example, the epistemic legitimacy we might impute to a piece of qualitative research built around interviews would often be denied by an economist or data scientist, even if conventions of academic civility often sweep the full implications of these clashes under the proverbial rug in interdisciplinary encounters (Fitzgerald and Callard 2015).

22 Scholarly denials of this privilege often take the form of what Sayer (1999) calls a PoMo flip. The conceptual structure is retained but inverted, such that a direct relationship between descriptions and the world is denied but as a totalizing claim which precisely embodies the epistemic privilege which is being repudiated: the claim that scholarly discourse doesn't map onto the world itself embodies the totalizing tendency of scholarly discourse. In doing so the specific question of *our* descriptions is evaded.

23 This is not unique to social media. For example, television allowed public events to be watched from private homes in a manner experienced as radically novel (Papacharissi 2010: 22). It's just that these innovations tend to fade into the background over time as features of renegotiated boundaries between public and private.

24 In this sense they are closer to policy sociology than public sociology. This has tended to be marginalized within Burawoy's public sociology but these technically inclined suggestions illustrate the role it might play once we dispense with the imperative to get beyond the ivory tower (Hartmann 2017).

25 The fact this involves what Marres (2012) calls an 'editing out' of technology is precisely why coming to terms with social media provides us with an opportunity to rethink the fundamental architecture of how we conceive of the political.

26 For example, a shared understanding of what is at stake in the exchange, norms concerning the conduct of the exchange or a reciprocal belief in the good intentions of those participating in it,

27 As Gregory and Singh (2018: 182–183) observe the dynamic characteristics which make a platform like Twitter attractive 'can also be a recipe for almost immediate (and public) miscommunication, with the speed of the platform potentially collapsing any chance for clarification, dialogue, or debate'.

28 Even if Boyns and Fletcher (2007) believe that Burawoy's intervention will only compound the problem.

29 There is a strategic case to be made for this in terms of the perceived authority of sociological knowledge but one which, we will argue in Chapter 8, increasingly breaks down in the face of political polarization and hostility towards expertise. Public sociology needs to find new bases for its own legitimation. The risk is that seeking purely normative ones would compound the collapse of legitimacy by explicitly embracing a militant identity (Holmwood 2007). This will be one of the key tensions we will explore going forward.

Chapter 5

[1] https://hcommons.org/.

Chapter 6

[1] To a certain extent it is inevitable that guidebooks and grey literature use this framing, as they seek to encourage and guide people in the use of platforms. But it does involve an unfortunate contraction of horizons when it comes to the problems encountered in the ensuing activity.

[2] This varies immensely between national systems and the account we offer here is an ideal type of marketization and the performance management which tends to go with it, with the intention of illustrating the core dynamic that is likely to be operative in relation to the metrics which digital platforms provide. It could be inferred from Robertson's (2019) analysis that this national variance is likely to diminish as a matter of managerial culture because global rankings exercise isomorphic pressures over institutions which increasingly operate within the same competitive (meta)field.

[3] Interestingly, Springer Nature doesn't, despite the fact Digital Science began as the technical division of Nature Publishing before being spun off as a separate company.

[4] The fact it relies on the RSS system which has long been speculated to be in decline compounds the problem. In their defence the list includes 14,000+ academic blogs but the issue is the opacity of this list rather than its size.

[5] For example, API changes for Pinterest and LinkedIn mean that these have been removed from the system. The closure of Google Plus further complicates scoring. In this sense it is far less stable than the traditional citational record.

[6] See Lupton (2014) for an empirical outline of what these fears look like, albeit one which massively over represents early adopters by being reliant on Twitter recruitment in the early 2010s.

[7] What we think of as an 'impact machine' has emerged rapidly within the system we operate within, incorporating research managers, impact consultants, professional trainers and impact champions in a rapidly emerging system built to encourage, evaluate and report on research impact (Jordan and Carrigan 2018a).

[8] This is consistent with what Van Dijck (2013) calls the 'popularity principle' around which social media platforms have been designed. We have focused on the interface between user cultures on social media and the framings of social media within the academy because of the risk that these can be mutually reinforcing, with problematic assumptions in the former being reflected by problematic assumptions in the latter to produce something that *feels* like common sense.

[9] This often goes hand-in-hand with an unwieldy dualism in which the performance of critique co-exists with objective complicity, leaving people in a situation where metrics matter objectively (in terms of career progression) and subjectively (in terms of perceived standing) but discussion of this dependence struggles to extend beyond the level of rehearsed grievances about the marketization of the academy (Fisher 2009, Bacevic 2019b).

[10] Drawing on Christopher Kelty's work on participation.

[11] We mean 'veilling' in Pickering's (2010) sense of rendering them unrepresentable even while we encounter them in practice.

[12] We mean this in Archer's (2000, 2003, 2007, 2012) sense but expanded through Carrigan's (2014, 2016, 2017a, 2018) work, which explores sociotechnical infrastructure as a condition *for* and object *of* reflexivity.

[13] In this sense writing in English is a provincialism masquerading as a universalism, offering the promise of overcoming territorial restrictions only through the para-territorial domination of the language.

[14] Thanks to an anonymous reader who flagged up how easily our argument could be misconstrued in this sense. Hopefully we've been sufficiently explicit that we're not rejecting the 'old' in favour of the 'new'.

[15] The Corpus Chronophage is a famous clock designed by John C. Taylor which adorns Corpus Christi College at the University of Cambridge. It depicts the chronophage eating the 59th second of every minute as part of an ornate clock which inevitably draws in a large crowd of tourists to (ironically) stop what they are doing and watch.

[16] For example, ensuring our breaks take longer than planned, producing a fear of missing out in relation to professional developments, the promise of a conversational break from solitary work or providing an intellectual satisfying focus for our procrastination from a project we are struggling with.

[17] Consider BuzzFeed's classification of 'LOL', 'OMG', 'Trashy', 'WTF' and 'Fail' with its established efficacy and data science pedigree (Abramson 2019: 36).

[18] While virality is foremost a commercial strategy, it's interesting to note the pleasure which staff at viral publishers reportedly find in achieving a viral hit (Abramson 2019: 115).

[19] This includes online gaming, online dating and newspaper comments sections as well as the more familiar social media platforms. However, these are all forms of platform in our sense of the term.

[20] A later study by the same organization with a slightly larger sample found 66 per cent and 41 per cent respectively a few years later (Duggan 2017). It would be interesting to explore how classification of harassment is developing with increasing awareness of the problem and what this mean for self-reporting in research such as this.

[21] The cases of figures who would once have languished in obscurity enjoying huge followings underscores the communicative opportunities that social media affords, but the politics emerging around what is coming to be called their 'deplatforming' reveals how these affordances are more ambiguous than might immediately seem to be the case. For example, the British far-right figure Tommy Robinson, real name Stephen Yaxley-Lennon, found himself banned from Facebook and Instagram in February 2019, where he had over 1 million followers, before being banned from Snapchat in April 2019. He had 413,000 Twitter followers when he was banned from the platform the year before. His YouTube account, with almost 400,000 subscribers, remains active at the time of writing but it has been placed under restrictions, having advertising suspended, which precludes him earning revenue from the channel, and being removed from YouTube's recommendation engine so users cannot find it unless they are deliberately searching for him. Ironically, each act of 'deplatforming', whether banning or restricting an account, contributed to a further increase in his media profile because it made front-page news in the UK, though it obviously prevented him from capitalizing on this visibility in order to increase his following in the way he once would have done.

[22] We recognize the concern of Gregory and Singh (2018) that this can be used to shut down the voices which the platforms opens up, rejecting as 'unruly' and 'uncivil'

what was formerly unheard. However, we still believe it is a useful shorthand to convey the perceived problem, even if we should be cautious about using it in a more analytical sense.

23   They are governed by rules and sanctions in the absence of normative agreement. See Archer (2016) for an extended discussion.

24   See Phillips (2015) for a thoughtful study of the complex figure of the 'troll' and how its fetishization in contemporary discourse belies the continuities between trolling culture and the perceived mainstream.

25   See Jordan (2017) for a comprehensive overview.

26   We use this term in a general way to encompass networks, teams, groups, collaborators and the other collective forms which collaboration takes within higher education.

27   See Donati and Archer (2015) for a detailed account of relational goods as emerging from collective activity, without being reducible to it. What is particularly useful about their account is their sensitivity to the motivational and coordinating function these goods serve for those involved. What we have done becomes our work and *we* share a commitment to it, even if we understand that work differently and it has different meaning for each of us.

28   This is another example of why exercising a scholarly influence over emerging metric cultures within higher education is so crucial because a dissemination-centric perspective is liable to squeeze funding for niche projects over time, even if these produce an immense amount of social and cultural value. There are some themes and topics which simply won't generate a large audience online, in spite of the potential for narrowcasting (Poe 2012). We need a language to defend their value.

29   As might be the case in a five-year funded project or a three-year funded project that is able to begin online engagement at an early stage.

30   Even if they involve funding, they are a form of research practice which is uniquely durable in the face of funding shifts, shortfalls and withdrawal.

31   In this sense, the 'content farm' is an expression of the competitive logic of digital visibility which warns where this might lead academics if pursued to extremes. We still lack an empirical understanding of the implicit and explicit criteria which academic blog editors use but their role, as well as it being recognized and taken seriously within the academy, seems crucial as a bulwark against the growth of academic content farms.

32   For example, editorial reflections on their own platforms, reflective blog posts about editorial practice, informal discussions with peers, formal reflections on digital scholarship in journal articles and formal discussions at conferences and workshops where they are cast as experienced experts.

Chapter 7

1   It should be stressed that platforms were not designed as surveillance devices. Zuboff (2019) makes a plausible argument that there is a sense in which we can talk about this data as being 'discovered'. It was produced as a by-product of existing systems and its deployment for optimization then advertising came later. This was at least true of the early platforms, even if the consolidation of the model *as* an influential framework means that systems are now designed with this exploitation in mind.

2   We would like to stress again that we are not saying legacy *publications* should be dispensed with. Our point is that some of the assumptions that surround

them, particularly what it means to be 'public', need to be rethought for the platform ecosystem.

3   It is an admittedly speculative hypothesis but we wonder how much of academic frustration with support staff when electronic infrastructure fails to work can be understood in terms of the disruption of a misleading sense of independent work: technology failure reveals the dependency of the autonomous individual on service provision by the university provision for even the most basic functions of their working life.

4   See McMillan Cottom (2017) for an illuminating account of the growth of these alternative providers in the US system and the political questions which they are generating.

5   Though a focus *solely* on the stagnant wages of university staff risks obscuring an even more problematic divide opening up between those with secure employment and the ever-expanding ranks of the academic precariat.

6   This category includes many pieces of software used online which we do not tend to think of as enterprise software, illustrating a blurring of boundaries between organizational customers and individual users, which is an interesting feature of the platform ecosystem.

7   This is why we identify them as a platform in the sense discussed in Chapters 2 and 3. They produce real time user data which *can* be leveraged into changing the system in a manner which is inherently opaque to the user and *may* be opaque to the client through which the user has subscription access.

8   Liable to be particularly problematic when we consider possible uptake in different national systems.

9   As opposed to reasoning about it in abstract terms, often though not exclusively in the guise of critique, before returning to a quotidian practice which is largely insulated from this reasoning. In a sense what we are talking about is a manifestation of the behaviour/attitude gap concerning the use of technology within higher education (Malpass et al 2007).

10 However, technological solutions to the problems of 'post-truth' tend to utilize the epistemology that culture warriors blame for this condition. For instance, as Galloway (2017: 117) observes, Facebook allows users to flag a story as fake and has introduced machine learning systems to identify potentially fake news. Both of these methods simply label a story as 'disputed' rather than 'fake', expressing the precise constructivist orientation which d'Ancona (2017) blames for our present predicament.

11 For example, sharing content as an expression of solidarity rather than of agreement with the factual claims made within it.

12 The capacity to cut through the thickets of distraction (Pettman 2016, Carrigan 2017a, Williams 2018).

13 Communication takes time and energy. This is even more true of the *strategic* communication which social media encourages from users.

14 What Burgess and Green (2018: 105) describe as 'meta-videos' on YouTube are a particularly interesting example of this when the affordances of the platform facilitate commentary *about* the platform that shape emerging norms *on* the platform.

15 It's striking how much resemblance there is between discussions of social media in different professional fields. For example, consider Bhola and Hellyer's (2016) account of dental training in comparison to a typical 'social media for academics' session encountered at a professional association conference.

16   Such a project will come closest to these conditions when there is a professional association with a legal grounding in relation to actors with a strong sense of professional identity. However, even in these cases, such as medicine, there is a tendency towards controversy simply because the costs of perceived malpractice are so high.

17   We should stress that we are not denying the cynicism which likely motivates a great deal of this activity, only stressing the significance of 'evidence' as a motif within it.

18   We don't mean this as a criticism in so far as that we recognize their necessity in order to isolate cognitive mechanisms. However, the techniques used to achieve this isolation inevitably entail some degree of removal from the normative gravity which characterizes our everyday existence and leads what we are doing to matter to us (Sayer 2011).

19   The period of alleged consensus on factfulness coincides with the development of what Crouch (2000) calls 'post democracy'. We cannot do justice to this claim here but our suggestion is that perceived agreement on the politically salient facts at hand inevitably involves the exclusion of voices outside of a narrow spectrum. This is why the decline of factfulness and the rise of populism go hand-in-hand: the integrity of the former depends on the exclusion of the latter.

20   Though of course one could suggest it's more a case of scanning them with satirical intentions rather than *reading* them in any substantial sense.

21   See Burrows (2018) for a useful overview of this intellectual tendency. Wendling (2018) provides a detailed introduction to the broader movement classified as the 'alt-right'. Neiwert (2017) exhaustively details the broader fortunes of radical right politics in the United States in terms of which the alt-right should be understood.

22   We prefer this term because it helps avoid the baggage which 'dialogue' carries, explored by us in Chapter 5. It also highlights the fact of *reaction as such*, the accumulation of these responses to sociological knowledge as well as the particular instances of it which might be salient for our purposes.

23   This is a trajectory which Google began prior to the social media firms we are discussing here, though the issues involved in search are slightly different (Vaidhyanathan 2012).

24   A similar outcome occurred when Google eventually withdrew its real names policy, with its attempted imposition on YouTube (via requiring commentators to have Google Plus) accounts being a particular source of contention.

25   This could be seen in terms of Archer's (1995) morphogenetic cycles in order to help us move beyond a simplistic valorization of either structure *or* agency.

Chapter 8

1   Thanks to Noortje Marres for introducing us to this phrase in a past conversation about the role of 'digital sociology' as a framing device in facilitating a particular sort of subdisciplinary conversation.

2   https://notesfrombelow.org/.

References

Abbott, A. (2014) *Digital Paper: A manual for research and writing with library and internet materials*. University of Chicago Press.

Abidin, C. (2018) *Internet Celebrity: Understanding fame online*. Emerald Publishing Limited.

Abramson, J. (2019) *Merchants of Truth: Inside the news revolution*. Random House.

Agger, B. (2007) *Public Sociology: From social facts to literary acts*. Rowman & Littlefield.

Ajibade, E. (1984) Difference. In: J. Berry (ed), *News for Babylon: The Chatto Book of West Indian-British Poetry*. Chatto & Windus, p 51.

Alexander, J. (2006) *The Civil Sphere*. Oxford University Press.

Allen, P. (2020) Political science, punditry, and the Corbyn problem. *British Politics*, 15(1): 69–87.

Alpaydin, E. (2016) *Machine Learning: The new AI*. MIT Press.

Anderson, C. (2006) *The Long Tail: Why the future of business is selling less of more*. Hachette UK.

Anderson, E. (2004) The cosmopolitan canopy. *The Annals of the American Academy of Political and Social Science*, 595: 14–31.

Andrejevic, M. (2013) *Infoglut: How too much information is changing the way we think and know*. Routledge.

Andrejevic, M., Hearn, A. and Kennedy, H. (2015) Cultural studies of data mining: Introduction. *European Journal of Cultural Studies*, 18(4–5): 379–394.

Apperley, T. and Parikka, J. (2018) Platform studies' epistemic threshold. *Games and Culture*, 13(4): 349–369.

Archer, M.S. (1988) *Culture and Agency: The place of culture in social theory*. Cambridge University Press.

Archer, M.S. (1995) *Realist Social Theory: The morphogenetic approach*. Cambridge University Press.

Archer, M.S. (2000) *Being Human: The problem of agency*. Cambridge University Press.

Archer, M.S. (2003) *Structure, Agency and the Internal Conversation.* Cambridge University Press.

Archer, M.S. (2007) *Making Our Way Through the World: Human reflexivity and social mobility.* Cambridge University Press.

Archer, M.S. (2012) *The Reflexive Imperative in Late Modernity.* Cambridge University Press.

Archer, M.S. (2016) Anormative social regulation: the attempt to cope with social morphogenesis. In: M.S. Archer (ed), *Morphogenesis and the Crisis of Normativity.* Springer, pp 141–168.

Arendt, H. (1967) *The Origins of Totalitarianism.* George Allen and Unwin.

Arendt, H. (1998) *The Human Condition.* Chicago University Press.

Aristotle (1885) *The Politics of Aristotle.* Vol. 2. Trans. W.A. Jowett. Clarendon Press.

Arribas Lozano, A. (2018) Reframing the public sociology debate: Towards collaborative and decolonial praxis. *Current Sociology,* 66(1): 92–109.

ASA (2011) David Brooks Award Statement. *American Sociological Association.* www.asanet.org/news-and-events/member-awards/excellence-reporting-social-issues-asa-award/david-brooks-award-statement

Augé, M. (1995) *Non-Places: Introduction to an anthropology of supermodernity.* Verso.

Auletta, K. (2018) *Frenemies: The epic disruption of the advertising industry (and why this matters).* HarperCollins.

Bacevic, J. (2017a) Solving the Democratic Problem. *Social Epistemology Review and Reply Collective,* 6(5): 50–52.

Bacevic, J. (2017b) Boundaries and barbarians: ontological (in)security and the [cyber?] war on universities. https://janabacevic.net/2017/03/08/boundaries-and-barbarians-ontological-insecurity-and-the-cyber-war-on-universities/

Bacevic, J. (2019a) With or without U? Assemblage theory and (de) territorialising the university. *Globalisation, Societies and Education,* 17(1): 78–91.

Bacevic, J. (2019b) Knowing neoliberalism. *Social Epistemology,* 33(4): 380–392.

Bacevic, J. (2019c) War on universities? Neoliberalism, intellectual positioning, and knowledge production in the UK. Doctoral dissertation, University of Cambridge.

Back, L. (2007) *The Art of Listening.* Berg.

Back, L. (2012) Live sociology: social research and its futures. *The Sociological Review,* 60: 18–39.

Back, L. (2016) Les Back: A Shared Sociology. Interviewed by Nasar Meer. *Sociology*, 50(5): 1023–1032.

Back, L. and Puwar, N. (2012) A manifesto for live methods: provocations and capacities. *The Sociological Review*, 60: 6–17.

Badgett, M.L. (2016) *The Public Professor: How to use your research to change the world.* NYU Press.

Baert, P. (2015) *The Existentialist Moment: The rise of Sartre as a public intellectual.* Polity.

Barlow, J.P. (2006) John Perry Barlow: Is Cyberspace Still Anti-Sovereign? *California Magazine.* CalAlumni Association. https://alumni.berkeley.edu/california-magazine/march-april-2006-can-we-know-everything/jp-barlow-cyberspace-still-anti

Barlow, J.P. ([1996] 2019) A declaration of the independence of cyberspace. *Duke Law & Technology Review*, 18(1): 5–7.

Barnes, T.J. and Wilson, M.W. (2014) Big data, social physics, and spatial analysis: The early years. *Big Data & Society*, 1(1): 1–14.

Bartlett, J. (2018) *The People Vs Tech: How the internet is killing democracy (and how we save it).* Random House.

Bauman, Z. (1998) *Work, Consumerism and the New Poor.* Open University Press.

Bauman, Z. (2000) *Liquid Modernity.* Polity.

Becker, H.S. (1986) *Writing For Social Scientists: How to start and finish your thesis, book, or article.* University of Chicago Press.

Becker, H.S. (2003) The politics of presentation: Goffman and total institutions. *Symbolic Interaction*, 26(4): 659–669.

Becker, H.S. (2007) *Telling About Society.* University of Chicago Press.

Beer, D. (2012) Open access and academic publishing: Some lessons from music culture. *Political Geography*, 8(31): 479–480.

Beer, D. (2013) *Popular Culture and New Media: The politics of circulation.* Springer.

Beer, D. (2014) *Punk Sociology.* Springer.

Beer, D. (2016a) *Metric Power.* Palgrave Macmillan.

Beer, D. (2016b) How should we do the history of big data? *Big Data & Society*, 3(1): 1–10.

Beer, D. and Burrows, R. (2007) Sociology and, of and in Web 2.0: Some initial considerations. *Sociological Research Online*, 12(5): 1–13.

Benjamin, W. (2007) *Illuminations.* Schocken Books.

Benjamin, W. (2014) *Radio Benjamin.* Verso Trade.

Bernays, E.L. (1961) *Crystallizing Public Opinion.* Liveright Publishing Corporation.

Bernays, E.L. (1977) *Public Relations*. University of Oklahoma Press.

Bernays, E.L. (2005) *Propaganda*. Ig Publishing.

Bhambra, G. (2016) Committing sociology: defending the public university. The Sociological Review blog. www.thesociologicalreview. com/committing-sociology-defending-the-public-university/

Bhaskar, R. (2010) *Reclaiming Reality: A critical introduction to contemporary philosophy*. Routledge.

Bhola, S. and Hellyer, P. (2016) The risks and benefits of social media in dental foundation training. *British Dental Journal*, 221(10): 609.

Bilton, N. (2013) *Hatching Twitter: How a fledgling start-up became a multibillion-dollar business & accidentally changed the world*. Sceptre.

Blau, J. and Smith, K.I. (2006) *Public Sociologies*. Rowman and Littlefield.

Blumer, H. (1972) Action vs. interaction: relations in public – microstudies of the public order by Erving Goffman, *Society*, 9: 50–53.

Boczkowski, P.J. and Papacharissi, Z. (eds) (2018) *Trump and the Media*. MIT Press.

Boland, T. (2018) *The Spectacle of Critique: From philosophy to cacophony*. Routledge.

Bookchin, M. (1974) *The Limits of the City*. Harper Torchbooks

Borden, I. (2002) *Another Pavement, Another Beach: Skateboarding and the Performative Critique of Architecture*. In: I. Borden, J. Kerr, A. Pivaro and J. Rendell (eds), *The Unknown City: Contesting architecture and social space*. MIT Press, pp 178–199.

Boudon, R. (1980) *The Crisis in Sociology*. Macmillan.

Bourdieu, P. (2000) *Pascalian Meditations*. Stanford University Press.

boyd, d. (2014) *It's Complicated: The social lives of networked teens*. Yale University Press.

boyd, d. (2017) When Good Intentions Backfire. Points. https://points.datasociety.net/when-good-intentions-backfire-786fb0dead03#.1igdjnd42

boyd, d. and Crawford, K. (2012) Critical questions for big data: Provocations for a cultural, technological, and scholarly phenomenon. *Information, Communication & Society*, 15(5): 662–679.

Boyns, D. and Fletcher, J. (2007) Reflections on public sociology: public relations, disciplinary identity and the strong program in professional sociology. In: L. Nichols (ed), *Public Sociology: The contemporary debate*. Transaction Publishers, pp 119–144.

Brock, T. and Carrigan, M. (2015) Realism and contingency: a relational realist analysis of the UK student protests. *Journal for the Theory of Social Behaviour*, 45(3): 377–396.

Brook, P. (1996) *The Empty Space*. Touchstone.

Brunton, F. (2013) *Spam: A shadow history of the internet*. MIT Press.

Bucher, T. (2013) The friendship assemblage: Investigating programmed sociality on Facebook. *Television & New Media*, 14(6): 479–493.

Bucher, T. (2017) The algorithmic imaginary: exploring the ordinary affects of Facebook algorithms. *Information, Communication & Society*, 20(1): 30–44.

Burawoy, M. (2002) Public sociologies and the grass roots. Speech to SWS Wrightsville Beach, 7 February.

Burawoy, M. (2004) The world needs public sociology. *Sociologisk Idsskrift*, 12: 255–272.

Burawoy, M. (2005) For public sociology. *American Sociological Review*, 70(1): 4–28.

Burawoy, M. (2008) Open letter to C. Wright Mills. In: K. Mitchell (ed), *Practising Public Scholarship: Experiences and possibilities beyond the academy.* John Wiley & Sons, pp 18–28.

Burawoy, M. (2011) On uncompromising pessimism: response to my critics. *Global Labour Journal*, 2(1): 73–77.

Burawoy, M. (2016) The neoliberal university: ascent of the spiralists. *Critical Sociology*, 42(7–8): 941–942.

Burawoy, M. (2017) On Desmond: The limits of spontaneous sociology. *Theory and Society*, 46(4): 261–284.

Burgess, J. and Green, J. (2009) *YouTube: Digital media and society series.* Polity.

Burgess, J. and Green, J. (2018) *YouTube: Online video and participatory culture.* John Wiley & Sons. 2nd edition.

Burrows, R. (2012) Living with the h-index? Metric assemblages in the contemporary academy. *The Sociological Review*, 60(2): 355–372.

Burrows, R. (2018) On neoreaction. The Sociological Review blog. www.thesociologicalreview.com/on-neoreaction/

Butler, J. (2015) *Notes Toward a Performative Theory of Assembly*. Harvard University Press.

Camp, J.T. and Heatherton, C. (2016) *Policing the Planet Why the Policing Crisis Led to Black Lives Matter.* Verso.

Canetti, E. (1962) *Crowds and Power.* Viking Press.

Caplan, R. and boyd, d. (2018) Isomorphism through algorithms: Institutional dependencies in the case of Facebook. *Big Data & Society*, 5(1), doi: 2053951718757253.

Carey, J. (1992) *The Intellectuals and the Masses: Pride and Prejudice among the Literary Intelligentsia 1880–1939.* Faber.

Carlson, N. (2015) *Marissa Mayer and the Fight to Save Yahoo!* Twelve.

Carmi, E. (2019) The hidden listeners: regulating the line from telephone operators to content moderators. *International Journal of Communication*, 13: 440–458.

Carrigan, M. (2011) There's more to life than sex? Difference and commonality within the asexual community. *Sexualities*, 14(4): 462–478.

Carrigan, M. (2013) Asexuality and its implications for sexuality studies. *Psychology of Sexualities Review*, 4(1): 6–13.

Carrigan, M.A. (2014) Becoming who we are: Personal morphogenesis and social change. Doctoral dissertation, University of Warwick.

Carrigan, M. (2016) The fragile movements of late modernity. In: M.S. Archer (ed), *Morphogenesis and the Crisis of Normativity*. Springer, pp 191–215.

Carrigan, M. (2017a) Flourishing or fragmenting amidst variety: And the digitalization of the archive. In: M.S. Archer (ed), *Morphogenesis and Human Flourishing*. Springer, pp 163–183.

Carrigan, M. (2017b) From ivory tower to glass tower. ChronicleVitae. https://chroniclevitae.com/news/1750-from-ivory-to-glass-tower

Carrigan, M. (2018) The evisceration of the human under digital capitalism. In: Al-I. Amoudi & J. Morgan (eds), *Realist Responses to Post-Human Society: Ex machina*. Routledge, pp 175–191.

Carrigan, M. (2019) *Social Media for Academics*. Sage. 2nd edition.

Carrigan, M. and Brumley, C. (2013) Combining journalism with academia: How to read a riot, LSE Impact Blog, 5 January. http://blogs.lse.ac.uk/politicsandpolicy/

Carrigan, M., Gupta, K. and Morrison, T.G. (2013) Asexuality special theme issue editorial. *Psychology & Sexuality*, 4(2): 111–120.

Caulfield, M. (2016) Maybe rethink the cult of virality? Hapgood. https://hapgood.us/2016/11/15/maybe-rethink-the-cult-of-virality/

Chambers, S. and Kopstein, J. (2001) Bad civil society. *Political Theory*, 29(6): 837–865.

Chang, J. (2009) It's a hip-hop world. *Foreign Policy*, 12 October. https://foreignpolicy.com/2009/10/12/its-a-hip-hop-world/

Chen, A. (2018) Why 'Uber for X' startups failed: The supply side is king. @andrewchen. https://andrewchen.co/why-uber-for-x-failed/

Christin, A. (2015) Web analytics in the workplace: What Amazon and web newsrooms have in common-and where they differ. LSE Impact Blog. https://blogs.lse.ac.uk/impactofsocialsciences/2015/10/09/what-amazon-and-web-newsrooms-have-in-common-and-where-they-differ/

Cinelli, M., Quattrociocchi, W., Galeazzi, A., Valensise, C.M., Brugnoli, E., Schmidt, A.L., Zola, P., Zollo, F. and Scala, A. (2020). The Covid-19 Social Media Infodemic. *Scientific Reports*, 10(1), 1–10.

Cohen, N. (2018) *The Know-it-Alls: The rise of Silicon Valley as a political powerhouse and social wrecking ball*. Oneworld Publications.

Cohen, P.N. (2019) Public engagement and the influence imperative. *Contemporary Sociology*, 48(2): 119–123.

Cohen, S. (1979) The last seminar. *The Sociological Review*, 27(1): 5–20.

Collins, P.H. (2011) Going Public: Doing the Sociology That Had No Name. In: D. Clawson, J. Misra, N. Gerstel, R. Zussman and R. Stokes (eds), *Public Sociology Fifteen Eminent Sociologists Debate Politics and the Profession in the Twenty-first Century*. University of California Press, pp 101–113.

Collins, R. (1998) The sociological eye and its blinders. *Contemporary Sociology*, (27)1: 2–7

Comunello, F., Mulargia, S. and Parisi, L. (2016) The 'proper' way to spread ideas through social media: exploring the affordances and constraints of different social media platforms as perceived by Italian activists. *The Sociological Review*, 64(3): 515–532.

Cooper, D. (2017) Concepts of 'applied and public sociology': Arguments for a bigger theoretical picture around the idea of a 'university third mission'. *Journal of Applied Social Science*, 11(2): 141–158.

Couldry, N. (2003) Media meta-capital: extending the range of Bourdieu's field theory. *Theory and Society*, 32 (5–6): 653–677.

Couldry, N. (2012) *Media, Society, World: Social theory and digital media practice*. Polity.

Couldry, N. (2014) Inaugural: A necessary disenchantment: Myth, agency and injustice in a digital world. *The Sociological Review*, 62(4): 880–897.

Couldry, N. (2015) The myth of 'us': digital networks, political change and the production of collectivity. *Information, Communication & Society*, 18(6): 608–626.

Couldry, N. and Van Dijck, J. (2015) Researching social media as if the social mattered. *Social Media+ Society*, 1(2): 1–7.

Couldry, N. and Hepp, A. (2018) *The Mediated Construction of Reality*. John Wiley & Sons.

Couldry, N., Fotopoulou, A. and Dickens, L. (2016) Real social analytics: A contribution towards a phenomenology of a digital world. *The British Journal of Sociology*, 67(1): 118–137.

Crick, B. (1962) *In Defence of Politics*. A&C Black.

Crow, G. (2005) Towards a sociology of endings. *Sociological Research Online*, 10(3): 1–10.

d'Ancona, M. (2017) *Post-Truth: The new war on truth and how to fight back*. Random House.

Daniels, J. and Thistlethwaite, P. (2016) *Being a Scholar in the Digital Age*. Policy Press.

Das, R. and Hodkinson, P. (2018) Paternal mental health and social media: Early field-work reflections on disclosure, affective coding and disconnection, Surrey Sociology blog. https://blogs.surrey. ac.uk/sociology/2018/06/18/paternal-men tal-health-and-social-media-early-fieldwork-reflections-on-disclosure-affective-coding-and-disconnection/

Davies, W. (2018) *Nervous States: How feeling took over the world.* Random House.

Davies, W. (2020) *This Is Not Normal: The collapse of liberal Britain.* Verso.

Davis, J. (1989) From 'Rookeries' to 'Communities': Race, Poverty and Policing in London, 1850–1985. *History Workshop Journal*, 27(1): 66–85.

Davis, M. (1992) *City of Quartz: Excavating the future in Los Angeles.* Vintage Books.

Dean, J. (2010) *Blog Theory: Feedback and capture in the circuits of drive.* Polity.

Delic, K.A. and Walker, M.A. (2008) Emergence of the academic computing clouds. *Ubiquity*, 2008(August): 1.

Derrida, J. (1992) Force of law: the 'mystical foundation of authority'. In: M. Rosenfeld, D. Gray Carlson and D. Cornell, *Deconstruction and the Possibility of Justice.* Routledge.

De Tocqueville, A. (1969) *Democracy in America.* New Anchor Books.

Dewey, J. (1927) *The Public and its Problems.* Henry Holt.

Doctorow, C. (2014) *Information Doesn't Want to be Free: Laws for the Internet Age.* McSweeney's.

Dolgon, C. (2017) *Kill It to Save It: An autopsy of capitalism's triumph over democracy.* Policy Press.

Donati, P. and Archer, M.S. (2015) *The Relational Subject.* Cambridge University Press.

Drezner, D.W. (2018) *The Ideas Industry: How pessimists, partisans, and plutocrats are transforming the marketplace of ideas.* Oxford University Press.

Du Bois, W.E.B (2003) *The Souls of Black Folk.* Barnes and Noble Classics.

Duggan, M. (2014) Online harassment. Pew Internet. www. pewinternet.org/2014/10/22/online-harassment/

Duggan, M. (2017) Online Harassment 2017. Pew Internet. www. pewinternet.org/2017/07/11/online-harassment-2017/

Dunn, J. (2005) *Setting the People Free: the story of democracy.* Atlantic Books.

Durkheim, E. (1982) *The Rules of Sociological Method.* Free Press.

Edelman (2018) 2018 Edelman Trust Barometer. Edelman. www. edelman.com/research/2018-edelman-trust-barometer

Egan, G. (2016) Why academics should NOT make time for social media. *Times Higher Education.* www.timeshighereducation.com/blog/why-academics-should-not-make-time-social-media

Erdt, M., Raamkumar, A.S., Rasmussen, E. and Theng, Y.L. (eds) (2018) *Altmetrics for Research Outputs Measurement and Scholarly Information Management.* Springer Singapore.

Erickson, F. (1986) Qualitative methods in research on teaching. In: M. C. Wittrock (ed), *Handbook of Research on Teaching.* Macmillan, pp 119–161.

Evans, A. (2017) Tinder as a methodological tool #Emergingdigitalpractices. Allegra lab. https://allegralaboratory.net/tinder-as-a-methodological-tool/

Evans, J. (2019) The new war on gender studies. The Conversation. https://theconversation.com/the-new-war-on-gender-studies-109109

Eyal, N. (2014) *Hooked: How to build habit-forming products.* Penguin.

Fanon, F. (1963) *The Wretched of the Earth.* Grove Press.

Fatsis, L. (2018) Becoming public characters, not public intellectuals: notes towards an alternative conception of public intellectual life. *European Journal of Social Theory,* 21(3): 267–287.

Fatsis, L. (2019a) Grime: criminal subculture or public counterculture? A critical investigation into the criminalisation of black musical subcultures in the UK. *Crime, Media, Culture,* 15(3): 447–461.

Fatsis, L. (2019b) Policing the beats: The criminalisation of UK drill and grime music by the London Metropolitan Police. *The Sociological Review,* 67(6): 1300– 1316.

Ferrell, L. (1993) *Crimes of Style: Urban graffiti and the politics of criminality.* Garland.

Fisher, M. (2009) *Capitalist Realism: Is there no alternative?* Zero Books.

Fisher, M. (2013) Exiting the vampire's castle. Open Democracy. www.opendemocracy.net/en/opendemocracyuk/exiting-vampire-castle/

Fisher, M. (2018) Abandon hope (summer is coming). In: D. Ambrose (ed), *K-punk: The collected and unpublished writings of Mark Fisher.* Repeater Books.

Fitzgerald, D. and Callard, F. (2015) *Rethinking Interdisciplinarity Across the Social Sciences and Neurosciences.* Palgrave.

Flyvbjerg, B. and Budzier, A. (2013) Why your IT project might be riskier than you think. *Harvard Business Review.* https://hbr.org/2011/09/why-your-it-project-may-be-riskier-than-you-think.

Foer, F. (2018) *World Without Mind.* Penguin.

Ford, M. (2015) *The Rise of the Robots: Technology and the threat of mass unemployment.* Oneworld publications.

Foucault, M. (1986) Of other spaces. *Diacritics*, 16(1): 22–27.

Frank, T. (1997) *The Conquest of Cool: Business culture, counterculture, and the rise of hip consumerism*. University of Chicago Press.

Frank, T. (2000) *Market Populism*. Vintage.

Frank, T. (2012) *Pity the Billionaire*. Random House.

Frank, T. (2016) *Listen, Liberal*. Scribe Publications.

Frank, T. (2018) *Rendezvous with Oblivion*. Metropolitan Books.

French, R.D. (2012) The professors on public life. *The Political Quarterly*, 83(3): 532–540.

Fromm, E. (2013) *To Have Or to Be?* Bloomsbury Academic.

Fuchs, C. (2012) *Social Media: A critical introduction*. Sage.

Gallagher, B. (2018) *How to Turn Down a Billion Dollars: The Snapchat story*. St. Martin's Press.

Galloway, S. (2017) *The Four: The hidden DNA of Amazon, Apple, Facebook and Google*. Random House.

Gane, N. and Back, L. (2012) C. Wright Mills 50 years on: the promise and craft of sociology revisited. *Theory, Culture & Society*, 29(7/8): 399–421.

Gans, H. (2016) Public sociology and its publics. *American Sociologist*, 47(1): 3–11.

Gans, H.J. (1989) Sociology in America: The discipline and the public. *American Sociological Review*, 54(1): 1–16.

Gerbaudo, P. (2012) *Tweets and the Streets*. Pluto Press.

Gerbaudo, P. (2019) *The Platform Party: The transformation of political organisation in the era of big data*. Pluto Press.

Gerlitz, C. (2016) What counts? Reflections on the multivalence of social media data. *Digital Culture & Society*, 2(2): 19–38.

Gerlitz, C. and Helmond, A. (2013) The like economy: Social buttons and the data-intensive web. *New Media & Society*, 15(8): 1348–1365.

Gerlitz, C. and Lury, C. (2014) Social media and self-evaluating assemblages: On numbers, orderings and values. *Distinktion: Scandinavian Journal of Social Theory*, 15(2): 174–188.

Giddens, A. (1991) *Modernity and Self-Identity: Self and society in the late modern age*. Stanford University Press.

Gillespie, T. (2010) The politics of 'platforms'. *New Media & Society*, 12(3): 347–364.

Gillespie, T. (2015) Platforms intervene. *Social Media+ Society*, 1(1).

Gillespie, T. (2018) *Custodians of the Internet: Platforms, content moderation, and the hidden decisions that shape social media*. Yale University Press.

Gilroy-Ware, M. (2017) *Filling the Void: Emotion, capitalism and social media*. Duncan Baird Publishers.

Gitelman, L. (ed) (2013) *Raw Data is an Oxymoron*. MIT Press.

Google (2019) AMP on Google. https://amp.dev/about/how-amp-works/

Gorwa, R. (2019) What is platform governance? *Information, Communication & Society*, 22(6): 854–871.

Green, J. (2017) *Devil's Bargain: Steve Bannon, Donald Trump, and the storming of the presidency*. Penguin.

Greenwald, G. (2014) *No Place to Hide: Edward Snowden, the NSA, and the US surveillance state*. Macmillan.

Gregory, K. and Singh, S. (2018) Anger in academic Twitter: sharing, caring, and getting mad online. *tripleC: Communication, Capitalism & Critique*. Open Access Journal for a Global Sustainable Information Society, 16(1): 176–193.

Guess, R. (2019) A republic of discussion: Habermas at ninety. *The Point Mag*. https://thepointmag.com/politics/a-republic-of-discussion-habermas-at-ninety/

Habermas, J. (1984) *The Theory of Communicative Action*. (Two Volumes) Beacon.

Habermas, J. (1989) *The Structural Transformation of the Public Sphere*. MIT Press.

Halford, S. and Savage, M. (2017) Speaking sociologically with big data: Symphonic social science and the future for big data research. *Sociology*, 51(6): 1132–1148.

Hall, G. (2016a) *Pirate Philosophy: For a Digital Posthumanities*. MIT Press.

Hall, G. (2016b) *The Uberfication of the University*. University of Minnesota Press.

Hancox, D. (2015) Skepta's mission. *The Fader*. 4 June. www.thefader.com/2015/06/04/skepta-cover-story-konnichiwa-interview

Hardin, G. (1968) The tragedy of the commons. *Science*, 162(3859): 1243–1248.

Harding, L. (2014) *The Snowden Files: The inside story of the world's most wanted man*. Guardian Faber Publishing.

Harney, S. and Moten, F. (2013) *The Undercommons: Fugitive planning and black study*. Minor Compositions.

Hartmann, D. (2017) Sociology and its publics: reframing engagement and revitalizing the field. *The Sociological Quarterly*, 58(1): 3–18.

Hashemi, M. (2016) A post-secular reading of public sociology. *Social Compass*, 63(4): 461–477.

Healy, K. (2017) Public sociology in the age of social media. *Perspectives on Politics*, 15(3): 771–780.

Henley, J. (2018) Digital Storytelling course. Guardian Masterclasses. London, February.

Hern, A. (2019) The strange world of TikTok: viral videos and Chinese censorship. Today in Focus. *The Guardian*. 7 October. www.theguardian.com/technology/audio/2019/oct/07/strange-world-tiktok-viral-videos-chinese-censorship

Hess, P. (2018) Sunsetting Klout. *Khoras Atlas*. https://community.khoros.com/t5/Atlas-Insights-Blog/Sunsetting-Klout/ba-p/473363

Hill, D.W. (2015) *The Pathology of Communicative Capitalism*. Springer.

Hirschman, A.O. (2002) *Shifting Involvements: Private interest and public action*. Princeton University Press

Hoffman, A.L. (2016) Facebook is worried about users sharing less – but it only has itself to blame. *The Guardian*. 19 April. www.theguardian.com/technology/2016/apr/19/facebook-users-sharing-less-personal-data-zuckerberg

Hoffman, R. and Casnocha, B. (2012) *The Start-up of You: Adapt to the future, invest in yourself, and transform your career*. Crown Business.

Holmwood, J. (2007) Sociology as Public Discourse And Professional Practice: A Critique Of Michael Burawoy. *Sociological Theory*, 25(1): 46–66.

Holmwood, J. (2010) Sociology's misfortune: disciplines, interdisciplinarity and the impact of audit culture. *British Journal of Sociology*, 61(4): 639–658.

Holmwood, J. and O'Toole, T. (2018) *Countering Extremism in British Schools? The Truth about the Birmingham Trojan Horse Affair*. Policy Press.

Holton, R.J. (1987) The idea of crisis in modern society. *British Journal of Sociology*, 38: 502–520.

Housley, W. (2018) Conversation analysis, publics, practitioners and citizen social science. *Discourse Studies*, 20(3): 431–437.

Hynes, M. (2016) Public sociology for an emergent people: the affective gift in Marina Abramović's The Artist is Present. *The Sociological Review*, 64(4): 805–820

Illich, I. (1973) *Tools for Conviviality*. Harper and Row.

Internet Live Stats (2019) Internet Live Stats. www.internetlivestats.com/

Internet World Stats (2019) Internet Usage Statistics: The Internet Big Picture. www.internetworldstats.com/stats.htm

Jacobs, J. (1961) *The Death and Life of Great American Cities*. Vintage Books.

Jacoby, R. (1987) *The Last Intellectuals: American Culture in the Age of Academe*. Basic Books.

Jenkins, J. (2013) *English as a Lingua Franca in the International University: The politics of academic English language policy*. Routledge.

Johnson, M.R., Carrigan, M. and Brock, T. (2019) The imperative to be seen: The moral economy of celebrity video game streaming on Twitch.tv. *First Monday*, 24(8).

Johnson, N.F., Leahy, R., Restrepo, N.J., Velasquez, N., Zheng, M., Manrique, P., Devkota, P. and Wuchty, S. (2019) Hidden resilience and adaptive dynamics of the global online hate ecology. *Nature*, 573(7773): 261–265.

Jordan, J. (2009) Reclaim the Streets. In: I. Ness (ed), *The International Encyclopedia of Revolution and Protest: 1500 to the present*, Wiley-Blackwell, p 2807.

Jordan, K. (2017) Understanding the structure and role of academics' ego-networks on social networking sites. Doctoral dissertation, The Open University.

Jordan, K. and Carrigan, M. (2018a) How was social media cited in 2014 REF Impact Case Studies? LSE Impact Blog. https://blogs.lse.ac.uk/impactofsocialsciences/2018/06/06/how-was-social-media-cited-in-2014-ref-impact-case-studies/

Jordan, K. and Weller, M. (2018) Academics and social networking sites: Benefits, problems and tensions in professional engagement with online networking. *Journal of Interactive Media in Education*, 2018(1), http://doi.org/10.5334/ jime.448.

Illich, I. (1971) *Deschooling Society*. Calder and Boyars.

Isin, E. and Ruppert, E. (2015) *Being Digital Citizens*. Rowman & Littlefield International.

Kaplan, J. (2015) *Humans Need Not Apply: A guide to wealth and work in the age of artificial intelligence*. Yale University Press.

Keegan, V. (2007) Will MySpace ever lose its monopoly? *The Guardian*. 8 February. www.theguardian.com/technology/2007/feb/08/business.comment

Kelty, C.M. (2020) *The Participant: A Century of participation in four stories*. University of Chicago Press.

Kennedy, H. and Moss, G. (2015) Known or knowing publics? Social media data mining and the question of public agency. *Big Data & Society*, 2(2).

Kennedy, H., Poell, T. and Van Dijck, J. (2015) Introduction: Special issue on Data and agency. *Data & Society*, 2(2).

Keucheyan, R. (2012) *Left Hemisphere: Mapping critical theory today*. Verso Books.

Kitchin, R. (2014) *The Data Revolution: Big data, open data, data infrastructures and their consequences*. Sage.

Klein, N. (2000) *No Logo*. Picador.

Klinenberg, E. (2018) *Palaces for the People: How to build a more equal and united society*. The Bodley Head.

Komljenovic, J. (2018) Big data and new social relations in higher education: Academia.edu, Google Scholar and ResearchGate. In: S. Sellar, R. Gorur and G. Steiner-Khamsi (eds), *World Yearbook of Education 2019: Comparative methodology in an era of big data and global networks*. Routledge.

Kornberger, M., Pflueger, D. and Mouritsen, J. (2017) Evaluative infrastructures: Accounting for platform organization. *Accounting, Organizations and Society*, 60, 79–95.

LaBelle, B. (2018) *Sonic Agency: Sound and emergent forms of resistance*. Goldsmiths Press.

Laclau, E. (2005) *On Populist Reason*. Verso.

Lanchester, J. (2015) The robots are coming. *London Review of Books*, 37(5): 3–8.

Lanier, J. (2014) *Who Owns the Future?* Simon and Schuster.

Lanier, J. (2018) *Ten Arguments For Deleting Your Social Media Accounts Right Now*. Henry Holt and Co.

Latour, B. (2005) *Reassembling the social: An introduction to actor-network-theory*. Oxford University Press.

Latour, B. and Weibel, P. (2005) *Making Things Public: Atmospheres of democracy*. MIT Press.

Lazega, E. (2015) Body captors and network profiles: A neo-structural note on digitalized social control and morphogenesis. In: M.S. Archer (ed), *Generative Mechanisms Transforming the Social Order*. Springer, pp 113–133.

Lazega, E. (2017) Networks and commons: bureaucracy, collegiality and organizational morphogenesis in the struggles to shape collective responsibility in new sharing institutions. In: M.S. Archer (ed), *Morphogenesis and Human Flourishing*. Springer, pp 211–237.

Le Bon, G. (1995) *The Crowd: A study of the popular mind*. Transaction Publishers.

Lee, U. (2015) Myspace makes a comeback. CBS News. www.cbsnews.com/news/former-social-media-giant-myspace-makes-a-comeback/

Lepecki, A. (2013) Choreopolice and choreopolitics. *The Drama Review*, 57(4): 13–27.

Lippmann, W. (1925) *The Phantom Public*. Harcourt Brace.

Little, D. (2012) Five years of understanding society. Understanding Society. 6 November. http://understandingsociety.blogspot.co.uk/2012/11/five-years-of-understandingsociety.html

Little, D. (2016) ANT-style critique of ABM. Understanding Society. http://understandingsociety.blogspot.co.uk/2015/12/ant-style-critique-of-abm.html

Losse, K. (2012) *The Boy Kings: A journey into the heart of the social network*. Simon and Schuster.

Lupton, D. (2014) Feeling better connected: Academics' use of social media. 10 June. www.canberra.edu.au/about-uc/faculties/arts-design/attachments2/pdf/n-and-mrc/Feeling-Better-Connected-report-final.pdf

MacIntyre, A. (2013) *After Virtue*. A&C Black.

Mahony, N. and Stephansen, H.C. (2016) The frontiers of participatory public engagement. *European Journal of Cultural Studies*, 19(6): 583–597.

Maile, S. and Griffiths, D. (eds) (2014) *Public Engagement and Social Science*. Policy Press.

Malpass, A., Barnett, C., Clarke, N. and Cloke, P. (2007) Problematizing choice: responsible consumers and sceptical citizens. In: M. Bevir and F. Trentmann (eds), *Governance, Consumers and Citizens: Agency and resistance in contemporary politics*. Palgrave MacMillan, pp 231–256.

Mandeville, B. (1970) *The Fable of the Bees*. Penguin.

Mantello, P. (2016) The machine that ate bad people: The ontopolitics of the precrime assemblage. *Big Data & Society*, 3(2), doi: 2053951716682538.

Margetts, H. (2017a) Political behaviour and the acoustics of social media. *Nature Human Behaviour*, 1(4): s41562-017.

Margetts, H. (2017b) Democracy is dead: long live democracy! Open Democracy. www.opendemocracy.net/en/author/helen-margetts/

Margetts, H. (2017c) Social media (and other platforms). Talk at Imagine 2027. Cambridge, November.

Marquand, D. (2004) *Decline of the Public: The hollowing out of citizenship*. Polity.

Marres, N. (2012) *Material Participation: Technology, the environment and everyday publics*. Springer.

Marres, N. (2017) *Digital Sociology: The reinvention of social research*. John Wiley & Sons.

Marres, N. (2018) Why we can't have our facts back. *Engaging Science, Technology, and Society*, 4: 423–443.

Martínez, A.G. (2016) *Chaos Monkeys: Inside the Silicon Valley money machine*. Random House.

Marwick, A.E. (2013) *Status Update: Celebrity, publicity, and branding in the social media age*. Yale University Press.

Mason, P. (2012) *Why it's Still Kicking Off Everywhere: The new global revolutions*. Verso.

Mason, P. (2016) *Post-Capitalism: A guide to our future*. Farrar, Straus and Girioux.

Mason, P. (2019) *Clear Bright Future: A radical defence of the human being*. Penguin UK.

Mayer-Schönberger, V. (2011) *Delete: The Virtue of Forgetting in the Digital Age*. Princeton University Press. https://press.princeton.edu/titles/9436.html

Mayhew, H. (2005) *The London Underworld in the Victorian Period: Authentic first-person accounts by beggars, thieves and prostitutes*. Dover Publications.

McAfee, A. and Brynjolfsson, E. (2017) *Machine, Platform, Crowd: Harnessing our digital future*. WW Norton & Company.

McArdle, A., and Erzen, T. (2001) *Zero Tolerance: Quality of life and the new police brutality in New York City*. New York University Press

McChesney, R.W. (2013) *Digital Disconnect: How capitalism is turning the Internet against democracy*. The New Press.

McDougall, W. (1927) *The Group Mind*. Cambridge University Press

McGettigan, A. (2013) *The Great University Gamble*. Pluto.

McGregor, R. (2010) *The Party: The secret world of China's communist rulers*. Penguin UK.

McIntyre, L. (2018) *Post-Truth*. MIT Press.

McMillan Cottom, T. (2015) 'Who the fuck do you think you are?': Academic engagement, microcelebrity and digital sociology from the Far Left of the matrix of domination. *Ada: A Journal of Gender, New Media, and Technology*, 7.

McMillan Cottom, T. (2017) *Lower Ed: The troubling rise of for-profit colleges in the new economy*. The New Press.

McNamee, R. (2019) *Zucked: Waking up to the Facebook catastrophe*. Penguin Press.

Medvetz, T. (2012) *Think Tanks in America*. University of Chicago Press.

Mellor, D. (2011) I refuse to be disillusioned. *SocofEd*, 18 April. https://socofed.wordpress.com/2011/04/18/i-refuse-to-be-disillusioned/

Merton, R. (1975) Structural analysis in sociology. In: P. Blau (ed), *Approaches to the Study of Social Structure*. Open Books.

Michels, R. (1932) Intellectuals. In: E. R. A. Seligman (ed), *Encyclopedia of the Social Sciences*. Macmillan, pp 118–126.

Miller, D., Costa, E., Haynes, N., McDonald, T., Nicolescu, R., Sinanan, J., Spyer, J., Venkatraman, S. and Wang, X. (2016) *How the World Changed Social Media*. UCL Press.

Mills, C.W. (1959/2000) *The Sociological Imagination*. Oxford University Press

Mollett, A., Brumley, C., Gilson, C. and Williams, S. (2017) *Communicating Your Research with Social Media: A practical guide to using blogs, podcasts, data visualisations and video*. Sage.

Morozov, E. (2019) Digital socialism? The calculation debate in the age of big data. *New Left Review*, (116): 33–67.

Mouffe, C. (2000) *The Democratic Paradox*. Verso.

Mouffe, C. (2005) *The Return of the Political*. Verso.

Müller, J.W. (2016) Capitalism in one family. *London Review of Books*, 38(23): 10–14.

Nagle, A. (2017) *Kill All Normies: Online culture wars from 4chan and Tumblr to Trump and the alt-right*. Zero Books.

Orben, A., Dienlin, T. and Przybylski, A.K. (2019) Social media's enduring effect on adolescent life satisfaction. *Proceedings of the National Academy of Sciences*, 116(21): 10226–10228.

O'Reilly, T. (2009) *What is Web 2.0*. O'Reilly Media, Inc.

Oreskes, N. and Conway, E.M. (2011) *Merchants of Doubt: How a handful of scientists obscured the truth on issues from tobacco smoke to global warming*. Bloomsbury Publishing USA.

Oswell, D. (2009) Yet to come? Globality and the sound of an infant politics. *Radical Politics Today*, 1(1): 1–18.

Pang, A.S.K. (2013) *The distraction addiction: Getting the information you need and the communication you want, without enraging your family, annoying your colleagues, and destroying your soul*. Hachette UK.

Papacharissi, Z. (ed) (2010) *A Networked Self: Identity, community, and culture on social network sites*. Routledge.

Papacharissi, Z. (2015) *Affective Publics: Sentiment, technology, and politics*. Oxford University Press.

Paolillo, J.C. (2018) The Flat Earth phenomenon on YouTube. *First Monday*, 23(12), http://dx.doi.org/10.5210/fm.v23i12.8251.

Parker, M. (2014) University, Ltd: Changing a business school. *Organization*, 21(2): 281–292.

Pariser, E. (2011) *The Filter Bubble: What the internet is hiding from you*. Viking.

Pasquale, F. (2015) The algorithmic self. *The Hedgehog Review*, 17(1): 30–46.

Pasquale, F. (2016) Two narratives of platform capitalism. *Yale Law & Policy Review*, 35: 309.

Pasquale, F.A. (2018) Tech platforms and the knowledge problem. *American Affairs*, II(2): 3–16.

Pausé, C. and Russell, D. (2016) Sociable scholarship: The use of social media in the 21st century academy. *The Journal of Applied Social Theory*, 1(1): 5–25.

Peele, J. (2019) *Us*. Monkey Paw Productions.

Pettman, D. (2016) *Infinite Distraction*. Polity.

Phillips, W. (2015) *This Is Why We Can't Have Nice Things: Mapping the relationship between online trolling and mainstream culture*. MIT Press.

Phillips-Fein, K. (2009) *Invisible Hands: The making of the conservative movement from the New Deal to Reagan*. W.W. Norton.

Phipps, A. (2014) The dark side of the impact agenda. *Times Higher Education*. www.timeshighereducation.com/comment/opinion/the-dark-side-of-the-impact-agenda/2017299.article

Pickering, A. (2010) *The Cybernetic Brain: Sketches of another future*. University of Chicago Press.

Plantin, J.C., Lagoze, C., Edwards, P.N. and Sandvig, C. (2018) Infrastructure studies meet platform studies in the age of Google and Facebook. *New Media & Society*, 20(1): 293–310.

Poe, M. (2012) What can university presses do? *Inside Higher Ed*. 9 July. www.insidehighered.com/views/2012/07/09/essay-what-university-presses-should-do

Putnam, R. (2000) *Bowling Alone: The collapse and revival of American community*. Simon and Schuster.

Putzel, J. (1997) Accounting for the 'dark side' of social capital: reading Robert Putnam on democracy. *Journal of International Development*, 9(7): 939–949.

Rainie, L. and Wellman, B. (2012) *Networked: The new social operating system*. MIT Press.

Reed, M.S. (2016) *The research impact handbook*. Fast Track Impact.

Reichelt, L. (2007) Ambient Intimacy. Disambiguity: Understanding Humans. www.disambiguity.com/ambient-intimacy/

Remler, D. (2014) Are 90% of academic papers really never cited? Reviewing the literature on academic citations. LSE Impact Blog. 23 April. http:// blogs.lse.ac.uk/impactofsocialsciences/2014/04/23/academic-papers-citation-rates-remler/

Rettberg, J.W. (2008) *Blogging*. Polity.

Riesman, D. (1950) *The Lonely Crowd: A study of the changing American character*. Yale University Press.

Roberts, D.E. (1999) Race, vagueness, and the social meaning of order-maintenance policing. *Faculty Scholarship at Penn Law*, p 589.

Robertson, S.L. (2019) Comparing platforms and the new value economy in the academy. *World Yearbook of Education 2019: Comparative Methodology in the Era of Big Data and Global Networks*. Routledge.

Robinson, W.I. (2018) The next economic crisis: digital capitalism and global police state. *Race & Class*, 60(1): 77–92.

Rogers, R. (2013) *Digital Methods*. MIT press.

Rojas, F. (2017) The Mccabe Query. OrgTheory.Net. https://orgtheory.wordpress.com/2017/09/29/the-mccabe-query/

Ronson, J. (2019) *The Butterfly Effect*. Audible Original Podcast.

Rorty, R. (1989) *Contingency, irony, and solidarity*. Cambridge University Press.

Rosenbaum, S. (2011) *Curation nation: how to win in a world where consumers are creators*. McGraw Hill Professional.

Rothbard, M. (1975) *The Political Thought of Étienne de la Boétie*. Free Life Editions.

Rudder, C. (2014) *Dataclysm: Who we are (when we think no one's looking)*. Random House Canada.

Runciman, D. (2018) *How Democracy Ends*. Basic Books.

Rushkoff, D. (2016) *Throwing rocks at the Google bus: How growth became the enemy of prosperity*. Penguin.

Sabarantam, M. (2017) Decolonising the curriculum: what's all the fuss about? SOAS Blog. www.soas.ac.uk/blogs/study/decolonising-curriculum-whats-the-fuss/

Sanders, S. (2017) Upworthy was one of the hottest sites ever. You won't believe what happened next. All Tech Considered, NPR. www.npr.org/sections/alltechconsidered/2017/06/20/533529538/upworthy-was-one-of-the-hottest-sites-ever-you-wont-believe-what-happened-next?t=1571156231344

Savage, M. and Burrows, R. (2007) The coming crisis of empirical sociology. *Sociology*, 41(5): 885–899.

Sayer, A. (1999) *Realism and Social Science*. Sage.

Sayer, A. (2011) *Why Things Matter to People: Social science, values and ethical life*. Cambridge University Press.

Scholz, T. (2016) *Uberworked and Underpaid: How workers are disrupting the digital economy*. John Wiley & Sons.

Schüll, N.D. (2014) *Addiction by Design: Machine gambling in Las Vegas*. Princeton University Press.

Scott, J. and Bromley, R.J. (2013) *Envisioning Sociology: Victor Branford, Patrick Geddes, and the quest for social reconstruction*. SUNY Press.

Seidman, S. (1998) *Contested Knowledge: Social theory in the postmodern era*. Blackwell.

Selvon, S. (1998) My girl and the city. In: O. Wambu (ed), *Empire Windrush: Fifty years of writing about Black Britain*. Victor Gollancz, pp 162–168.

Selwyn, N. and Stirling, E. (2016) Social media and education… now the dust has settled. *Learning, Media and Technology*, 41(1): 1–5.

Sennett, R. (2002) *The Fall of Public Man*. Penguin.

Sennett, R. (2008) *The Craftsman*. Yale University Press.

Seymour, R. (2019) *The Twittering Machine*. Indigo Press.

Shenk, D. (1997) *Data Smog: Surviving the information glut*. HarperCollins.

Shephard, K., Brown, K., Guiney, T., Deaker, L. and Hesson, G. (2018) Exploring the use of social media by community-engaged university people. *Innovations in Education and Teaching International*, 56(5): 558–568.

Shirky, C. (2007) *Here Comes Everybody: The power of organizing without organizations*. Penguin.

Shirky, C. (2009) *Cognitive Surplus: Creativity and generosity in a connected age*. Penguin UK.

Simmel, G. (1904) The sociology of conflict. *American Journal of Sociology*, 9(4): 490–525.

Simmel, G. (1949) The sociology of sociability. *American Journal of Sociology*, 55(3): 254–261.

Simmel, G. (1969) The metropolis and mental life. In: R. Sennett (ed), *Classic Essays on the Culture of Cities*. Prentice-Hall, pp 47–60.

Simmel, G. (1997) *Simmel on Culture: Selected Writings*. Edited by D. Frisby and M. Featherstone. Sage.

Skeggs, B. (2019) The forces that shape us: The entangled vine of gender, race and class. *The Sociological Review*, 67(1): 28–35.

Skocpol, T. (2003) *Diminished Democracy: From membership to management in American civic life*. University of Oklahoma Press.

Sloterdijk, P. (2012) *The Art of Philosophy: Wisdom as a practice*. Columbia University Press.

Smith, C. (2003) *Moral, Believing Animals: Human personhood and culture*. Oxford University Press.

Solnit, R. (2006) Democracy should be exercised regularly, on foot. *The Guardian*. 6 July. www.theguardian.com/commentisfree/2006/jul/06/comment.politics

Sontag, S. (1982) *Against Interpretation and Other Essays*. Octagon Books.

Srnicek, N. (2017) *Platform Capitalism*. Polity.

Srnicek, N. and Williams, A. (2015) *Inventing the Future: Postcapitalism and a world without work*. Verso.

Statista (2019) Number of registered members on Goodreads from May 2011 to July 2019 (in millions). www.statista.com/statistics/252986/number-of-registered-members-on-goodreadscom/

Statista (2020) Internet usage worldwide – Statistics & Facts. www.statista.com/topics/1145/internet-usage-worldwide

Stein, A. and Daniels, J. (2017) *Going Public: A guide for social scientists*. University of Chicago Press.

Stewart, B.E. (2018) Academic Twitter and academic capital: Collapsing orality and literacy in scholarly publics. In: D. Lupton, I. Mewburn and P. Thomson (eds), *The Digital Academic: Critical Perspectives on Digital Technologies in Higher Education*. Routledge, pp 79–93.

Stone, B. (2013) *The Everything Store: Jeff Bezos and the age of Amazon*. Random House.

Stone, B. (2017) *The Upstarts: How Uber, Airbnb and the killer companies of the new Silicon Valley are changing the world*. Random House.

Stones, R. (2012) Structuration. *The Wiley-Blackwell Encyclopedia of Globalization*. Wiley-Blackwell.

Storch, R. (2008) The plague of the blue locusts: police reform and popular resistance in Northern England, 1840–57. *International Review of Social History*, 20(1): 61–90.

Streeck, W. (2011) Public sociology as a return to political economy. *Transformations of the Public Sphere*. https://publicsphere.ssrc.org/streeck-public-sociology-as-a-return-to-political-economy/

Strittmatter, K. (2018) *We Have Been Harmonised: Life in China's Surveillance State.* HarperCollins.

Stuart, E., Thelwall, M. and Stuart, D. (2019) Which image types do universities tweet? *First Monday*, 24(3).

Taplin, J. (2017) *Move Fast and Break Things: How Facebook, Google, and Amazon have cornered culture and what it means for all of us.* Pan Macmillan.

Tarde, G. (2006) *L'Opinion et la Foule*. Editions du Sandre.

Tarnoff, B. and Weigel, M. (2018) Why Silicon Valley can't fix itself. *The Guardian*. 3 May. www.theguardian.com/news/2018/may/03/why-silicon-valley-cant-fix-itself-tech-humanism

Taylor, A. (2014) *The People's Platform: Taking back power and culture in the digital age*. Random House.

Taylor, C. (1985) *Philosophical Papers: Volume 2, philosophy and the human sciences*. Cambridge University Press.

Taylor, C. (1989) *Sources of the Self: The making of the modern identity*. Harvard University Press.

Taylor, C. (2004) *Modern Social Imaginaries*. Duke University Press.

Taylor, R. (1990) Modes of Civil Society. *Public Culture*, 3(1): 95–118.

Thiel, P. and Masters, B. (2014) *Zero to One*. Penguin Random House.

Thompson, J.B. (1995) *The Media and Modernity: A social theory of the media*. Polity.

Thompson, J.B. (2005) *Books in the Digital Age: The transformation of academic and higher education publishing in Britain and the United States*. Polity.

Thompson, J.B. (2010) *Merchants of Culture: The publishing business in the twenty-first century*. Polity.

Thrift, N. (2005) *Knowing Capitalism*. Sage.

Townsley, E. (2006) The public intellectual trope in the United States. *The American Sociologist*, 37(3): 39–66.

Treviño, A.J. (2013) C. Wright Mills as designer, craftsman and stylist. In: *C. Wright Mills and the Sociological Imagination*. Edward Elgar Publishing.

Trotter, W. (1908) Herd instinct and its bearing on the psychology of civilised man. *The Sociological Review*, 1(3): 227–248.

Tufekci, Z. (2013) 'Not this one': Social movements, the attention economy, and microcelebrity networked activism. *American Behavioral Scientist*, 57(7): 848–870.

Tufekci, Z. (2014a) Engineering the public: Big data, surveillance and computational politics. *First Monday*, 19(7).

Tufekci, Z. (2014b) Capabilities of movements and affordances of digital media: paradoxes of empowerment. DML Central. https://clalliance.org/blog/capabilities-of-movements-and-affordances-of-digital-media-paradoxes-of-empowerment/

Tufekci, Z. (2017) *Twitter and Tear Gas: The Power and fragility of networked protest*. Yale University Press

Turkle, S. (2016) *Reclaiming conversation: The power of talk in a digital age*. Penguin.

Turkle, S. (2017) *Alone together: Why we expect more from technology and less from each other*. Hachette UK.

Turner, F. (2006) *From Counterculture to Cyberculture: Stewart Brand, the Whole Earth Network, and the rise of digital utopianism*. University of Chicago Press.

Turner, G. (2010) *Ordinary People and the Media: The demotic turn*. Sage.

Uprichard, E. (2008) Children as 'being and becomings': Children, childhood and temporality. *Children & Society*, 22(4), 303–313.

Urry, J. (2013) *Societies Beyond Oil: Oil dregs and social futures*. Zed Books.

Vaidhyanathan, S. (2012) *The Googlization of Everything (and why we should worry)*. University of California Press.

Vaidhyanathan, S. (2018) *Antisocial Media: How Facebook disconnects us and undermines democracy*. Oxford University Press.

Van Dijck, J. (2013) *The Culture of Connectivity: A critical history of social media*. Oxford University Press.

Van Dijck, J. and Poell, T. (2018) Social media platforms and education. In: J. Burgess, A. Marwick and T. Poell (eds), *The SAGE Handbook of Social Media*. Sage, pp 579–591.

Veblen, T. (1994) *The Theory of the Leisure Class*. Penguin.

Vis, F. (2016) Research Resilience: Why academics and funders alike should care about #RIPTwitter. LSE Impact Blog. https://blogs.lse. ac.uk/impactofsocialsciences/2016/02/09/research-resilience-why-academics-and-funders-alike-should-care-about-riptwitter/

Vitale, A.S. (2017) *The End of Policing*. Verso.

Vogel, P. (2017) The conservative dark-money groups infiltrating campus politics. Media Matters for America. www.mediamatters.org/james-okeefe/conservative-dark-money-groups-infiltrating-campus-politics

Vogelstein, F. (2013) *Battle of the Titans*. HarperCollins UK.

Vostal, F. (2014) Thematizing speed: between critical theory and cultural analysis. *European Journal of Social Theory*, 17(1): 95–114.

Vostal, F. (2016) *Accelerating Academia: The changing structure of academic time*. Springer.

Wade, L. and Sharp, G. (2013) Sociological images: blogging as public sociology. *Social Science Computer Review*, 31(2): 221–228.

Watters, A. (2014) *The Monsters of Education Technology*. Hack Education. http://monsters.hackeducation.com/

Watters, A. (2015) *The Revenge of the Monsters of Education Technology*. Hack Education. http://monsters.hackeducation.com/

Watters, A. (2016) *The Curse of the Monsters of Education Technology*. Hack Education. http://monsters.hackeducation.com/

Weber, M. (1994) *Political Writings*. Cambridge University Press.

Weller, M. (2011) *The Digital Scholar: How technology is transforming scholarly practice*. Bloomsbury.

Weltevrede, E., Helmond, A. and Gerlitz, C. (2014) The politics of real-time: A device perspective on social media platforms and search engines. *Theory, Culture & Society*, 31(6): 125–150.

Wendling, M. (2018) *Alt-right: From 4chan to the White House*. PlutoPress.

Wikipedia (2019) List of social networking websites. https://en.wikipedia.org/wiki/List_of_social_networking_websites

Williams, J. (2018) *Stand Out of Our Light: Freedom and resistance in the attention economy*. Cambridge University Press.

Williams, M., Sloan, L. and Brookfield, C. (2017) A tale of two sociologies: Analyzing versus critique in UK Sociology. *Sociological Research Online*, 22(4): 132–151

Williamson, B. (2018) Silicon startup schools: technocracy, algorithmic imaginaries and venture philanthropy in corporate education reform. *Critical Studies in Education*, 59(2): 218–236.

Williamson, B. (2019) The platform university: a new data-driven business model for profiting from HE. WonkHE. https://wonkhe.com/blogs/the-platform-university-a-new-data-driven-business-model-for-profiting-from-he/

Winlow, S. and Hall, S. (2013) *Rethinking Social Exclusion: The end of the social?* Sage.

Wood, D.M. and Monahan, T. (2019) Platform surveillance. *Surveillance & Society*, 17(1/2): 1–6.

Woodcock, J. (2017) *Working the Phones: Control and resistance in call centres*. Pluto Press.

Woodcock, J. (2018) Digital labour in the university: understanding the transformations of academic work in the UK. *TripleC*, 16(1): 129–142.

Wu, T. (2010) *The Master Switch: The rise and fall of information empires*. Vintage.

Ylijoki, O. (2016) Organising Logic: Project time versus process time in the accelerated academy. LSE Impact Blog. https://blogs.lse.ac.uk/impactofsocialsciences/2016/03/23/project-time-versus-process-time-in-accelerated-academy/

Žižek, S. (1989) *The sublime object of ideology*. Verso.

Žižek, S. (2009) *In Defense of Lost Causes*. Verso.

Žižek, S. (2018) *Like a Thief in Broad Daylight: Power in the era of post-humanity*. Penguin.

Zuboff, S. (2019) *The Age of Surveillance Capitalism: The fight for a human future at the new frontier of power*. Profile Books.

Zuckerman, E. (2017) Managing decentralized publication and curation. *Parameters*. https://parameters.ssrc.org/2017/02/imagining-decentralized-publi cation-and-curation/

Index

References to endnotes show both the page number and the note number (197n17).